A CLASH
OF
THRONES

THE POWER-CRAZED
MEDIEVAL KINGS, POPES
AND EMPERORS OF EUROPE

ANDREW RAWSON

The History Press

First published 2015

The History Press
The Mill, Brimscombe Port
Stroud, Gloucestershire, GL5 2QG
www.thehistorypress.co.uk

British Library Cataloguing in Publication Data.
A catalogue record for this book is available from the British Library.

ISBN 978 0 7509 6228 5

Typesetting and origination by The History Press
Printed in Great Britain

CONTENTS

INTRODUCTION

Welcome to the biggest group of warriors, conquerors, philanderers, murderers and back-stabbers you are ever likely to meet. The power-mad medieval kings of Europe.

Starting with the Great Schism in 1054 and ending with the discovery of the New World in 1492, we see how kings and princes used military campaigns and political intrigue to secure their own power and usurp everyone else's. From conquests to civil wars, and through marriages and alliances, discover how kingdoms grew into the countries we recognise today and learn how some were overrun.

See how the popes and antipopes used God to sway kings' decisions and influence the power struggles across the continent. Hear about the threats from the Islamic infidels without and heretical religions within, and see how Crusades in the name of God brutally put down anyone who challenged the all-powerful Catholic Church. From the Holy Roman Emperor to the Knights Templar, and many more, powerful men and organisations all vied to promote their own brand of Christianity.

Learn about the princesses and queens who had to marry, forging alliances that satisfy a king's desire for increasing power while he chased women in court to satisfy his lust for the pleasures of the flesh. Find out how some wives used their wits and femininity to influence their husbands and their barons to change the balance of power in the royal courts. Also hear about the contrived reasons for royal divorces and the political fallout from the break-ups. Encounter some of the royal bastards who helped their fathers consolidate their power and others who plotted to kill so they could take the throne for themselves.

Murder, campaigns, politics, intrigue, torture, marriage: you had to be master of them all to become a successful king. Battles, poisoning, plague, illness, accidents: you had to avoid them all to remain a successful king. Here are their stories woven together in a light-hearted way. Enjoy the lives and struggles of the most important people in medieval Europe as they played the real game of thrones.

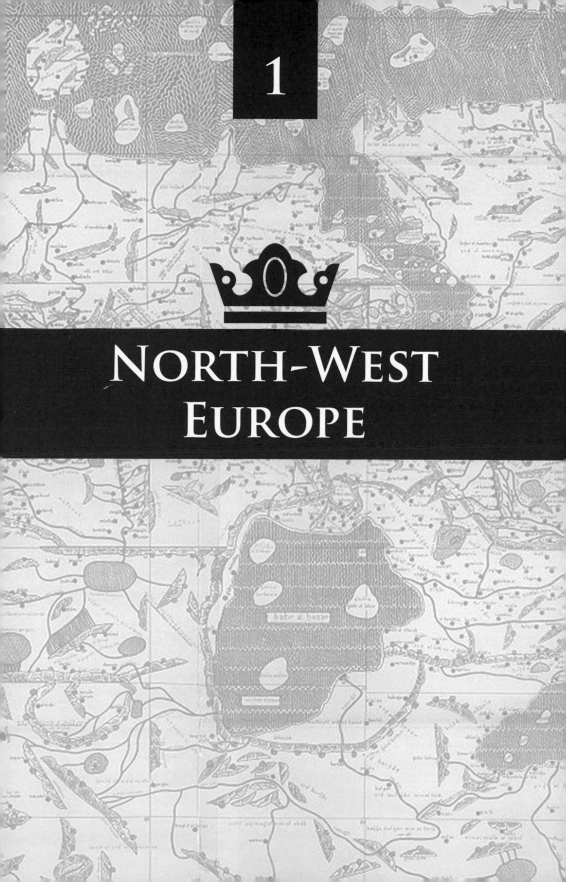

1

NORTH-WEST EUROPE

FRANCE WAS A FEUDAL STATE and the seizure of England by the Norman Duke William led to the conquest of Ireland in 1183 and Wales a century later. France and England would alternately make alliances through marriage and make war as a result of these marriages. The England-based Angevin Empire extended to rule Wales as well as large parts of Ireland and France. Most of the French territories would soon be lost.

There would be constant battles along the way between the Scottish and the English, with Scotland relying on France at times, resulting in a mutual assistance pact in 1295. Scotland acquired the Western Isles from Norway in 1266, followed by the Orkney and Shetland Islands after 1468.

THE KINGDOM OF FRANCE

Henri I became King of the Franks when the French crown lands were at their smallest, encompassing only what is now the region Île-de-France, and the rest of the country was run by dukes. He twice failed to capture Normandy from Duke William the Bastard and then met Emperor Henry III to discuss Lorraine. The emperor fled when he proposed hand-to-hand combat to decide ownership. Following his father's death, Young Philippe I was crowned in 1060 with his mother Anne as regent. Philippe first captured Flanders from Robert the Frisian at the Battle of Cassel in 1071 and then made peace with William of Normandy (also known as 'the Conqueror').

Philippe had a son with Bertha of Frisia and then divorced her in 1092, declaring that she was too fat when what he really wanted to do was to marry his mistress, Bertrade, daughter of Simon de Montfort I. Pope Urban II excommunicated Philippe, so he refused to support the First Crusade. Urban lifted the excommunication when Philippe promised to leave Bertrade, but he kept returning to her and became known as 'the Amorous'.

Louis VI the Fat was crowned in 1108 and he was primarily occupied with fighting 'robber barons' who were stealing his income in Normandy. His son Philippe was crowned co-king in 1129, but the disobedient teenager was riding through Paris when a pig made his horse rear and throw him; he died the following day.

Instead, teenage Louis VII, a pious man, succeeded his Fat father, but his wife Eleanor of Aquitaine disliked his devout ways and said she had 'thought to marry a king, only to find she'd married a monk'. She liked it even less when he vowed to go on a Crusade.

Louis VII and his army reached the Holy Land in 1148 after escaping an ambush near Laodicea. Eleanor asked Louis to support her uncle, Raymond of Antioch, but he divorced Eleanor and headed to Jerusalem to fight alongside Conrad and Baldwin instead. Louis VII returned home in 1149, when their siege of Damascus ended in disaster, having spent his fortune. Meanwhile, Eleanor married Henry Plantagenet, giving the future King Henry II of England the duchy of Aquitaine, and a furious Louis VII was defeated when he attacked him.

Louis VII eventually had a son with his third wife in 1165, and Philippe II was crowned in 1180. Although Henry II of England continued to expand his territories along the north and west coast of France, there was trouble brewing in England. Henry made the mistake of giving his overseas territories to his eldest son, Henry the Young King. His brother Richard, future Lionheart, allied with Philippe to get his revenge.

The jealousy was reversed when Richard was recognised as heir to Henry's lands and Philippe was later made feudal lord of Henry's French lands in 1189. Henry II died shortly afterwards, but the power struggle was interrupted when the Third Crusade was launched. Philippe reluctantly joined Richard I of England and Emperor Friedrich I, but he returned to France after they recaptured Acre. Richard was captured in Austria on the way home, accused of murdering King Conrad of Jerusalem. He was eventually ransomed and returned in 1194 only to find Philippe and John had joined forces to recover Normandy. Richard tried to recover his lands, only to be killed in a skirmish in 1199.

John was crowned King of England but he ignored a summons to Paris to answer a charge so Philippe seized England's lands in France. Philippe had more than tripled the size of his kingdom and would be known as 'Augustus' in homage to the Roman Caesar. But Pope Innocent III was annoyed that Philippe was busy fighting English troops in northern France rather than stamping out the Cathar heresy in the south, so he excommunicated John in 1213 for interfering with Church matters. Innocent also urged Philippe to invade England, seize John and put his own son Louis on the English throne. John repented by turning England over to the pope and it was returned as a papal fief. An Anglo-Flemish-German coalition failed to recover John's French fiefs, and while John fled to England, Philippe defeated Otto IV of Germany at the Battle of Bouvines in 1214.

While Philippe had been successful in military matters, he had trouble at home. Isabelle died in childbirth and he hated his second wife Isambour of Denmark so much that he imprisoned her in a convent rather than crown her. He declared himself divorced but Pope Celestine III refused an annulment because Isambour insisted the marriage had been consummated. To make matters worse, Thomas I of Savoy kidnapped and married Philippe's bride-to-be Margaret of Geneva en route to Paris, claiming the king was already betrothed. Philippe married Agnes of Merania instead, but Pope Innocent III again declared the union void and placed France under an interdict. Louis finally took Isambour back in 1213.

Louis VIII the Lion succeeded his father in July 1223 and concentrated on reinforcing the Albigensian Crusade against the Cathar heretics. Young Louis IX was crowned in 1226 aged 12, with his mother as regent. He expelled the country's Jewish moneylenders, confiscated their property and used it to finance the Seventh Crusade when he came of age. Louis captured Damietta in 1249 only to be captured at the Battle of Fariskur, and was forced to give up the city to pay his ransom.

Louis was leading the Eighth Crusade to the Holy Land when the Byzantine Emperor Mikhaël VIII proposed joining the Roman and Latin Churches (at that time they were two separate entities) in order to win the support of the pope, in response to hostility from Louis's younger brother, Charles of Sicily. Charles suggested Louis attack Tunis instead, to strengthen his position in the Mediterranean. Louis took up the suggestion only to die in North Africa in 1270. Louis's son, Philippe III the Bold, concluded a truce with the Emir in Tunis and returned to France to be crowned, taking his father's bones with him.

Pope Martin IV excommunicated Peter III of Aragon for starting the War of the Sicilian Vespers in 1282 and gave Aragon to Philippe's son, Charles, Count of Valois. Philippe and Charles went to claim the kingdom, supported by James II of Mallorca, but they were beaten at the Battle of the Col de Panissars in 1285. Philippe then died of dysentery, having nearly bankrupted France. Philippe IV, the Fair, inherited Navarre through his wife, Joan, in 1284 and inherited France from his father Philippe the Bold a year later. Edward I of England was a vassal to Philippe but his brother, Edmund Crouchback, agreed all Edward's overseas lands could be exchanged in return for his own territories in 1293. But Philippe defaulted on the deal and instead offered the hand of his daughter, Isabella, to Edward's son to ensure peace.

Philippe was defeated at the Battle of the Golden Spurs in Flanders in 1302 but he soon forced the Flemish to accept peace. His debts to the Knights Templar increased and though he expelled and disinherited 100,000 Jews to raise money in 1306, he still did not have enough to pay them off. Instead, Philippe used his influence over Pope Clement V, who had just moved from Rome to Avignon, to arrest the Templars as heretics. On Friday 13 October 1307, hundreds of French Templars were arrested and they were soon being tortured and executed. Their leader, Jacques de Molay, was burned at the stake in 1314 and he cursed the king and the pope from the flames. Pope Clement V died a month later while Philippe died in a hunting accident, six months later.

Louis X the Quarreler had inherited Navarre from his mother in 1305 and was crowned King of France in 1314. He immediately faced a revolt in Flanders and a scandal in Paris. His wife Marguerite and sisters-in-law Blanche and Juana were arrested for adultery in the Tour de Nesle affair. Marguerite and Blanche were imprisoned and their lovers were executed while Juana was found innocent. Louis wanted his marriage annulled and Marguerite conveniently died soon after; he married Clémence five days later.

Louis drank too much cold wine and died after a strenuous game of indoor tennis in 1316, so his brother Philippe became regent to the pregnant Clémence. Her son, Jean the Posthumous, only lived a few days and some believed that Philippe, who would be King Philippe V the Tall, had poisoned the baby. The majority of the nobility opposed his coronation. Pope John XXII called for a Crusade in 1320 but the recruitment drive turned into a violent anti-Semitic uprising which Philippe had to stamp out. He would die in the summer of 1321.

The French king Charles IV the Fair helped his uncle, Charles of Valois, capture Aquitaine from the English in the 1324 War of Saint-Sardos. Charles's sister Isabella went to France on behalf of her husband, Edward II of England, to negotiate a peace. But Isabella hated her spouse and started a relationship with the exiled Roger Mortimer. She betrothed her son to a local count's daughter and used her dowry and a loan from her brother to raise a mercenary army. Isabella invaded England and deposed Edward, who was murdered in 1327, earning a reputation as the She-Wolf of France. Isabella then encouraged her young son, Edward III, to make peace with Charles but only Aquitaine was returned to England.

Charles died without a male heir, and while Charles of Valois's son, Philippe VI the Fortunate, was crowned, Isabella claimed the throne for her son. Philippe started his reign by giving Navarre to its rightful heiress, the future Joan II, and then took in David II of Scotland in 1334 and declared himself champion of Scottish interests. Philippe accused Edward of rebellion and disobedience in 1337 and seized Aquitaine, starting the Hundred Years War between England and France.

The French fleet was destroyed at the Battle of Sluys in 1340, so Philippe played a waiting game against the cash-strapped Edward. The first major clash at Crécy in 1346 ended with an injured Edward defeating Philippe. The Black Death struck in 1348, killing one-third of France's population, including Philippe's wife, Joan the Lame, the brains behind the throne. Philippe married Blanche of Navarre, a union that alienated many people because she had been betrothed to his son. Philippe died soon afterwards.

There were rumours that Philippe's successor, John II the Good, was having a relationship with Charles de La Cerda, the Constable of France, which scandal resulted in the murder of de La Cerda. The Hundred Years War then flared up and John was captured at the Battle of Poitiers in 1356 by Edward III's son, the Black Prince. John's son Louis was held as a replacement hostage in Calais while his father was released and attempted to raise the huge ransom. Louis escaped in 1363 but John voluntarily returned to England, where he died in captivity.

Charles V the Wise was the first heir to the French throne to call himself the *Dauphin* but there were rumours he was illegitimate. The Black Prince refused to visit Paris to answer charges about his rule of Gascony, so Charles called him disloyal and declared war in 1369. The English were soon defeated, and while Charles recovered most of France, the Black Prince fled to England and died. The Church was split in 1376, with half of Europe supporting the pope in Rome and the rest supporting the antipope in Avignon. It did not matter to Charles, because a festering abscess killed him, the result of an attempt to poison him thirty years earlier.

Charles VI the Beloved drew his sword when a leper grabbed his horse on campaign in Brittany in 1392. He had killed several servants before he was overpowered and the incident marked the start of his madness. Soon Charles the Mad could not remember his own name, his status or his wife. He sometimes refused to bathe or change his clothes and the doors of his apartments were sealed to keep him safe. Charles's uncles, Philippe of Burgundy and Jean of Berry, dismissed all of Charles's advisers and even murdered the king's brother, Louis I of Valois, when he demanded the throne in 1407.

Seeking to benefit from the instability of the French throne, Henry V of England made a claim for the French crown and invaded, defeating the French army at Agincourt in 1415. Four of Charles's sons died childless while the mad king claimed his fifth son (also Charles) was illegitimate. So he signed the 1420 Treaty of Troyes, which recognised Henry as his successor and married him to his daughter, Catherine. Young Charles sought refuge in the south of France, having failed to defeat the English in the north.

Both Henry V and Charles VI died in 1422, allowing Charles VII to claim the throne ahead of young Henry VI of England.

Orleans was under siege when the teenage Joan of Arc announced she had a divine mission in 1429. A disguised Charles met her, expecting to uncover her scam, but she bowed before him and said, 'God give you a happy life, sweet King!' Joan inspired the king to claim his inheritance and he broke the Siege of Orleans and turned the tide of the war. Charles was crowned *de jure* king after winning the Battle of Patay in 1429, but the Burgundians captured Joan and handed her over to the English. Charles VII did nothing to save her and she was burned at the stake in 1431. The Treaty of Arras would bring the Burgundians over to the French side, meaning that Charles the Victorious had recovered all of France apart from Calais.

Charles refused to give his son, Louis, the powers of the *Dauphin* and banished him after he quarrelled with his mistress, Agnès Sorel, in 1446. They never met again. Five years later, Louis wed Charlotte of Savoy, who was just 9 years old, without his father's consent, resulting in war between them. When Philippe of Burgundy offered to support Louis, Charles warned him that he was 'giving shelter to a fox who will eat his chickens'. Charles fell ill in 1458 but Louis refused to visit his father until he heard he was dying.

He then rushed to be by his side, not to make peace with Charles, but to be crowned ahead of his brother.

Louis IX the Cunning used plots and conspiracy to get his way and was known as the 'Universal Spider'. Edward IV of England invaded France in 1475 so Louis paid him to renounce his claim and leave, ending the Hundred Years War. Louis bragged he had driven the English out with pâté, venison and wine. Philippe of Burgundy gave money in exchange for territories so Louis could go on Crusade. So Philippe's son, Charles, and the king's brother, also Charles, formed the League of the Public Weal, hoping to protect their inheritance. The ensuing rebellion ended with the death of Charles of Burgundy and an end was put to the Burgundian Wars at the Battle of Nancy in 1477.

Louis died in 1483 and his teenage son, Charles VIII the Affable, was crowned with his older sister Anne as regent. He was betrothed to Margaret, daughter of the Holy Roman Emperor Maximilian. But when Maximilian married the young Anne of Brittany by proxy (without seeing her) and without Charles's permission, Charles retaliated by invading Brittany and married Anne himself instead, her marriage to Maximilian being annulled by the pope. The unhappy bride took two beds to her wedding to make her point.

Charles made treaties with Austria and England while recruiting a large army to face the emperor. Pope Innocent VIII also offered Naples to Charles after expelling Alfonso II in 1489, only to form the League of Venice when he became too powerful. Charles was defeated at the Battle of Fornovo in 1495 and he died three years later after hitting his head on a door lintel on his way to play a game of tennis!

THE ENGLISH KINGDOM AND THE ANGEVIN EMPIRE

At the start of this period England covered the same area as today, with Wales to its west and Scotland to its north, but the first threats came from Norway and France across the seas.

Edward the Confessor had been raised in exile in Normandy and he was crowned in 1042. Ten years later, his father-in-law, Godwin, assembled an army so Edward banished him. Edward favoured the Normans in his court so the English barons invited Godwin back to challenge him, until threat of a Norwegian invasion rallied the English and Danes behind Edward. The deeply religious king, known as 'the Confessor', died early in 1066.

Edward's brother-in-law, Harold Godwinson, was crowned Harold II, but he immediately faced an invasion in northern England by his brother Tostig and Harald of Norway. He defeated them at Stamford Bridge but then had to march south to face a challenge from William of Normandy, who claimed Edward had promised him the throne back in 1051. William the Bastard also had the support of Emperor Henry IV and Pope Alexander II.

William defeated and killed Harold near Hastings and although Edgar the Aetheling, Edward's intended heir, staged a rebellion and was proclaimed king, he was never crowned. Instead, William the Conqueror was crowned on Christmas Day and then returned across the Channel to defend Normandy. English nobles captured York with Danish help in 1069, but the Normans bribed the Danes to leave. Malcolm III of Scotland also invaded England, but William's counter-attack resulted in the 1072 Treaty of Abernethy and the handing over of Malcolm's eldest son as a hostage.

William died in 1087, leaving England to his younger son William Rufus and Normandy to his elder son Robert. Ruling as William II, William Rufus expanded his power into the north of England but turned his attentions to Normandy when Robert went on Crusade in 1096. He died following a hunting accident in the New Forest in 1100 and his brother Henry was crowned. Henry defeated Robert at the Battle of Tinchebray in France and imprisoned his older brother in 1106; he died in captivity.

Henry I sealed the peace with Scotland through his marriage to Matilda of Scotland, but the succession was plunged into turmoil when his legitimate sons William and Richard drowned when the *White Ship* sank in the English Channel in 1120. His daughter Matilda, Empress of the Holy Roman Empire by marriage, was declared heir, but after Henry died from eating too many fish in 1135 her cousin, Stephen of Blois, seized the throne. Matilda invaded England in 1139 and Stephen was soon captured, plunging the country into a civil war known as 'the Anarchy'. Although the Empress Matilda ruled for a few months, her arrogance antagonised her supporters and Stephen was released in exchange for her illegitimate half-brother, Robert of Gloucester. Matilda retired to Normandy when Robert died in 1147, leaving the throne in dispute.

Matilda's eldest son, Henry, had been given Normandy and he invaded England in 1149 and 1153. After Stephen's son died young, the Treaty of Wallingford nominated Matilda's son Henry to inherit the throne after Stephen's death as Henry II. Stephen died in 1154 and Empress Matilda died in 1167. The Archbishop of Canterbury refused to crown Stephen's son, Eustace, because Pope Alexander III had declared against him. Eustace died while plundering Church lands in 1153 and his death was seen as a sign from God. Instead, Henry II inherited the Angevin Empire under the Treaty of Wallingford, and it covered England and large parts of what is now France. He soon fell out with the Archbishop of Canterbury, Thomas Becket, who was murdered in 1170. Three years later, his sons Henry, Richard and Geoffrey joined their mother, Eleanor of Aquitaine, in a rebellion against their father. France, Scotland, Flanders and Boulogne would also join in before the Great Revolt was settled. Henry had invaded Ireland and the 1175 Treaty of Windsor provided lands there for his faithful youngest son, John. Henry and Geoffrey rose up again in 1183, but their rebellion ended when young Henry died while pillaging monasteries across France. Meanwhile, Philippe II of France had convinced Richard that his father would crown John king. Philippe and Richard rebelled and defeated Henry in 1189. Henry retired and died from a bleeding ulcer.

Succeeding his father, Richard I immediately went on Crusade, leaving others to rule England, and he took over the Third Crusade after Philippe II left. He defeated Saladin at the Siege of Acre and the battles of Arsuf and Jaffa and though he failed to reconquer Jerusalem, he would be known as 'the Lionheart'. Although Richard concluded the Treaty of Jaffa in 1192, he was suspected of assassinating King Conrad of Jerusalem and was taken prisoner by Leopold V in Austria. He was handed over to Emperor Henry VI in 1193, and while Philippe of France failed to seize Richard's French possessions, Queen Eleanor stopped Richard's brother John invading England. Richard was released when a huge ransom was paid. Philippe warned everyone, 'look to yourself, the devil is loosed', and John fled to the French court. Richard was recrowned and he recovered all his lands before dying while fighting a rebellious baron in France in 1199. The Lionheart spoke no English, had spent only a few months in England and left no heir.

Henry II's youngest son, John, was crowned and although Philippe II of France recognised his Angevin lands under the 1200 Treaty of Le Goulet, he seized northern France only four years later. Pope Innocent III wanted Philippe to stamp out the Cathar heresy in the south of France and he excommunicated John in 1213 for stopping him. Innocent also urged Philippe to invade England, but John repented and turned England over to the pope; it was returned as a papal fief.

An Anglo-Flemish-German coalition failed to recover John's French fiefs and Philippe defeated Otto IV of Germany at Bouvines in 1214 while John was putting down a rebellion in England. The English barons forced their king to sign Magna Carta, to reduce his powers, in 1215. John ignored the treaty, so the English barons offered the throne to Philippe's son, Prince Louis, and he was proclaimed king and soon controlled half of England. John died of dysentery in 1216 and supporters of his young son, Henry III, quickly defeated Louis and the rebel barons.

Henry assumed power in 1227, and while he accepted Magna Carta, he made poor choices of friends and advisers. He launched campaigns against France in 1230 and 1242, both of which failed. He also spent money trying to make his son the King of Sicily. The 1258 Provisions of Oxford and the 1259 Provisions of Westminster reduced his powers. Henry renounced them in 1262, so the barons rebelled under Simon de Montfort and captured their king. He escaped and defeated and killed de Montfort at the Battle of Evesham in 1265.

Edward I was a tall man who was known as 'Longshanks'. He had accomplished little on his Crusade to the Holy Land when he heard of his father's death in 1272 and he returned to England. Edward subjected Wales to English rule in 1283 after a series of rebellions, but Scotland resisted and he became known as 'Hammer of the Scots'. His son was crowned Edward II in 1307 and Scotland fought back, freeing themselves from English control following Robert the Bruce's victory at Bannockburn in 1314.

Edward was victorious in a civil war in 1322 but his wife, Isabella of France, led an invasion of England four years later. He renounced the throne in favour of his son Edward and was imprisoned, but he could not be legally deposed or executed. The barons agreed to depose the king at a secret meeting chaired by Roger Mortimer and he was forced to abdicate in 1327 before he was allegedly murdered by having a red-hot poker pushed into his anus.

Isabella and Mortimer controlled young Edward III and made an unpopular peace with the Scots under the Treaty of Northampton. Edward executed Mortimer and sent his mother into retirement when he came of age in 1330. He then successfully campaigned against Scotland in 1333. He declared himself heir to the French throne through his mother four years later, precipitating the Hundred Years War. He overran Brittany in 1342 and was victorious at the Battle of Crécy in 1346.

The Black Death struck in 1348, curtailing military activities for several years, but Edward the Black Prince, son of Edward III, won the Battle of Poitiers in 1356 and the Treaty of Brétigny returned large parts of French territories. Later military failures, compounded by the return of the plague, forced Edward III to surrender most of these gains to Charles V of France under the 1375 Treaty of Bruges. Edward retired to Windsor, leaving the throne in the hands of Edward the Black Prince, but Edward died a year before his father, resulting in the succession of his young son, Richard II.

Richard II is famous for having personally stopped the Peasants' Revolt in 1381, when he was still just a teenager, by meeting the rebels outside London.

However, he became dependent on a circle of favourites, many of whom were put to death by the 'Merciless Parliament' of 1388; in retaliation he executed or exiled many parliamentary leaders over the next two years.

Richard seized the lands of his uncle, powerful nobleman John of Gaunt, when he died in 1399. John's son Henry of Bolingbroke raised an army, invaded England and deposed. Richard plotted to recover his throne, but he was probably murdered in prison and Henry, now King Henry IV, put his body on display to prove he was dead.

Henry IV faced a plague in 1400, followed by a revolt in Wales. He then defeated a revolt by the Percy family at the Battle of Shrewsbury in 1403 and executed many of the rebels. Henry regained control of the country but he was dogged by illness and his son Henry assumed control of the country before he died in 1413.

Henry V immediately laid claim to the French crown and sailed for France to capture Harfleur. The *Dauphin* refused his offer of personal combat, so Henry defeated the French army at the Battle of Agincourt in 1415. Charles VI of France recognised Henry V as regent and heir apparent to the French throne under the 1420 Treaty of Troyes and married him to his daughter, Catherine of Valois.

Henry went on to capture Normandy only to die in 1422, just before Charles, leaving his infant son, Henry VI, King of England and disputed King of France.

During Henry VI's infancy, the Cardinal Beaufort and the Duke of Gloucester were his regents in England, while the Duke of Bedford represented him in France. The dual regency was difficult to maintain and the *Dauphin* and Jeanne d'Arc weakened English rule in France until Normandy was lost in 1450.

Richard, Duke of York was made Protector when Henry VI fell ill and a civil war between the Yorkist and Lancastrian factions had broken out before he recovered two years later – the Wars of the Roses. This was a struggle to decide whether the succession should stay with the male line or pass through the female line. Henry's queen, Margaret of Anjou, was determined to fight for her husband's and son's Lancastrian cause. The Duke of York was killed at the Battle of Wakefield in 1460 and his son Edward, Duke of York defeated the Lancastrians at the Battle of Towton in 1461. Then London opened its gates to the Yorkist forces and Edward was crowned Edward IV – the first Yorkist king.

Henry fled to Scotland but was captured in 1465 and imprisoned in the Tower of London. Edward was then forced to flee to the continent and Henry VI was restored to the throne by the kingmaker, the Earl of Warwick. His son Edward was defeated and killed by the former Edward IV at the Battle of Tewkesbury in 1470 and then Warwick was killed at the Battle of Barnet. Edward IV regained the throne and Henry died in suspicious circumstances in the Tower. Order was restored in England and peace was made with Louis XI of France at Picquigny in 1475, finally ending the Hundred Years War begun under Edward III.

Edward had secretly married Elizabeth Woodville, the first consort to be crowned queen, and their young son succeeded him as Edward V in 1483. Edward IV's brother, Richard, Duke of York immediately arrested and executed his nephew Edward V's protectors, Earl Rivers and Richard Grey. Edward protested, so Richard, Duke of York imprisoned him and his brother in the Tower of London. Richard then produced evidence that Edward IV had been contracted to marry another woman before he married Elizabeth, making the boys illegitimate. He was was crowned Richard III and the 'Princes in the Tower' were never seen again; they are presumed to have been murdered.

The sole heir, Prince Edward, died soon after Richard III's ascent to the throne. Richard's reign was beset by rebellion from the start, and in the final chapter of the Wars of the Roses, Henry Tudor landed with French troops in Wales and defeated and killed the king at the Battle of Bosworth in 1485, ending the war once and for all. Crowned Henry VII, he restored the stability of the English monarchy by marrying Edward IV's daughter, Elizabeth of York, in 1486, uniting the houses of York and Lancaster. While peace returned to England, the new Tudor king was troubled by the pretenders Perkin Warbeck and Lambert Simnel, who impersonated the murdered princes.

THE KINGDOMS OF IRELAND

There were several kingdoms in Ireland, the main ones being Uí Néill (Ulster), Connacht, Mide (Meath), Munster and Leinster. By tradition Ireland as a whole was ruled by a High King, but in reality this position was far from secure, with the rulers of the respective kingdoms fighting for superiority. As 'High King with opposition', to maintain power you would have to control at least the three Viking cities: Dublin, Waterford and Limerick. Only a 'High King without opposition' would be able to march his army anywhere in Ireland. It was to this that Ireland's rulers aspired.

Donnchadh was the King of Munster. His strength was based on the towns of Limerick and Cork, in the south-west of Ireland. But Aed of Connacht attacked him in the 1050s, and he later lost Dublin and Limerick to Diarmait of Leinster. Donnchadh of Munster was defeated in the Galtee Mountains and deposed in 1063; he died on a pilgrimage to Rome the following year. Diarmait of Leinster was killed fighting Conchobar of Mide in 1072.

Toirdelbach had succeeded Donnchadh, his uncle, as King of Munster, and having fought on behalf of Leinster, he was then given Dublin after Diarmait died in battle. Conchobar of Mide and his wife were murdered the following year and Toirdelbach was then able to ravage Mide and Connacht in a bid to consolidate his rule over all Ireland, while his sons Muirchertach and Diarmait ruled Dublin and Waterford and deposed Ruaidri of Connacht. They then defeated his replacement, Ua Ruairc, at the Battle of Monecronock in 1082. But war broke out while Toirdelbach was raiding Mide and he fell ill and died in 1086.

Following his father's death, Muirchertach banished his brother Diarmait from Munster, so he could be sole king. Muirchertach then established his control of Leinster, Tara and Dublin before killing Domnall of Mide and declaring himself High King of Ireland in 1101.

Arnulf de Montgomery of Wales married Muirchertach's daughter to form an alliance against the English, but their combined forces were defeated by Henry I of England. Instead they turned on Magnus Barefoot of Norway, who had recently landed in Ireland with a large army. Arnulf then tried to seize Muirchertach's throne, so Muirchertach snatched his daughter back and married her to one of his cousins. Around the same time, Muirchertach captured Ulster and then married a daughter to Magnus's son, Sigurd, in 1102 to secure his position. But Magnus was killed in an ambush as he prepared to head back to Norway and the marriage was cancelled. Diarmait briefly seized power while Muirchertach was ill but the latter regained control of Munster and captured his brother; Muirchertach died in 1119.

Domnall, King of Connacht, was born of a dynastic alliance between the ruling family of Connacht and Mor, sister of Muirchertach. But he was deposed in 1106 by his brother Tairrdelbach, with the help of Muirchertach, who went on to secure his position as High King for many years and established the city of Galway in 1124.

Tairrdelbach had over twenty sons by his many wives. Ruaidri of Connacht knew he was not his father's favourite, and he went to great lengths to secure his position as heir, blinding one of his brothers and arresting three others, while also seeking to prove his status with raids against his father's enemies. As a result of his machinations Ruaidri became King of Connacht without opposition following his father's death.

However, he was not High King of Ireland as his father had been; that position was claimed by Muircheartach Mac Lochlainn, King of Tyrone. Ruaidri of Connacht undermined Muircheartach Mac Lochlainn by capturing Munster. Muircheartach Mac Lochlainn and sixteen of his closest followers were murdered as a result of hostilities with the King of Ulster in 1166.

Ruaidri conquered Leinster in 1167 and took many hostages, but the exiled King Diarmait of Leinster returned with Anglo-Norman support in 1169 and captured most of Leinster. Henry II of England followed to assert his rule and he was welcomed by the rebels. The 1175 Treaty of Windsor left Ruaidri with the west of Ireland, while Henry gave the east to his young son, John. Ruaidri's son Muirchertach led an Anglo-Norman raid into Connacht in 1177 and was blinded by his father for his disobedience. Ruaidri abdicated in 1183, but would return to power briefly in 1185 and 1189.

THE KINGDOMS OF WALES

Wales covered a similar area to modern Wales. Gruffydd ap Llywelyn became self-appointed king in 1055 and annexed parts of England before Harold Godwinson defeated him in 1063. He was murdered by his own men because they wanted to secure peace with England. Wales reverted to the kingdoms of Gwynedd in the north, Powys in the centre and Deheubarth in the south.

The Kingdom of Gwynedd

Bleddyn ap Cynfyn had seized power with the support of Harold Godwinson after his half-brother Gruffydd was murdered, only to be defeated in battle in 1073. He was succeeded by his cousin Trahaearn ap Caradog. However, Gruffudd ap Cynan, a rival claimant to the throne, returned from an Irish campaign and, with the support of Rhys of Deheubarth, killed Trahaearn at the Battle of Mynydd Carn in 1081.

Gruffudd ap Cynan was captured by the Norman Earl of Chester, Hugh the Fat, after meeting him to discuss an alliance, but he escaped and allied himself with Cadwgan of Powys to revolt against the Normans. They were forced to flee to Ireland when the Normans bribed the Norse fleet they had hired to leave. Gruffudd and Cadwgan recovered their kingdoms the following year and agreed a border with England's new king, Henry I, with Pura Wallia (the principality of Wales) under Welsh control and Marchia Walliae (the Welsh Marches) under English control.

Henry I and Alexander I of Scotland invaded Gwynedd and Powys in 1116 with the excuse that Gruffudd ap Cynan was sheltering rebels. Gruffudd made peace and retired. Henry I died in 1136 and the kingdoms of Gwynedd, Deheubarth and Powys allied following the execution of Gwenllian, Gruffudd's daughter and wife of the Prince of Deheubarth. They routed the Normans at the Battle of Crug Mawr in 1136 and Gruffudd died knowing his realm would not 'go to the flames' of any invaders.

Owain Mawr (Owain the Great) succeeded his father in 1137. Despite the fact that they had previously fought together against the Normans, Owain quickly became embroiled in a dispute with his brother Cadwaladr. Anarawd of Deheubarth was murdered by Cadwaladr's men just before his wedding to Owain's daughter. In punishment Owain stripped Cadwaladr of his lands.

Henry II of England and his allies, including Cadwaladr, invaded Owain's territory in 1157; Henry was nearly killed in an ambush and then his navy was defeated. Cadwaladr, with the backing of Henry I, forced Owain to reinstate him. However, on the deaths of Madog of Powys and his son Llywelyn in 1160, Owain was able to annex part of Powys and extend his power to the east. He then formed a new alliance with Rhys of Deheubarth and ambushed Henry's army, forcing it to withdraw, while a mercenary

Norse navy failed to harass the Welsh coast. A revengeful Henry II captured and mutilated the sons of Owain and his allies.

Owain died in 1170 leaving the crown to Hywel, his second son. He had become heir after Rhun, Owain's eldest and favourite son, died mysteriously in 1146. Hywel's half-brothers, Dafydd and Rohdri, defeated and killed him at the Battle of Pentraeth in 1170. They then turned on one another, with Dafydd exiling his brother Maelgwn to Ireland and imprisoning Rhodri. He sought to rule Gwynedd alone, and married Henry's illegitimate half-sister Emma to make peace with England. Rhodri escaped in 1175 and the two brothers eventually agreed to divide Gwynedd between them; he was forced into exile on the Isle of Man in 1190.

Llywelyn – son of Iorwerth ab Owain Gwynedd, Owain's eldest legitimate son – defeated Dafydd in 1194 and ceased his lands, and when Rhodri died in 1195 he was able to reunite the Kingdom of Gwynedd. He became known as Llywelyn the Great.

Llywelyn married John's illegitimate daughter, Joan, to restore peace with England in 1205. Relations between them deteriorated, however, after Llywelyn allied with the barons who forced John to sign Magna Carta in 1215. Llywelyn signed the 1218 Treaty of Worcester with Henry III to consolidate his territories, but hostilities with the English lords in the Welsh Marches continued until the 1234 Peace of Middle established a lasting truce.

Llywelyn took great care to ensure that his legitimate and favourite younger son, Dafydd, would succeed him, rather than his older but illegitimate son Gruffudd, though Gruffud would be given some lands to rule. This was controversial, as Welsh custom held that the eldest child should succeed his father whether or not he was legitimate.

Llywelyn suffered a severe stroke in 1237, and Dafydd took up his role as successor eagerly, imprisoning his half-brother Gruffudd and confiscating his lands. Henry III of England invaded Gwynedd in 1241 and the Treaty of Gwerneigron forced Dafydd to give up lands and hand over his half-brother Gruffudd as a hostage. Gruffudd would die trying to escape from the Tower of London climbing down a knotted sheet.

Dafydd successfully campaigned against the English occupation, but he died in 1246, leaving no children; Gruffudd's sons Owain and Llywelyn divided the realm. Henry III demanded that their brother Dafydd be given lands when he reached maturity in 1255, hoping to destabilise the kingdom. Llywelyn rejected the idea and defeated and imprisoned Dafydd and Owain at the Battle of Bryn Derwin, thereby reuniting Gwynedd once more.

Other Welsh principalities united behind Llywelyn to campaign against England, and as the English Barons' Revolt reached its climax at the Battle of Lewes in 1264, Llywelyn allied with the victorious rebel Simon de Montfort. A peace between England and Wales was formalised under the 1267 Treaty of Montgomery, following the death of de Montfort. The King of England recognised the title Prince of Wales, while the Welsh princes became vassals of Llywelyn.

The principality of Wales ended following the death of Henry III in 1272. His successor Edward I, who wanted to rule the whole of Great Britain, declared Llywelyn 'a rebel and disturber of the peace'. An English army broke Wales's unity in 1282 and Llywelyn was forced to sign the Treaty of Aberconwy. The death of Llywelyn's wife, Eleanor de Montfort, daughter of the rebel earl, in childbirth caused him to have a nervous breakdown and he then rejected the offer of a pension and an estate in England. Llywelyn was killed in an ambush and although his brother Dafydd was proclaimed Prince of Wales, the kingdom disintegrated and his family was captured in 1283. Llywelyn became known as Llywelyn the Last.

Wales became incorporated into England's kingdom under the Statute of Rhuddlan and Dafydd was hung, drawn and quartered and his children were imprisoned for life. Although Welsh rebellions continued after 1284, the title Prince of Wales was retained by the sovereign until it was awarded to his son, Prince Edward.

The Kingdom of Powys

Bleddyn ap Cynfyn and his brother Rhiwallon had taken the thrones of Gwynedd and Powys following the death of their half-brother Gruffyd ap Llewelyn. They successfully defended their thrones again Gruffydd's sons at the Battle of Mechain in 1070 to retain his position, but Rhiwallon was killed and Bleddyn was left to rule alone, until his death at the hands of Trahaearn of Gwynedd in 1075. While Gwynedd was lost to Trahaearn, the Kingdom of Powys was divided between Bleddyn's sons Maredudd, Cadwgan and Iorwerth.

Iorwerth supported the English king and handed over his brother Maredudd to Henry I, but the lands which he had been promised in return were not forthcoming.

Civil war then broke out when Cadwgan's son, Owain, raped and abducted Nest, daughter of the King of Deheubarth and wife of Gerald of Pembroke. The Normans bribed Owain's Welsh enemies to attack him, and Iorwerth was able to drive Owain out of Powys and briefly regained his position as ruler. Owain's ally, Madog Ap Rhirid, retaliated by having Iorwerth killed in a burning building, and Cadwgan was restored to his throne and recalled Owain from exile. However, the alliance was to turn sour and Madog Ap Rhirid later murdered Owain's father Cadwgan. Owain took the throne, and when his uncle Maredudd captured Madog Ap Rhirid, Owain avenged his father's death by blinding Madog Ap Rhirid. Owain was eventually to be killed by Nest's husband while putting down a rebellion in Deheubarth.

He was succeeded by Maredudd, who raided England. King Henry retaliated, seizing most of Powys. Maredudd was succeeded by his son Madog ap Maredudd in 1132, who regained most of his lands after supporting Henry II's attacks on Gywnedd in 1157. Madog died in 1160 and his son died soon after, so their lands were split into the much smaller territories Fadog Powys and Wenwynwyn Powys, with a portion being appropriated by Owain Mawr of Gwynedd.

The Kingdom of Deheubarth

Maredudd reclaimed Deheubarth following the death of Gruffydd in 1063. He immediately faced a Norman invasion but was given an English estate for not resisting. He died in battle in 1072. His brother Rhys was defeated by Traehaern of Gwynedd, only to be killed by Caradog of Gwent in 1078. He was succeeded by his cousin Rhys, who faced attacks by Cadwgan of Powys in 1088 and from Maredudd's son, Gruffydd. Rhys was killed by the Normans in the Battle of Brecon in 1093 and Deheubarth was under their rule until 1155, with his son Gruffydd ap Rhys in opposition.

In 1136, with Gruffydd ap Rhys absent in Gwynedd, his wife Gwenllian, the strikingly beautiful daughter of the King of Gwynedd, had raised and army and led them in battle against Norman raiders. She was defeated, captured and executed. In response, Gruffydd joined the King of Gwynedd to defeat the Normans at the Battle of Crug Mawr in 1136. He died soon afterwards.

His son Anarawad was murdered on Cadwaladr's orders just before he married Owain's daughter. Anarawad's brother, Cadell, was ambushed and badly injured by Normans while out hunting and he would die on a pilgrimage to Rome. A third son, Rhys ap Gruffydd, thus ruled from 1155. However, in 1158 he was forced to submit to Henry II and then had to fight for his lands. He made peace with England in 1171, but when Richard I became king, Rhys took the opportunity to attack the Normans once more.

Rhys ap Gruffydd died during an epidemic in 1197, and his sons Gruffydd and Maelgwn quarrelled until Gruffydd died in 1201. Maelgwn lost lands to Gwynedd before he died in 1230 and Deheubarth became subject to Gwynedd after Maelgwn's younger brother Rhys was mortally wounded in battle in 1234.

THE KINGDOM OF SCOTLAND

At the start of this period, Scotland controlled the lowlands area known as Alba, while the islands and Highlands belonged to Norway.

Macbeth the Red King killed Duncan I the Diseased in 1040. Duncan's wife fled, taking her children with her, but Duncan's son Malcolm Canmore (meaning 'big head') returned and killed Macbeth at the Battle of Lumphanan in 1057. Macbeth's stepson Lulach the Foolish was crowned, but he was assassinated only a few months later and Malcolm

Canmore became Malcolm III of Scotland. He made a truce with the Scandinavian-controlled Highlands by marrying Ingibiorg, invaded Northumbria and, now a widower, married Edward the Confessor's daughter Margaret to seal the peace with England.

But England's situation changed when William of Normandy invaded and defeated Harold II at Hastings in 1066. Malcolm captured Cumbria and 'harried' the north of England until 1072, while Edward the Confessor's son Edgar took control of the rest of the north of England with Danish help. Malcolm arranged peace between William and Edgar, handing over his son Duncan as a hostage to seal the deal. William II of England reclaimed the north of his country in 1091. Malcolm invaded England again when Edgar fled to Scotland, but subsequently made peace when William II marched north.

Malcolm was killed and his second son Edward was mortally wounded at the Battle of Alnwick in 1093. Malcolm's widow Margaret died of grief a few days later and Donald III the Fair, the dead monarch's brother, exiled Malcolm's sons and took the throne. Malcolm's son Duncan had grown up in the English court since he was given as a hostage to William I, but he raised an army by promising Scottish titles. He captured the throne from his uncle but the Scottish considered him too English; Duncan II was ambushed and killed in 1094 and Donald took the throne once more.

Duncan's brother, Edgar the Valiant, returned with another English army and captured Donald, possibly blinding and imprisoning him. Edgar concentrated on securing southern Scotland (the area known as Alba) but he died (possibly murdered) in 1107.

Neither Donald nor Edgar left any sons, so another of Malcolm's sons was crowned Alexander I. He married Henry I of England's illegitimate daughter, Sybilla, and then joined the king on his campaign into Wales in 1114. Alexander became known as 'the Fierce' after putting down an uprising by the 'men of the Isles'. He died in 1124.

David, yet another of Malcolm's sons, living in exile in the English court, claimed the Scottish throne with Henry's support but he was king 'in little more than name'. Alexander's son, Malcolm, led a rebellion while David was visiting Henry in 1130, but David returned with an English army and imprisoned his nephew.

Anarchy broke out in England following Henry I's death in 1135. David switched his support to Henry's daughter, the Empress Matilda, after his son Henry was insulted at Stephen of Blois's court. David then attacked the north of England only to be defeated at the Battle of the Standard in Yorkshire in 1138. Although Matilda seized England, the civil war continued as David raided further south. Both son and father died in 1153, leaving David's young grandson, Malcolm IV, to inherit the throne. His pro-English attitude was scorned – even more so when he did not stop Henry of England taking back Cumbria and Northumbria. The last straw came when he joined an English campaign into France in 1159. He returned to find Scotland in rebellion. Malcolm IV 'the Maiden' died of an illness in 1163, aged only 24.

William I the Lion was the brother of Malcolm IV and succeeded him on the throne. His flag was a red lion on a yellow background and it would become Scotland's royal standard. After failing to retake Northumbria from the English, William joined the revolt against Henry II, led by Henry's wife and sons, in 1173. During the Battle of Alnwick the following summer, William charged the English shouting, 'Now we shall see which of us are good knights.' He was captured and taken to Normandy, and Scotland was occupied.

William I was released after agreeing to acknowledge Henry and to pay for an army of occupation, but the Scots rebelled against the Treaty of Falaise. Henry II had also chosen William's bride, a low-status relative called Ermengarde. The hated treaty ended in 1189, after William gave money for Richard the Lionheart's Crusade and Scotland regained its independence.

Richard the Lionheart's successor, King John, secured his northern regions by moving an army towards Scotland in 1209 and William I betrothed his only son to King John's young daughter Joan to maintain the peace.

William died in 1214 and his teenage son Alexander II joined the English barons revolting against King John. When Prince Louis of France arrived in England to attempt to claim the English throne from John, Alexander marched south from Scotland to pay homage to Louis. But when John died and his young son Henry was a popular replacement, Louis and Alexander returned home.

England and Scotland agreed the Treaty of York in 1237, defining their common border, and Alexander was in the process of securing the Western Islands when he died in 1248.

Alexander II's 7-year-old son Alexander III succeeded his father. He was betrothed to the young daughter of Henry III, but the Justiciar of Scotia and the Earl of Menteith argued over the regency until Menteith kidnapped the king; they shared control.

Alexander claimed the Western Isles when he reached his majority, provoking retaliation from Norway, who had traditionally ruled there. Håkon IV of Norway launched an expedition to the islands, but Alexander dragged out the talks, preventing Håkon from sailing home before winter, and the Norwegian king died in the Orkneys. Håkon's successor agreed to sell the Isle of Man and the Western Isles under the 1266 Treaty of Perth.

Alexander III's son died in 1284 so he made his granddaughter his heir – Margaret, Maid of Norway, daughter of Eric II of Norway and Margaret of Scotland. Nonetheless he remained desperate for a male heir, so he married a French noblewoman, Yolande of

Dreux, and was delighted when she fell pregnant. After a drunken night in Edinburgh Castle, he rode alone to give his spouse a surprise birthday visit, only to fall from his horse and break his neck en route. Yolande lost their child and Margaret, Maid of Norway took the throne, but died en route from Norway to her new realm in 1290, ending the line of William I.

In the absence of an heir, four guardians were appointed to rule Scotland while thirteen candidates were considered, with Edward I of England as the arbitrator. This was known as 'the Great Cause'. The result of these deliberations was that John de Balliol, great-grandson of David, brother of William I the Lion, was inaugurated on St Andrew's Day 1292.

Edward I immediately demanded an alliance. Instead John de Balliol signed a treaty of mutual assistance with France (the forebear for the Auld Alliance). In response Edward I invaded Scotland and defeated John at Dunbar in 1296. He ripped the Scottish arms from John's surcoat, earning John the name 'Empty Coat'. John was imprisoned in the Tower of London for three years and then allowed to go to the Continent, leaving the crown of Scotland and the Great Seal of Scotland behind. He would never return to Scotland.

A period of uncertainty followed, in which Scotland was once more ruled by guardians. One of these was William Wallace, who held the position until he was defeated in battle in 1298. He was executed in 1305 for rebelling against Edward I's rule.

He was succeeded by Robert the Bruce and John Comyn, but this alliance soon broke down. Robert and John Comyn allied once more against the English king, but Comyn betrayed Robert the Bruce. As a result of this Robert killed John Comyn in 1306 and was excommunicated by the pope. Robert seized the throne six weeks after Comyn's death, but he was defeated in battle by Edward I and forced into hiding. He returned to win the Battle of Loudoun Hill in 1307 and then regained prestige for Scotland by defeating Edward II at Bannockburn in 1314. Robert invaded the north of England while his brother Edward invaded Ireland, hoping to start an uprising. Pope John XXII recognised Robert as king while the Franco-Scottish alliance was renewed in the Treaty of Corbeil in 1326. Edward III finally renounced all claims to Scottish sovereignty under the Treaty of Northampton.

Robert died in 1329, leaving the throne to his 5-year-old son David II, who was already married to Edward II's daughter Joan. Scotland's pride was dented when Edward III defeated their army at Dupplin in 1332 and crowned the pretender, Edward Balliol. David's supporters launched a surprise attack on the Balliol as he slept, and he fled half-naked to England. He returned with an army but was defeated at Halidon Hill in 1333.

David and Joan had been sent to France for their safety; they returned in 1341. David invaded England only to be captured at the Battle of Neville's Cross in 1346. Following this defeat David was imprisoned for eleven years. He was released in 1357 to raise his ransom. He attempted to pay his dues by promising Scotland to Edward after his death, or by handing over a son. Edward rejected this because he wanted money. David promised to pay but was unable to raise the money, so he began protracted negotiations for peace with England instead, to appease the English king.

David II died in 1371, leaving the throne to his nephew, Robert II. Robert recaptured southern Scotland from England by 1384 and then obtained Scotland's inclusion in an Anglo-French peace. But his son John was impatient for the throne and he staged a coup before defeating the English at the Battle of Otterburn in 1388.

Robert II died in 1390 and John was crowned as Robert III. To his brother Robert's disgust, he handed control to his son David when he fell ill in 1399, resulting in a fraternal quarrel. David was murdered in his uncle's castle in 1402, and though Robert was cleared of responsibility for his death, there were concerns for Robert III's other son, James.

In 1406, young James was en route to France when his ship was involved in a clash with his uncle's supporters and forced to anchor off Bass Rock Island in the Firth of Forth. He was rescued a month later, but the new ship was captured by pirates who took James to Henry IV of England for a reward. Robert III died after learning of his son's imprisonment.

James, now James I of Scotland, would be held for eighteen years, during which time his cousin Murdoch Stewart was governor of Scotland. James developed a respect for the English, even serving with Henry V in his 1420–21 campaign against the French. Hostages were eventually sent as a ransom and on his return, in a bid to assert his authority, James executed Governor Murdoch and his sons, and then arrested Alexander, Lord of the Isles. He also forgot about the hostages in England and spent the ransom money on fine buildings instead. As such, he was not altogether popular. One who turned against James was Robert II's son and James's uncle, Walter Stewart. He had the king assassinated in 1437 – he was killed trying to escape his attackers along a sewer tunnel under Blackfriars Monastery. Walter then tried to kill James's wife Joan, but Joan, although injured, escaped and reached her son in Edinburgh Castle and his position as successor was secured. Walter and Sir Robert Graham, the assassin, were beheaded the day after young James II was crowned.

Joan married Sir John Stewart in 1439 and the lieutenant general, the Earl of Douglas, placed them both under house arrest while James was transferred to Sir Alexander Livingston's custody. After the Earl of Douglas died, his two young sons were invited to dine with James in Edinburgh Castle. They were then beheaded in what would be called 'the Black Dinner'.

James executed Alexander and his son when he came of age in 1449 and then stabbed the Earl of Douglas to death, living up to his nickname 'Fiery Face' (referring to a facial birthmark). He would defeat the new Earl of Douglas at the Battle of Arkinholm in 1455 but his downfall was his love of artillery. James was killed when a gun exploded as he lit the powder.

A young James III was crowned in 1460 and his marriage to Margaret of Denmark ended the annual tribute Scotland had been paying for the Western Isles. The Orkney and Shetland Islands were also part of the dowry but James annexed the islands rather than acknowledging the arrangement. James had married his sister to Sir Alexander Boyd, but Alexander and his family were executed and the marriage was declared void when he challenged the king.

James's brother, John, died suspiciously in 1480 and his other brother, Alexander, fled to France accused of treason. He returned to Scotland with the Duke of Gloucester (the future Richard III of England) in 1482, arrested James and became lieutenant general. But James bribed his way to freedom and Alexander fled to France. He would be killed jousting in Paris in 1485. Rebels wishing to depose James III seized his young son, James, and used him as their figurehead to rally support. James III was killed at the Battle of Sauchieburn in 1488, leaving a teenage James IV as king, and a guilty one at that. He paid penance for his father's death by wearing a cilice chain (a weighted metal chain) around his waist every Lent.

James eventually brought the Lord of the Isles under control. He then invaded England in 1496 on behalf of Perkin Warbeck, who claimed to be one of the English 'Princes in the Tower', in a challenge against Henry VII. He would establish good relations with England after Warbeck was executed.

2

SCANDINAVIA

S CANDINAVIA SLOWLY EMERGED FROM THE pagan Viking era with the establishment of royal authority and the arrival of Christianity. Norway owned the Scottish Western Isles (the Outer Hebrides) until 1266 and the Orkney and Shetland Islands until 1469. Sweden established rule in what is now Finland in the 1100s and the area became part of Sweden in 1249. Denmark was slowly mortgaged to German princes until the Black Death arrived in 1349 and the high mortality rate allowed the survivors to become strong again.

Norway, Sweden and Denmark alternately fought and then married to ally with each other. That is, until they entered the Kalmar Union under Queen Margaret I of Denmark in 1397, in which they were supposed to be treated equally. But Denmark was clearly the senior partner while Sweden kept trying to reassert its independence.

THE KINGDOM OF NORWAY

Norway occupied the western side of the Scandinavian Peninsula (not the northern regions of modern Norway) and the islands surrounding Scotland. Magnus the Good defeated a challenge by Sweyn Estridsson at Lyrskov Heath in 1043. Sweyn allied with Harald Hardrada so Magnus made his uncle co-king and together they drove Sweyn out. Harald had fought as a mercenary in Russia and the Byzantine Empire and he made a claim for the Danish throne after he was crowned king in 1046. Tostig, exiled brother of the English king Harold Godwinson, invited Harald the Hard Ruler to claim the English throne, so he invaded northern England in 1066, only to be killed at the Battle of Stamford Bridge.

Magnus had been crowned king before Harald left for England, but he gave south-east Norway to his teenage brother Olaf when he returned. Olaf ruled all Norway after Magnus died of an illness and he founded the city of Bergen in 1070. He made peace with Denmark by marrying Sweyn, King of Denmark's daughter and married his half-sister to Svend's son. Olaf, known as 'the Peaceful', also made a truce with William the Conqueror of England. Olaf died in 1093.

From 1093, Olaf's illegitimate son Magnus III Barefoot ruled the south from Viken, while his cousin Håkon ruled the north from Trondheim. But Norway's barons rebelled against Magnus. Magnus stopped their uprising and hanged Håkon's adoptive father, Tore pa Steig, who was behind the rebellion.

Magnus was left in control of all Norway when Håkon died in 1095 and he raided the Orkneys, the Hebrides, the Isle of Man and Anglesey before leading campaigns into Sweden. The Danish king Eric Evergood initiated peace talks among the three Scandinavian monarchs and Magnus married Margaret, daughter of King Inge of Sweden, to seal an alliance.

Magnus invaded Ireland and had just forced King Muirchertach to recognise Norwegian control of Dublin when he was ambushed and killed in 1103. Norway was left to his three illegitimate sons: teenage Sigurd I returned from Ireland to rule the south and Eystein ruled the north; they both acted as regent for their brother Olaf, who died of illness while still a teenager.

Eystein stayed at home but Sigurd went on Crusade to Jerusalem and helped King Baldwin of Jerusalem to conquer Sidon. He returned via Constantinople, exchanged his ships for horses and rode back across Europe, arriving back in Norway in 1111. Eystein died in 1123, leaving no male heir until a young man named Harald Gille arrived from Ireland, declaring that he was an illegitimate son of Magnus Barefoot. Though the claim was proved by a trial by fire, Harald agreed not to claim Norway's throne.

Sigurd died in 1130, leaving several illegitimate sons – in an age when competence decided who was king rather than legitimacy. It was Magnus IV the Blind who prevailed, and he divided the country with Harald Gille.

He later defeated Harald at the Battle of Farlev in 1134. He then disbanded his army for the winter and was sheltering in Bergen when the exiled Harald returned with Danish support. Harald captured Magnus and had him blinded and castrated, and cut off his leg before sending him to a monastery.

Another of Magnus Barefoot's sons, Sigurd the Noisy, then murdered Harald in his bed and made the blinded Magnus IV his co-king to legitimise his rule. But the barons accused Sigurd and Magnus of murdering their king and they were defeated at the Battle of Minne by supporters of Harald's son, the infant Inge the Hunchback. Sigurd and Magnus rallied Danish support only to be defeated at the naval Battle of Holmengrå in 1139; Magnus was killed, Sigurd was captured. Sigurd was scalped, flayed and his limbs and spine were broken by hammers. He was then hanged, decapitated and his body thrown down a scree of rocks for good measure.

Harald left four sons: the aforementioned Inge the Hunchback, Sigurd the Mouth, Eystein and Magnus. The latter died young in 1145, leaving the other three to squabble over power. Inge the Hunchback murdered Sigurd the Mouth at a peace meeting in Bergen in 1155, accusing him of planning to dethrone him. Eystein had missed the meeting so his men deserted him and he was captured and executed by Inge in 1157. Sigurd's and Eystein's supporters united behind Sigurd's young son, Håkon II, known as 'the Broad Shouldered'. Håkon's supporters killed Inge near Oslo in 1161.

But it was not long before Håkon II was killed in turn by a new contender, Erling Skakke, at the Battle of Sekken in 1162. Inge the Hunchback's supporters now rallied behind Erling's young son, Magnus, instead. His supporters were called the Heklungs (the Hoods) because of their connection with the Church. Magnus V was crowned King of Norway in 1161. However, Eystein's grandson, Olav the Unlucky, was proclaimed king while Erling and Magnus were visiting Denmark. Erling was heading back to regain control when he was ambushed at Rydjokul, barely escaping with his life. Olav the Unlucky was defeated at the Battle of Stanger in 1168, and he fled to Denmark, where he died the following year.

Sigurd II's son, Sverre, came to Norway in 1177 and became leader of the Heklungs' rivals, the Birkebeiners (the 'Birch Legs', because they used birch bark for shoes). Sverre's power base increased after Erling was killed at the Battle of Kalvskinnet in 1179, but Magnus still had Danish support on his side. Sverre twice defeated the Heklungs on land, at the battles of Ilevollene and Nordnes, and then destroyed two of his fleets. Magnus was drowned at the Battle of Fimreite in 1184, ending the Heklungs' struggle for Norway.

Magnus's son, Sigurd, raised support in the Orkney and Shetland Islands but the 'Isle Beards', as they were known, were defeated at the Battle of Florvåg in 1194 and teenage Sigurd's corpse was displayed in Bergen to prove he was dead.

Sverre expected to be crowned, but the Bishop of Stavanger excommunicated the king slayer with Pope Celestine III's support. Although Pope Innocent III later sent a letter annulling the excommunication, the bishop bearing it pawned it en route and then died under suspicious circumstances. The pawnbrokers delivered a fake letter to Sverre, but he himself was accused of forgery and Norway was placed under an interdict. Innocent told Sweden and Denmark to depose Sverre but he calmly bought them both off.

The Baglers were Sverre's new enemy. They controlled the Viken region in the southeast of Norway, with Inge as their leader and Oslo as their capital. They then invaded Birkebeiner territory, burnt Bergen and forced Sverre to flee, so he rallied support and defeated the Baglers' fleet in Strindafjord in 1199. Sverre died of illness and Inge was murdered by his own men in 1202.

Sverre had declared that the illegitimate Håkon was his only son on his deathbed – he was crowned Håkon III, and his reign was brief but troubled. He prevented his father's queen, Margareta, returning to Sweden and took her daughter Kristina from her, to stop them challenging his position. When he died in 1204 following a bloodletting, Margareta was accused of poisoning him. She was found guilty when one of her men failed a trial by fire, so she fled to Sweden.

As Håkon had no children, his 4-year-old nephew Guttorm was proclaimed king, with Håkon the Crazy — a grandson of Sigurd the Mouth — as his regent. But the infant king died shortly afterwards and Håkon's fiancée, Swedish noblewoman Kristina Nikolasdotter, was accused of poisoning him. Håkon was considered unsuited to be crowned. Instead, Guttorm was succeeded by Håkon's brother Inge II, leader of the Birkebeiner faction, with Håkon taking a prominent position under him.

Erling Stonewall declared himself Magnus's illegitimate son and Valdemar II of Denmark sent an army to Norway to support him. Erling passed a trial to become the Bagler's leader and challenger to Inge. Erling attacked Nidaros Castle during the wedding of Inge's sister and Inge swam the Nidelva River to escape. Erling died in 1207 and his successor, Philip, agreed a compromise with Inge serving as senior king while Håkon ruled the west and Philip ruled the east.

Inge and Håkon agreed a legitimate son would inherit both their lands, only to fall out when Håkon had a legitimate son and Inge had an illegitimate son. However, this never came to pass, as Håkon died in 1214 and Inge took over his lands. Both Philip and Inge died in 1217, leaving the succession in turmoil once more.

Håkon III had died in January 1204. A few months later his mistress Inga of Varteig gave birth to a son, also named Håkon, who she claimed was Håkon's illegitimate son. Unfortunately, they were in enemy territory, which put them in danger, and two Birkebeiner warriors had to ski through a blizzard with the infant Håkon, pursued by Baglers, to deliver him to Inge.

While there were several claimants for the throne of Inge II following his death in 1217, after Inga passed a trial to prove her son's legitimacy Håkon became the frontrunner. One of the other candidates, Inge's half-brother Earl Skule Bårdsson, settled for acting as his regent. Håkon was crowned Håkon IV, and married Skule's daughter, Margret, in 1225.

Håkon reunified the Birkebeiners and the Baglers but he had to put down an uprising by a new Bagler pretender, Sigurd Ribbung. Skule would also proclaim himself king in 1239 so Håkon IV had him executed and in order to strengthen his own postion declared his young son, also Håkon, co-ruler. They became known as Håkon the Old and Håkon the Young respectively. This strong move effectively ended Norway's civil wars.

Håkon the Young became embroiled in a war against Denmark in 1256 only to die soon after. Håkon the Old retaliated by abducting Princess Ingeborg from a monastery in 1261 and marrying her to his son Magnus, aiming to claim the inheritance of her murdered father, Christopher of Denmark. Around the same time, Greenland submitted, Iceland was captured and the Hebrides were retaken. Håkon the Old had extended Norway's territory to the largest it had ever been.

Håkon the Old visited Scotland in 1262 to negotiate ownership of the Western Isles but Alexander III of Scotland prolonged the talks. Håkon was forced to spend the winter in the Orkneys, where his fleet was destroyed by storms and he himself died.

Håkon the Old's son Magnus was proclaimed king under the law of succession of the oldest legitimate son and became known as 'the Law Mender'. He sold the Hebrides and the Isle of Man to Scotland, while Scotland recognised Norwegian rule over the Shetlands and Orkneys under the 1266 Treaty of Perth.

Magnus died of illness in 1280, and while he was succeeded by his young son, Eirik II, his mother and the barons wielded the power.

Eirik became known as 'the Priest Hater' because of his difficult relations with the Church; he also became known for claiming others' territories. Eirik married Margaret of Scotland in 1281, but she died in childbirth two years later. Their daughter Margaret would be infant Queen of Scotland from 1286 to 1290, and Eirik would try to claim Scotland through his daughter. Similarly, Eirik allied with outlawed Danish nobles accused of murdering Erik V of Denmark and tried to claim the latter's lands through the lineage of his mother Ingeborg, who was daughter of King Erik IV of Denmark. Eirik II later married Isabel Bruce, sister of Robert the Bruce, but they had a daughter rather than the hoped-for son, thwarting his plan to seize Scotland.

With no direct heir, Eirik was succeeded by his brother, Håkon V, in 1299. He moved the Norwegian capital from Bergen to Oslo. He had just one legitimate daughter, who was married to the brother of the King of Sweden. Their son was to succeed his grandfather when Håkon V died in 1319.

Magnus VII of Norway was also Magnus IV of Sweden. Unfortunately his decision to make his favourite courtier, Bengt Algotsson, Duke of Finland and Viceroy of Scania was unpopular with adversaries; they called him 'the Caresser' and spread rumours that he was homosexual, a mortal sin at the time. His son Håkon VI was given the Norwegian throne in 1343, while his father continued to rule in Sweden.

Håkon became co-ruler of Sweden with Magnus in 1362 after Eric died. In 1363 he married Margaret, daughter of Valdemar IV of Denmark, but relations with his father-in-law were strained. This conflict lasted until Valdemar died in 1375.

A group of exiled Swedish noblemen deposed father and son in Sweden in favour of Albert of Mecklenburg in 1363, leading to years of war between the factions, but Magnus and Håkon were unable to retake the Swedish throne from Albert.

Young Olaf II became King of Norway when his father died in 1380, with his mother as regent. Olaf died suddenly as a teenager, possibly from poisoning, in 1387, and his mother continued to rule alone. Albert had mocked Margaret, calling her 'King Pantsless' when the nobles promised her the regency, but when Albert's army of mercenaries invaded Norway in 1389 it was routed and Albert was imprisoned, leaving 'King Pantsless' as ruler of the three Scandinavian kingdoms by 1397.

Margaret had adopted her grand-nephew Boguslaw. She renamed him Eric of Pomerania and hailed him King Eric III of Norway in 1389. She remained overall ruler of the three kingdoms in the Kalmar Union until she died on board her ship in Flensburg harbour in 1412. The Norwegian nobility incited peasant rebellions to undermine Eric II's rule and he turned to piracy after he was deposed in 1440.

Christopher the Bavarian then ruled Norway from Denmark, but his reign was blighted by famine and he was called the 'Bark King' when his people were forced to eat ground tree bark mixed with flour.

Christopher's death in 1448 resulted in the partial break-up of the union. Charles of Sweden was crowned King of Norway but renounced his claim six months later, after Denmark and Norway decided to elect the same ruler from among Christopher's legitimate sons. Christian I ruled from Denmark until 1481, but he struggled to bring Norway under his rule because it wanted to be an independent kingdom.

THE KINGDOM OF SWEDEN

At this time Sweden occupied the eastern side of the Scandinavian Peninsula and the west coast of modern-day Finland (on the north-east coast of the Baltic Sea).

The early history of the Swedish throne is not well known. Anund Jacob was King of Sweden from 1022 until around 1050. He became known as 'the Coal-Burner' because he razed so many of his opponents' houses to the ground. His successor, Emund the Bad, was so called because he supported an English missionary called Osmundus instead of Sweden's pagan priests. His son-in-law Stenkil became king in 1060 and he promoted Christianity.

Following his death there were two contenders for the throne: his son, Eric Stenkilsson, and Eric the Pagan. They died fighting one another over the crown in 1067. After their deaths the throne was taken by Håkan the Red in Gothenland and Anund Gårdske. But Anund Gårdske was deposed in around 1070 after refusing to make sacrifices at the Uppsala Temple and Håkan the Red then ruled alone for a decade.

Stenkil's sons Inge the Elder and Halsten came to power after Håkan the Red. Inge the Elder was a devout Christian who refused to respect Sweden's traditional practices. He cancelled animal sacrifices at the temple and was stoned by the Swedish people and forced to abdicate in favour of his brother-in-law Sweyn the Sacrificer. Sweyn took the throne and reintroduced the pagan rituals. He sentenced the Englishman Bishop Eskil to death by stoning to try to stop the spread of Christianity. Sweyn was burnt to death when Inge set his home on fire in 1087. Inge re-established Christianity across Sweden but he was at war with Norway until 1101.

Inge's son, Ragnvald, died before he could succeed his father on the throne. Instead Inge's nephews Inge the Younger and Philip, sons of his brother Halsten, were crowned co-kings in 1110, but Philip died in 1118.

Inge the Younger is believed to have fought off a Norwegian invasion in 1123, but died shortly afterwards. There were suspicions that his wife Ulvhild had poisoned his drink. She went on to marry the Danish king, Nils Svensson, and then the Swedish king, Sverker the Elder.

His successor was Ragnvald – little is known about him. He was elected king by the Upplanders and strengthened his position when he was acknowledged by the East Gothlanders. His arrogant attitude earned him his nickname, Knaphövde, the name of a large drinking vessel – a reference to his empty-headedness. The Geats of West Gothland murdered him in 1126 and elected a Danish prince called Magnus the Strong in his place. He was a grandson of Inge the Elder.

Magnus I was ousted by a rival, Sverker I Clubfoot, who conquered his lands and then invaded the new Republic of Novgorod, a medieval Russian state, in 1142, ending a century of peace. Sverker was murdered at a Christmas Day service in 1156, possibly by the pretender Magnus Henriksson – another of Inge the Elder's grandsons.

Eric IX the Lawgiver then took the throne. He consolidated Christianity in Sweden but the nobles hated paying tax to the Church, so they supported his Danish rival Magnus Henriksson, who held power in Gothland. He had Eric dragged from his horse, tortured and beheaded after a church service in 1160 – only to meet his own grisly end, murdered by Charles's men at the Battle of Örebro in 1161, after only the briefest of reigns.

Charles VII of Sweden reigned from 1161, until Canute I, the son of Eric IX the Lawgiver, returned home after ten years in exile and murdered Charles in 1167. He then defeated Sverker I's sons in 1173 and proclaimed himself king. He built a castle on the island of Stockholm in 1187 and the surrounding settlement would soon grow into the country's capital.

Sverker II the Younger had been raised in Denmark after Canute I murdered his father Charles VII, and Canute IV of Denmark supported him, hoping to destabilise Sweden. Sverker was chosen as the next king when Canute I died in 1196 and he returned home and exiled Canute's four young sons to Norway. They would return with an army in 1205, but three were killed during Sverker's victory at the Battle of Älgarås. The fourth, Eric X the Survivor, defeated Sverker with Norwegian support at the Battle of Lena in 1208. Sverker raised Danish support but was defeated and killed at the Battle of Gestilren in 1210. Eric X married Princess Richeza to make peace with Denmark, but he died of fever in 1216, leaving his wife pregnant.

Sverker's teenage son John took the throne, despite Rome's objections, but he died aged 21, unmarried and childless. Eric the Survivor's young posthumous son, Eric XI the Lame, was crowned but his supporters were defeated by Canute II the Tall at the Battle of Olustra in 1229 and Eric fled to Denmark.

When Canute died Eric returned as king, but he had no sons and so he was succeeded by his nephew, Valdemar IV, in 1250. However, Valdemar's father held the real power and continued to rule even after Valdemar came of age.

Valdemar was married to Sofia, daughter of Eric V of Denmark, but he had an affair with her sister, Jutta, and she had a child in 1272. Jutta was locked in a convent while Valdemar visited Rome to ask Pope Innocent IV for absolution. Sofia's father was outraged and helped Valdemar's brothers Magnus and Eric defeat Valdemar at Hova in 1275. Sofia was made to return to Denmark and Magnus was elected king.

Magnus III was known as 'Barn Lock' because he introduced a law which meant that the yeomanry did not have to grant free hospitality to travelling nobles and bishops; the shout 'peasants, lock your barns' was heard when they approached. Valdemar briefly seized southern Sweden in 1277 but Magnus captured him in 1288 and he was 'imprisoned' – living in comfort with the company of mistresses.

Magnus III died two years later and his young son Birger became king with the Lord High Constable of Sweden as his guardian; he was soon married to Princess Martha of Denmark. A noble called Torgils supported Birger in a feud against his brothers, dukes Erik and Valdemar, but was later beheaded as a gesture of peace when the brothers acknowledged Birger as king.

The peace did not last long. During the feast of the Håtuna games in 1306, dukes Erik and Valdemar imprisoned Birger. The Danish king soon forced them to release the king, but he had to give up the royal domain while Erik and Valdemar were married to Norwegian princesses. Birger secured his revenge when he arrested Erik and Valdemar during the Nyköping banquet and starved them to death in the castle dungeons in 1317. But their supporters succeeded in ousting the king the following year, exiling him to Denmark and executing his son Magnus.

Mats Kettilmundsson was regent until Duke Erik's infant son Magnus IV was crowned king in 1319, but the Norwegian noble Erling Vidkunsson ruled Sweden until Magnus came of age in 1331.

Magnus broke his alliance with Novgorod in 1348 but his invasion of the province was stopped when the plague swept across the country. His sons, Erik and Håkon, had been elected heirs of Sweden and Norway, but the Swedish nobles wanted Magnus replaced because he made his favourite courtier Duke of Finland and Viceroy of Scania. Magnus had agreed Håkon could be his co-ruler of Norway, but an impatient Erik rebelled in 1357 and forced Magnus to share Sweden with him. Erik accused his mother Blanche of poisoning him when he fell ill soon afterwards but she died too. They were both victims of the plague.

The Swedish Council of Aristocracy, banished by Magnus during Eric's rebellion, visited Albert of Mecklenburg, Magnus IV's nephew, looking for his support in 1363. Albert invaded and was proclaimed King of Sweden while Magnus fled to Norway. It was the start of eight years of civil war. Magnus was imprisoned following the Battle of Gataskogen in 1365, but Albert was becoming increasingly unpopular and an alliance of Håkon's Norwegian forces and the Danish under Valdemar IV besieged him in Stockholm in 1371; Albert was victorious, but a peace treaty was signed as a result of which Magnus was released and returned to Norway in 1374; unfortunately he drowned en route when his ship sank.

Albert had secured the throne but he had been forced to make huge concessions to the Swedish nobility. The tide turned against him once again in 1389, and the Swedish Council of Aristocracy turned to Margaret of Denmark for help. She defeated and captured Albert at the Battle of Asle and took control of Stockholm.

Sweden was under Danish control for forty-five years, ruled by Margaret I until 1412 and then by Eric of Pomerania until mine workers and peasants, led by nobleman Engelbrekt Engelbrektsson, rebelled against his high taxes in 1434. But the Swedish nobility hijacked the rebellion and threw their support behind leading nobleman Karl Knutsson, who was to become Charles VIII. Engelbrekt was assassinated in 1436 but he became a national hero as public protector and opponent of the Kalmar Union.

Sweden was once more under Danish rule and Christopher the Bavarian ruled until 1448, while Bengt and Nils Jonsson acted as his co-regents under the Kalmar Union. Charles VIII was crowned when Christopher died but the Danish elected Christian while Norway elected Charles. Christian wanted the Norwegian crown but Charles refused to step down, so Sweden and Denmark went to war.

Charles increased taxes and confiscated Church property until nobleman Erik Axelsson and Archbishop Jons Bengtsson forced him into exile in 1457. Christian I replaced him but he too argued with the archbishop, so Bengtsson excommunicated him. Christian retaliated by imprisoning the archbishop. When the exiled Charles XIII Christian was forced to abdicate. In a bid to recover power he made peace with Archbishop Bengtsson who took up his cause. Archbishop Bengtsson twice defeated Charles's mercenary army. Although Christian I once again became King of Sweden, the archbishop held the real power. Dissatisfaction with the archbishop's reign led to Erik Axelsson being elected regent, but he later avowed his support for Charles XIII, who retook the throne once more.

Archbishop Bengtsson died 'poor and exiled, regretted by no one, hated by many, and feared by all'.

Charles XIII died in 1470, leaving a young son, Charles, by his mistress Kristina, whom he had married on his deathbed. Although Prince Charles had been legitimised, the Swedish government appointed Sten Sture as their regent instead. Sten Sture refused Danish demands for reunion and defeated Christian I's Swedes and Danes at the Battle of Brunkeberg in 1471. Sten also faced a Russian invasion of Finland in 1495 and the Swedish nobility had deposed him by the time it had been turned back. Christian I's son, John of Denmark and Norway, worked with Russia to undermine Sten Sture, and the Russo-Swedish War began in 1496. John defeated Sten Sture with support of the Swedish nobility at the Battle of Rotebro in 1497 and his coronation reunited the Kalmar Union countries once more.

THE KINGDOM OF DENMARK

At this time Denmark occupied the Danish Peninsula, the southern tip of modern Sweden and the islands in between, at the entrance to the Baltic Sea.

King Magnus the Good had wanted to split his kingdom between his sons, with Harald to inherit Norway and Sweyn to inherit Denmark, but the brothers fought. Sweyn nearly captured Harald in 1050 and then barely escaped with his life at the naval Battle of Niså in 1062. They made peace and recognised each other's claims two years later. Sweyn then joined Edgar Atheling's invasion of England in 1069. While they captured York, Sweyn accepted money from William the Conqueror to leave Edgar and return home. He made a second unsuccessful attempt to capture England in 1074.

On one occasion Sweyn was apparently ridiculed by his guests during New Year's Eve celebrations so he murdered them in church the following day. He then dressed in sackcloth and cast himself face down in front of Roskilde Cathedral so that Bishop Vilhelm would lift his excommunication.

While Sweyn fathered over twenty children, five of them future kings, only one was legitimate – Svend Svendsen, who died young. Instead he was succeeded by one of his illegitimate sons, Harald III Hen, who deplored the Danish customs of trial by combat and ordeal by fire; instead he had his men swear oaths to prove their allegiance.

Harald's brother, Canute had gone into exile following Harald's succession, but came out of exile when Harald died in 1086 to take the throne as Canute IV. Canute believed the crown of England belonged to him and made plans to invade; the expedition was thwarted by the threat of invasion of Danish territory in Schleswig by the Holy Roman Emperor Henry IV. Canute's brother Olaf was exiled after asking if the invasion could be delayed further to let his people collect their harvest. Canute postponed the invasion until the following year, but the peasants rebelled and he and his brother Benedict were murdered while taking refuge in a church. Canute would later become the patron saint of Denmark.

Thus, in 1086, Olaf I, a fourth son of Sweyn's, was recalled from Flanders to take the throne and his younger brother Niels took his place in exile. But Denmark was struck by famine, which the people considered a divine punishment for the killing of Canute, and Olaf, who had earned the nickname 'the Hunger', died in suspicious circumstances.

The famine ended when Eric I Evergood was crowned in 1095, which was taken as a divine sign. Unfortunately, his reputation was tarnished when he drunkenly murdered four men at a feast. He went on an expiatory pilgrimage to the Holy Land only to fall ill and die in Cyprus in 1103.

The fifth son of Sweyn, Niels, was duly recalled from Flanders and crowned, but it was his wife, Margaret, daughter of Inge I of Sweden, who made all the decisions until she died. Niels's son, Magnus, was King of Sweden; Denmark unsuccessfully went to war to defend Magnus when he was dethroned in 1130, and Magnus returned the favour when his father faced rebellion in 1131.

Eric, Eric I's illegitimate son, had been elected anti-king and although his rapid retreat in the face of multiple defeats by Magnus earned him the nickname 'Harefoot', he was renamed Eric the Memorable after he killed Magnus at the Battle of Foteviken in 1134. Niels retreated, seeking refuge with Emperor Lothar III of Germany. En route he was warned not to enter the former rebel city of Schleswig, and famously replied, 'Should I fear tanners and shoemakers?' He should have heeded the warning because he was promptly killed in the town.

Eric II the Memorable was proclaimed king. He promptly murdered his half-brother, Harald the Spear, who had returned to attempt to claim the throne, as well as all Harald's sons except one, Olaf. Eric was an unpopular ruler and a nobleman called Sorte Plov planned to assassinate him in 1137. He asked permission to speak to Eric and then kicked off the block of wood covering his spear tip and stabbed the king. Eric's nephew, Eric, stepped forward to kill the assassin only to be told, 'Put away thine mace, young Eric. A juicy piece of meat hath fallen in thine bowl!' The murder had made him king.

Eric III the Lamb was challenged by Eric's surviving son, Olaf, until his death in battle near Helsingborg in 1141. Five years later Eric III abdicated, probably through illness, leaving no legitimate heir.

From 1146, Canute V ruled Jutland and Sweyn III ruled Zeeland. Canute was the son of Magnus of Sweden and grandson of King Niels, while Sweyn was the illegitimate brother of Eric III the Lamb. A third claimant was Valdemar, Duke of Schleswig, a grandson of Eric I. He helped Sweyn banish Canute from Jutland and then exiled Sweyn when he refused to hand over the lands he was promised as a reward. But Sweyn visited his childhood friend Emperor Friedrich Barbarossa and returned from Germany in 1157 with the military might of Henry the Lion, a powerful German prince, behind him.

The three claimants decided in principle to split Denmark in three. Sweyn called a meeting to discuss the details, but he had no plans to share power: Canute was murdered and an injured Valdemar escaped what became known as 'the Blood Feast of Roskilde'. Valdemar won the Battle of Grathe Heath a few weeks later while Sweyn was killed by peasants when his horse became bogged in a marsh. Valdemar spent the next twenty-five years rebuilding Denmark.

Canute VI, son of Valdemar, had been co-ruler with his father from 1170, and following his father's death he was crowned king in 1182. Almost immediately he went on the rampage after defeating a peasant uprising at the Battle of Dysjcbro.

In 1184, the Holy Roman Emperor Friedrich Barbarossa sent Canute a reminder that his father Valdemar had promised to acknowledge him as overlord; Canute ignored the request. Enraged, Friederich ordered Bogislaw of Pomerania to invade but his fleet was routed by Bishop Absalon at Rugen, leaving Canute ruling a vast area of northern Europe. Canute allowed his young brother, Prince Valdemar, to rule southern Denmark but his protector, Bishop Valdemar, plotted to overthrow the king and make it look like Prince Valdemar had planned the conspiracy. The prince and the bishop were imprisoned, and when Count Adolph of Rendsburg invaded southern Jutland to rescue the bishop he too was captured, during the Battle of Stellau in 1201. Canute imprisoned the count in the cell next to the bishop, so they could talk.

Canute's wife, Gertrude, had chosen a life of celibacy, so Canute eventually released his brother Valdemar to succeed him. The Teutonic Knights asked for Danish help in the eastern Baltic in 1219 but the Estonian chiefs raided the Danish camp after agreeing to acknowledge Valdemar II. Legend says a red cloth with a white cross drifted from the sky and a voice was heard to say, 'When this banner is raised on high, you shall be victorious!' The Danes won, Valdemar became known as 'the Victorious' and the

Estonian people were forcibly baptised. Valdemar ordered a new fortress called Tallinn (which translates as Danish Castle) to be built and the legendary banner was adopted by Denmark; it is Europe's oldest flag.

Count Henry I of Schwerin abducted Valdemar and his eldest son while they were out hunting in 1223. In response, Denmark declared war on the Holy Roman Empire but was defeated by Albert II of Orlamunde at the Battle of Mölln in 1225. The Danes had to agree to pay a ransom, promise not to seek revenge and acknowledge German territories. Pope Honorius III told Valdemar he could ignore the oath, but Valdemar's counter-attack was defeated at the Battle of Bornhöved in 1227. Valdemar continued hunting until he was killed in an accident in 1231.

Valdemar's eldest son predeceased him, and so his second son succeeded him as Eric IV. Eric was known as 'Plough Penny' because his taxes were determined by the number of ploughs a man owned. He also wanted to tax the Church but confiscated its properties instead when he was threatened with excommunication. Eric's brother Abel of Schleswig tried to win his independence until their sister, Sophie, arranged a truce between them. Abel later offered Eric hospitality while he was campaigning in Holstein in 1250 but a chamberlain imprisoned the king, took him out in a boat and beheaded him.

Abel swore he had not murdered his brother but most thought he had and said 'Abel by name, Cain by deeds'. Sicko Sjaerdema led a rebellion of Frisia's peasants against rising taxes. Abel defeated them and killed their leader near Eiderstedt in 1252. Eric's other brother, Christopher, blamed Abel for his brother's death and asked Pope Innocent IV to canonise Eric, to exclude Abel's sons from the succession. When that failed, Abel's son, Valdemar, was imprisoned while Christopher was crowned.

Archbishop Jacob Erlandsen excommunicated Christopher because he taxed the Church and then threatened to excommunicate any bishop who anointed his young son prince. Christopher had the archbishop paraded in chains around the country wearing a fool's cap with a fox tail before he was imprisoned. Valdemar's widow then stirred up a rebellion and Christopher was forced to flee to southern Jutland, where Abbot Arnfast murdered him in 1259 with poisoned communion wine. He had served it as revenge for mistreating Archbishop Jakob and oppressing the Church. Christopher's allies would call him 'Christ's sacrifice'.

Christopher's son, a young Eric V, was crowned king with his mother Margaret as regent. He immediately faced trouble. A Wendish army raided Copenhagen and Skane until its chief, Jarimar, was murdered by an irate farmer's wife and his men returned home. Archbishop Erlandsen repeatedly conspired to take Eric's throne while Duke Valdemar rebelled in southern Jutland, and Eric and Margaret were captured at the Battle of Lo Heath in 1261. All royal properties in southern Jutland had to be handed over to secure their release.

Eric became known as 'Clipped Coin' because he 'short-changed' his people, and he was eventually forced to sign a charter limiting his authority in 1282. Several nobles swore to murder him. Their informer found him camped in a church barn while hunting in Viborg in 1286. The assassins crept in dressed as Franciscan monks and stabbed him to death.

His son was crowned Eric VI. As he too was a young king, his mother ruled on his behalf, and her first act was to excommunicate and exile nine men for the murder of her husband, following a questionable trial. They built forts in Norway and raided Denmark. Later, when Eric was old enough to rule alone, he faced another challenge from the ambitious Archbishop Jens Grand. Grand famously declared, while under arrest by Eric, 'I would rather the king sliced me apart joint by joint than submit to his commands.' He escaped captivity and fled to Rome; in response Pope Boniface VIII excommunicated Eric and put Denmark under interdict until he apologised.

Eric spent his money on tournaments while the peasants starved and hundreds were hung from Copenhagen's walls when they rebelled in 1312. The nobles then joined the uprising, hanging anyone who refused to support them inside their houses. Eric sold crown property to pay his debts and died in 1319, leaving the country with no money and no heir.

Eric's brother Christopher went into exile when Eric died, but the barons recalled him to rule because they wanted a weak king. He inherited a bankrupt country, had virtually no power and was unable to tax the Church or nobles, so he taxed his German territories and the peasants instead. Christopher asked his son Eric to attack northern Germany but his troops deserted him and Prince Eric was captured.

Christopher abdicated in 1326 and the German and Danish nobles wanted young Valdemar V of Schleswig to rule with his uncle, Gerhard III of Holstein, the biggest mortgage holder of Denmark, as regent. But there was a law that prevented the same person from ruling both Schleswig and Denmark, so Christopher was restored as a puppet monarch of a mortgaged country under Gerhard III of Holstein in 1329. Eric was released in 1330 but he was forced to marry Elizabeth, the sister of Count Gerhard III. This union was dissolved when Christopher joined forces with Gerhard's cousin and rival Count Johan of Holstein-Plön and attacked Gerhard at Vordingborg. Eric was mortally wounded and Christopher II was imprisoned following the Battle of Lohede (or Danevirke) in 1331. 'The king who mortgaged Denmark to the Germans' died soon afterwards and the peasants pleaded for Magnus IV of Sweden to rule them. He accepted and Denmark ceased to be a formal kingdom.

In 1340 a Jutland squire Niels Ebbesen assassinated Count Gerhard III and Christopher's son was proclaimed Valdemar IV 'the New Dawn'. But he only controlled a small area of Jutland.

Valdemar married Helvig of Schleswig, who later had his mistress Tove murdered. He used the dowry from this marriage and higher taxes to pay Denmark's debts, while the Bishop of Roskilde gave him Copenhagen for his capital. He also sold Danish Estonia to the Teutonic Knights to raise further funds. By capturing or buying the rest of the country's castles, Valdemar forced the Germans out of Danish lands and made Denmark a nation once again.

Valdemar's Crusade to Lithuania in 1346 failed and he was then censured by Pope Clement VI for going on a pilgrimage to Jerusalem without Rome's approval. The beaching of a ship with a dead crew on the coast of northern Jutland in 1349 marked the arrival of the Black Death, which killed half the population of Denmark in two years. Valdemar took advantage of the deaths of his enemies to inherit, capture or buy up lands. A number of nobles paid a visit in 1358 and told him they disagreed with his methods, so he bribed fishermen to murder them as they sailed back to Jutland.

In 1362, Valdemar captured Countess Elisabeth of Holstein-Rendsburg as she journeyed to marry Håkon VI of Sweden. Archbishop of Lund declared this betrothal void because Håkon was already engaged to Valdemar's young daughter, Margaret. Elisabeth was held in a convent and Valdemar convinced Magnus of Sweden to stick to their marriage agreement, but the Swedish nobles rebelled and forced Magnus to abdicate.

Valdemar was concerned about the growth of the Hanseatic League, an alliance of merchants and trading towns which was increasingly dominating northern Europe. He was right to be worried; he was forced out of Denmark by an alliance between the League, Norway and Sweden in 1368. He was allowed to return after promising the League a say in Denmark's succession.

Following his father's death, young Olaf II was crowned King of Denmark in 1376 and King of Norway from 1380, with his mother Queen Margaret as his regent. But the teenage king died unexpectedly in 1387, maybe from poison, and Margaret became queen of the two countries. When Albert of Sweden was taken prisoner in 1389, Margaret became ruler of all three Scandinavian kingdoms.

Margaret had adopted her grand-nephew Boguslaw and he was renamed Eric of Pomerania when he was hailed King of Norway in 1389. He was also named King of Denmark and Sweden in 1396 but Margaret remained ruler of the three kingdoms. The three Councils of the Realms met at Kalmar in 1397 to discuss the union of Scandinavia.

They were divided on the issue, but they nonetheless paid homage when Eric came of age and Margaret remained ruler of Scandinavia throughout her life.

An impostor declared himself King Olaf in 1402; many Scandinavians did not believe the young king had died, and rallied to the cause. 'Olaf' was presented to Queen Margaret, but he could speak no Danish and on questioning admitted he was in fact the son of Prussian peasants. A mock crown was placed on his head and he was burnt at the stake. Margaret died on board her ship in Flensburg harbour in 1412.

Eric of Pomerania's rule was opposed in Denmark and he retired to his castle and 'went on strike' when the Danish nobility refused to crown him. All three Scandinavian countries had deposed him by 1440 and he made his living from piracy.

Christopher the Bavarian was elected puppet king of all three countries from 1440. A peasant rebellion defeated the nobles at St Jorgen's Hill in 1441 and its leader, Eske Brock, was killed and pieces of his dismembered body were sent to the towns as a warning. Christopher retaliated by overrunning the rebel camp at Husby Hole. He made Copenhagen the capital of Denmark but the rest of his reign was blighted by famine.

The death of Christopher in 1448 precipitated the break-up of the union. Sweden elected Charles as their king while Denmark chose Christian, resulting in struggles between their supporters. Charles was also crowned King of Norway but had to renounce his claim six months later. Denmark and Norway finally signed a treaty requiring them to elect the same ruler from the king's legitimate sons. Christian would rule until 1481. Denmark was the base of his power and he struggled to bring Norway and Sweden under his rule. John wanted to restore the Kalmar Union and increase Danish power but Norway and Sweden challenged his rule.

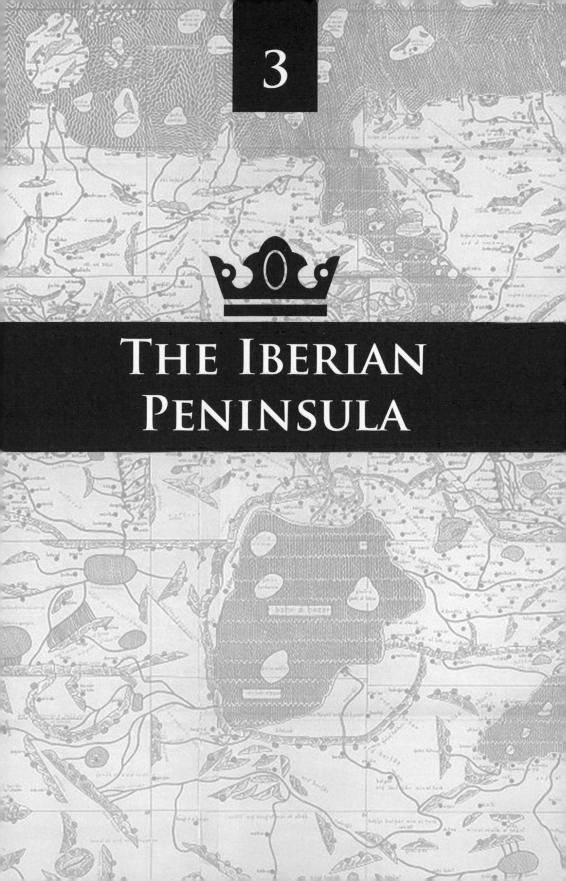

3

THE IBERIAN PENINSULA

I T WOULD TAKE OVER 400 years for the combined armies of Portugal, Castile and Aragon to capture the peninsula from the Muslims. In the meantime, the Christian kingdoms fought, allied and inter-married, rarely getting involved in the rest of Europe. Only Aragon would spread its influence across the Mediterranean Sea.

THE KINGDOM OF PORTUGAL

The County of Portugal covered the northern half of modern-day Portugal; the southern part was under the rule of the Almoravid Berbers. It bordered Galicia to the north and Castile to the east.

Henrique, Count of Portugal died in 1112 and his widow, Theresa of León, married a Galician count. Theresa and Henrique's young son, Afonso, was exiled but he rebelled when he came of age and defeated his stepfather at the Battle of São Mamede in 1128. He then imprisoned his mother in a monastery. Afonso declared himself independent of Alfonso VII, Emperor of all Spain, and became known as Portugal's founder. His soldiers proclaimed him their king following their victory against the Moors at the Battle of Ourique in 1139. He confirmed his independence from León by beating Alfonso VII of Castile at the tournament of Arcos de Valdevez in 1141. He allied with Aragon and then with Castile under the Treaty of Zamora so that he could seize Santarém and Lisbon from the Moors, doubling the size of his territories.

Afonso married his daughter, Urraca, to Fernando II of León around 1165, but his fortune turned four years later, when he fell from his horse and was captured by his son-in-law's soldiers. Afonso had to surrender part of Galicia to León as a ransom. His son, Sancho, married Afonso II's sister, Dulce, in 1174 so that Aragon and Pope Alexander III would recognise Portugal's independence.

Sancho I was crowned in 1185 and attacked the Moors to the south rather than trying to reclaim Galicia. He became known as 'the Populator' because he established new towns with Fleming and Burgundian immigrants. He also populated the royal household with nineteen children.

Afonso II the Fat, Sancho's eldest surviving son, became king in 1212, and while he made peace with Castile, he was forced to exile his troublesome brothers and sisters. Pope Honorius III excommunicated him for spending Church money and he died before he could pay it back. His teenage son Sancho II the Pious also failed to pay, concentrating instead on capturing Almohad strongholds south of Lisbon, ignoring the arguments between the country's merchants and the clergy. Pope Innocent IV told the Portuguese barons to replace Sancho, so his brother Afonso the Bolognian was invited from France to take the throne and Sancho the Pious went into exile in 1247.

Afonso III divorced his first wife so he could marry Beatrice, Alfonso X's illegitimate daughter, sealing an alliance with Castile. But the peace ended when Portugal conquered the Algarve because the area had been paying tribute to Castile. Alfonso X claimed the area and the resulting war lasted until the 1267 Treaty of Badajoz determined the border between Castile and Portugal. Afonso had twenty children, one more than his grandfather, and he was excommunicated for taxing the Church, the same as his father.

Dinis I succeeded his father Afonso III. He issued market licences to raise taxes and was named the Farmer King. He granted asylum to the Knights Templar, who sought to escape persecution in France, in 1307, creating the Order of Christ to continue the disbanded religious order. Dinis favoured his illegitimate son over his legitimate son when he died in 1325 and Afonso IV the Brave was forced to exile his illegitimate brother Afonso Sanches to secure his succession.

Afonso the Brave married his daughter María to Alfonso XI of Castile and his son Pedro to Alfonso's ex-wife, Constance. He invaded Castile when he discovered his daughter was being mistreated but María intervened to end the war. Pedro imprisoned Constance after she gave birth to their son, and instead he lived with his mistress, Inês, instead, much to his father's disgust.

Castile was plunged into a civil war when Alfonso XI died in 1350 and Portugal welcomed exiled Castilian barons. Pedro gave them important positions, angering his father, and their animosity increased when Pedro married his mistress after Constance died. Afonso was concerned for his grandson's life, so he imprisoned Inês in 1355 and had her murdered. Pedro retaliated by devastating areas of the country.

Pedro was forgiven on his father's deathbed in 1357 and legend has it that he seated Inês's body on a throne and made the barons kiss her hand in homage, while claiming their four children were legitimate. He then handed over Castilian prisoners in exchange for Inês's assassins and cut out their hearts. Pedro frequently acted as judge in court and became known as 'the Just' or 'the Cruel', depending on the outcome.

Pedro's legitimate son, Fernando I the Handsome, was crowned in 1367, but he was challenged by his illegitimate uncle, Enrique II of Castile, until Pope Gregory XI stepped in. Fernando had been betrothed to Leonora of Castile but he forced his lover, Leonor Teles, to divorce her husband so they could marry.

John of Gaunt, 1st Duke of Lancaster, asked Fernando for help to seize the Castilian throne but they failed. John continued to stake his claim after Enrique II died, but Fernando made peace with Castile by marrying his daughter, Beatrice, to Enrique's successor Juan I of Castile.

Fernando died leaving no heir in 1383, plunging Portugal into a two-year crisis. His illegitimate brother, João I the Good, was declared king but Juan of Castile invaded with French help, claiming the throne through his marriage to Beatrice. England sided with Portugal and they defeated the Castilians at the Battle of Aljubarrota. João then married John of Gaunt's daughter, Philippa, to seal the Anglo-Portuguese alliance. João I died of the plague in 1433.

Portugal had conquered Ceuta on the North African coast in 1415, giving it access to the Mediterranean Sea and expanding Portuguese interests. João's successor, his son Duarte the Eloquent, pursued Portuguese interests in Africa. He is notable for having financed his brother Henrique the Navigator's exploration of Africa's west coast.

The new Portuguese city of Ceuta, however, was becoming isolated – the African trading caravans had switched to Tangier following the Portuguese invasion. The situation worsened when Henrique the Navigator's army was captured in Morocco in 1437. Duarte had to give up Ceuta and hand over his brother Fernando as a hostage to get his army back.

Duarte died of the plague in 1438 and Fernando died in captivity in 1443. Duarte's young son, Afonso V, came to the throne and his uncle Pedro quickly replaced his unpopular mother, Leonor, as regent. Pedro strengthened his position by making Afonso marry his daughter, Isabel, and then plotted against the king when he came of age until he was defeated and killed at the Battle of Alfarrobeira in 1449.

Pope Nicholas V granted Afonso V the right to reduce 'Saracens, pagans and any other unbelievers' to slavery in two bulls that would later be used as justification for future colonialism and the slave trade. Afonso V had conquered the North African coast by 1458 and supported Henrique the Navigator's further exploration of the continent's Atlantic coast. He became known as 'Afonso the African'.

Enrique IV of Castile had been childless for many years and was believed by many to be impotent. When his wife, Afonso's sister Juana of Portugal, had a daughter, she was assumed to be illegitimate. Afonso married his niece, Juana 'la Beltraneja', in 1475, hoping to claim the throne of Castile, but the Church frowned on her because of the rumours surrounding her parentage. Instead, it seemed Isabel of Castile would inherit, and so Isabel's husband, Fernando II of Aragon, and Afonso met in the Battle of Toro in 1476. The outcome was indecisive, and Afonso turned to Louis XI of France for support. The campaign for the throne of Castile fell apart when Louis XI backed out of their alliance.

Disillusioned by his failure to win Castile, Afonso retired to a monastery, leaving Portugal to his paranoid son João II, who executed, murdered or exiled anyone who conspired against him. He executed the Duke of Braganza, he stabbed the Duke of Viseu to death, and imprisoned and poisoned the Bishop of Evora. But he became known as 'the Perfect Prince' for he invested in explorations of the Guinea coast, which found enough gold to clear the county's debts. Although Bartolomeu Dias navigated the Horn of Africa to reach Asia in 1488, João turned down Cristoforo Colombo when he suggested sailing across the Atlantic to find an easier route to Asia.

João had signed the 1479 Treaty of Alcáçovas with Castile and Aragon, ending the War of the Castilian Succession. It meant all claims to each other's thrones were void and the New World would be divided between Spain and Portugal (the Treaty of Tordesillas confirmed the division in 1494). The Treaty of Alcáçovas also agreed the marriage of Fernando and Isabel of Castile's daughter, Isabel, to João II's son Afonso, making him heir to Portugal, Castile and Aragon if Fernando and Isabel's son Juan died. But Fernando and Isabel played every diplomatic trick to dissolve the wedding until Afonso died in a mysterious riding accident in 1491. The king and queen were suspected because Afonso's Castilian valet was never to be seen again, but nothing was proved and their throne was safe.

THE KINGDOMS OF GALICIA AND LEÓN

Galicia occupied the north-west corner of the Iberian Peninsula (including what would later become Portugal), with León to the east. Castile was to the east of León and the Almoravids held al-Andalus, the territory to the south.

Castile, León and Galicia were divided into three kingdoms following the death of Fernando I of León in 1065. García II was given Galicia but his brothers, Sancho of Castile and Alfonso of León, forced him into exile and partitioned his kingdom. The reunited kingdom was passed to Alfonso the Brave when Sancho was assassinated and García returned home expecting to regain his kingdom. Instead he was imprisoned until his death in 1090.

Alfonso the Brave died in 1109 and the young future Alfonso VII of León-Castile-Galicia was crowned King of Galicia in 1111, after his mother took the united throne following her divorce from Aragon's Alfonso the Warrior. He was crowned King of León and Castile when his mother died in childbirth in 1126. Afonso I of Portugal recognised Alfonso as liege in 1137 but the latter had to confirm Portugal's independence and hand over southern Galicia after losing the tournament of Arcos de Valdevez in 1141. Alfonso led a series of Crusades against the moderate Almoravids but had to agree a peace treaty with the fanatical Islamists called the Almohads in 1146. He joined the Siege of Almería after Pope Eugene III preached the Second Crusade and signed the 1151 Treaty of Tudilén with Ramón Berenguer, King of Aragon, agreeing conquest zones. Alfonso VII died returning from an expedition to retake Almeria in 1157.

Alfonso had left León and Galicia to his son Fernando II, but Fernando's brother Sancho of Castile invaded and they had to make peace at Sahagún in 1158. Sancho then died and Fernando took advantage of the Castilian civil war that broke out after the crowning of Sancho's infant son, Alfonso VIII.

Following a new truce, Fernando captured lands from Portugal, whose king Afonso I was injured falling from his horse as he fled from battle. Peace was secured when Fernando married Afonso's daughter, Urraca, and Fernando II and Afonso then fought side by side against the Moors. They fell out in 1175 and the marriage was then annulled, using the excuse that they were cousins.

In 1179 the Treaty of Cazola was signed which redefined the spheres of interest on the Iberian Peninsula. Fernando took little notice of the agreement and allied with the Almohads to attack Portugal instead.

The ailing Fernando II did not like his eldest son, so he married his lover Urraca López de Haro, hoping to legitimise their two sons.

Despite his efforts, Alfonso IX was crowned in 1189 and became known as 'the Slobberer' because he foamed at the mouth during his frequent fits of rage. He seized Extremadura from Portugal and organised the Cortes of León in 1188, the first parliament with people's representation to be held in Western Europe.

The Almohads defeated Castile at the Battle of Alarcos in 1195 and Alfonso IX was excommunicated by Pope Celestine III for taking the opportunity to attack Castile. He also divorced his first wife, Teresa of Portugal, so he could marry Princess Berengaria of Castile, securing peace. But Pope Innocent III ruled the marriage invalid and placed Galicia and León under interdict because Alfonso had married a cousin. They stayed together until he returned to Teresa in 1204, inviting an attack by Castile.

Alfonso left his kingdom to Teresa's daughters, Sancha and Dulce, hoping to keep Galicia and León independent, but Berengaria's son, Fernando, contested the will and he paid his half-sisters to give up their claim. Fernando III of Castile was crowned in 1230, uniting Galicia and León with Castile.

The Kingdom of Castile

Fernando I was Count of Castile from 1029 and King of León from 1037. Castile occupied the central northern area of the Iberian Peninsula, with León to the west and Navarre to the east. The Almoravids held the territories to the south.

Fernando defeated his brother García Sanchez III of Navarre at the Battle of Atapuerca in 1054 and crowned himself Emperor of Spain, becoming known as Fernando the Great. The Muslim *taifa*s (petty kings) paid to stop him raiding their territory but he used the money to finance further incursions. Fernando fell ill during a raid in 1065 and returned home to divide his kingdom between his sons, giving Castile to Sancho, Galicia to García and León to Alfonso.

Sancho II the Strong defeated his cousins Sancho IV of Navarre and Sancho of Aragon in the War of the Three Sanchos in 1068. He then defeated his brother Alfonso of León at the Battle of Llantada, but three years later they joined forces to take Galicia from their younger brother García. Sancho had to beat Alfonso again, with El Cid's support, at the Battle of Golpejera and then exiled him, adding León to his lands. Sancho was besieging his rebellious sister, Urraca, in the castle of Zamora in 1072 when a Zamoran noble, Vellido Dolfos, disguised himself as a deserter and entered Sancho's camp to assassinate him.

Alfonso claimed Sancho's crown, becoming Alfonso IV the Brave, and imprisoned his brother García when he returned from exile. He proclaimed himself Emperor of Spain in 1077 only to be defeated and injured fighting the Almoravids at the Battle of Sagrajas in 1086. Alfonso pronounced his illegitimate son Sancho heir, but he died after the Battle of Uclés and his daughter Urraca became Empress of Spain in 1109.

Urraca married Alfonso I of Aragon, creating an alliance between Castile and Aragon, but they separated after only a year because he physically abused her, starting a war which resulted in Aragon allying with Portugal. A truce was declared in 1112, when an annulment was brokered between Urraca and Alfonso. Urraca then used her femininity and her body to make allies amongst her barons and thus recovered Asturias, León and Galicia while Alfonso took part of Castile. She also made sure her young son Alfonso VII rather than her lover, Pedro González de Lara, succeeded her. Urraca died in childbirth in 1126.

Alfonso VII the Emperor of all Spain agreed the Peace of Tamara with Aragon but he made a claim on the kingdom when Alfonso the Warrior died without descendants in 1134. The Aragonese nobles took the Warrior's brother from his monastery and crowned him instead. Although Alfonso the Emperor retaliated by capturing Zaragoza, he failed to make Navarre and Aragon submit. Alfonso also tried to dominate Afonso I of Portugal, but Afonso beat him at the tournament of Arcos de Valdevez in 1141, confirming Portugal's independence.

Alfonso was returning from an expedition in 1157 when he was killed in the Sierra Morena mountains.

Sancho III the Desired inherited Castile and Toledo from his father, but his only contribution was to found the Order of Calatrava before he died a year later in 1158. A squire escaped with the infant Alfonso VIII on his horse, stopping the barons seizing the heir to the throne, but they continued to challenge the young king until he came of age.

Alfonso VIII, known as the Noble, allied Navarre, Galicia, Portugal and Aragon and the 1179 Treaty of Cazola redefined their zones of expansion. A peace treaty was brokered with the Almohads but he soon broke it only to be defeated at the Battle of Alarcos in 1195. Pope Innocent III called for a new Crusade and the Castilians, Aragonese, Navarrese and Franks allied to defeat the Almohads at the Battle of Las Navas de Tolosa in 1212.

His young son Enrique inherited the throne of Castile in 1214 with his sister Berengaria as regent. Enrique I married Mafalda, Sancho I of Portugal's daughter, to secure an alliance, but Pope Innocent III annulled the union because they were cousins. The teenage Enrique was killed by a falling roof tile in 1217 and Berengaria hid his death until she had secured the throne for her son, Fernando III.

She also betrothed him to Emperor Friedrich Barbarossa's granddaughter, Elisabeth. Fernando paid Alfonso of León's daughters, Sancha and Dulce, for their throne in 1230 and the Treaty of las Tercerias united León and Castile.

Caliph Abdallah al-Adil shipped the Almohad army across to Morocco to seize power in North Africa in 1224. Fernando helped his rival al-Bayyasi of Baeza capture Jaen, Granada and Cordoba, and was given frontier castles as a reward. Al-Bayyasi was murdered in an uprising and al-Andalus was left in the hands of local emirs. Fernando took advantage of the chaos to make large advances over the next twenty years, capturing Seville and Cordoba.

Ferdinand's son Alfonso X the Wise was crowned in 1252 and immediately invaded Portugal, forcing Afonso III to surrender. Alfonso made him marry his illegitimate daughter Beatrice and promised the land would be given to their heirs. Alfonso then supported Henry III of England's war against Louis IX of France and married his sister Eleanor to Henry's son, Edward, gaining a powerful ally.

When William II of Holland died in 1256, Alfonso won the election for the King of the Romans but he never travelled to Germany to be crowned emperor.

Pope Gregory X deposed Alfonso when his expensive and complicated intrigues ruined Castile's economy and sparked a rebellion.

Alfonso's eldest son, Fernando, had been killed fighting the Moors at the Battle of Écija in 1275 and he wanted to leave the throne to his infant grandson Alfonso. But his surviving son, Sancho, objected and the ensuing civil war resulted in Alfonso having to accept him as his heir. Alfonso X wanted to unite his kingdom with a Crusade but he was denounced when he allied with the Moors and he died, defeated and deserted, in 1284.

Sancho IV was immediately challenged by his brother Juan, so he executed hundreds of his brother's supporters and imprisoned Juan. Juan revolted with the support of the Marinid tribes of Morocco, when he was released, but Sancho IV, who was known as el Bravo – 'the Brave' – drove them back to North Africa.

Castile was in anarchy when Sancho's young son Fernando IV was crowned in 1295, and his mother, María, had to hide him until he came of age. He became known as Fernando the Summoned because he sentenced two brothers to death and they said he would answer for his crime in the next world. He did not have to wait long to find out if they were right. He captured Gibraltar from the Moors in 1309, but died aged only 17, while preparing to raid Granada.

Alfonso XI's father, Fernando IV, and his mother had both died when he was an infant. His great uncles Juan and Pedro died fighting in Granada and then his grandmother María died while he was a child. His great-uncle Philippe and two uncles called Juan ruled Castile, León and Galicia until he came of age in 1325. He executed anyone who opposed him without a trial and was known as 'the Avenger'. His reign saw the kingdom extended to the Straits of Gibraltar after the Battle of Río Salado in 1340, and he conquered Algeciras in 1344.

Alfonso ignored his wife María of Portugal, having only two children with her but ten with his mistress, Eleanor de Guzmán. He died when an epidemic swept his camp during the Siege of Gibraltar in 1350.

After Alfonso's death, María, mother of the new king, teenage Pedro, convinced him to execute his stepmother, Eleanor, for being involved in Enrique of Trastámara's rebellion.

Pedro was betrothed to Joan, daughter of Edward III of England, but she died en route, so he married his lover, María, in secret in 1353. Although his mother forced him to divorce and marry Blanche instead, he had four children with María. Pedro the Cruel executed many opponents and some say he murdered his wife in 1361.

Castile began the prolonged War of the Two Pedros against Pedro IV of Aragon and Enrique of Trastámara in 1356. Enrique seized the throne in the Castilian Civil War in 1366 and Pedro the Cruel fled with his treasury to Portugal, only to be turned away by his uncle Pedro I. Then he went to Galicia and joined Edward the Black Prince, son of Edward II of England, who helped him retake his throne following the Battle of Nájera in 1367.

Pedro failed to pay the English mercenaries and the allies turned on each other. Castile was defeated when Pedro invaded the English domains north of the Pyrenees and Edward the Black Prince left the Iberian Peninsula. Pedro was trapped in Montiel fortress in 1369 by Enrique of Trastámara so he offered Enrique's messenger a bribe to help him escape. Enrique offered the messenger more money and he was led to the king's tent, and stabbed Pedro to death.

John of Gaunt claimed the throne of Castile because he was married to Pedro's daughter, Constance. He borrowed money to fight alongside Fernando I of Portugal in the Fernando Wars, which dragged on inconclusively from 1369 to 1382. Enrique then went to war against Portugal and England in the Hundred Years War, in which John of Gaunt persisted over his claim to the Castilian throne. The War of the Two Pedros finally ended with the 1375 Treaty of Almazan but only because the Black Death had devastated both sides' armies.

Juan I was crowned in 1379 and he betrothed his infant son Enrique to Fernando of Portugal's young daughter Beatrice, ending the Fernando Wars. But Juan married Beatrice himself after his wife, Eleanor, died in childbirth. When Fernando of Portugal died in 1383, Juan believed he had a right to the throne but his invading army was defeated at the battles of Trancoso and Aljubarrota in 1385. The Portuguese Cortes proclaimed João of Aviz to be their king, foiling Juan's plans, and he was killed in a horse riding accident in 1390, leaving his teenage son, Enrique the Infirm, as King of Castile.

Enrique was married to Catherine of Lancaster to stop her father, John of Gaunt, pursuing his claim to the throne. He was sick all his life and died in 1406, leaving his infant son, Juan II, to inherit the throne, with his mother Catherine and his uncle Fernando of Aragon as co-regents. Juan would be king for forty-nine years but he was very dependent on advisers until his second wife, Isabel of Portugal, dismissed them all. Juan helped place Yusuf IV on the throne of Granada in 1431, and received an annual tribute in return.

Enrique IV was crowned in 1454, having defeated Aragon at the Battle of Olmedo. Some believed his daughter Juana 'la Beltraneja' was actually Beltrán de la Cueva's daughter, and the rumours were confirmed when his wife Joan had two other illegitimate children. Enrique had also divorced his first wife, Blanche II, stating witchcraft had prevented them consummating the marriage. Her virginity was confirmed, and while prostitutes confirmed Enrique was sexually capable, the nickname 'the Impotent' stuck.

Enrique named his half-sister Isabel as his successor on the condition that he could arrange her marriage. Her first betrothal was to Fernando, Juan II of Navarre's youngest son, at the age of 6. But Juan inherited Aragon when his brother Alfonso died childless in 1458, so he did not need Castile's support. Isabel was then secretly betrothed to Juan of Navarre's wayward eldest son, Carlos, but he was thrown in prison by his father and died there. Isabel was next betrothed to the important Castilian noble Pedro Giron to mitigate civil war, but Pedro fell ill and died. Queen Isabel of Portugal tried to get her to marry Alfonso V of Portugal on two occasions but she refused. She also rejected a union with Louis XI of France's brother, Charles of Valois.

Juan of Navarre secretly arranged a second betrothal to his son Fernando, her first love, and Isabel took matters into her own hands in 1469. She left Enrique's court, pretending to visit her brother's tomb, while Fernando crossed Castile disguised as a servant so they could meet up and marry in secret.

Isabel succeeded Enrique in 1474 and although there were plots to usurp her, Portugal gave up its claim to the throne of Castile under the 1479 Treaty of Alcáçovas. The Atlantic Ocean and overseas territories were also divided, cutting Spain out of the Atlantic and Guinea's gold.

Castile invaded what remained of al-Andalus in 1482 and ten years later Muhammad XII surrendered the region and gave Isabel and Fernando the keys to Granada. The Alhambra Decree of March 1492 forced 40,000 Jews to leave Spain, while a similar number converted to Christianity. Isabel and Fernando then brought the country under Roman Catholicism through the Inquisition.

Queen Isabel agreed to sponsor Cristoforo Columbo's voyage across the Atlantic Ocean and he landed on San Salvador Island in the Galápagos Islands on 12 October 1492. He returned the following year with natives, gold and promises of a New World, opening the door to Spain's Golden Age of exploration and colonisation. However, the Portuguese did not want the Spanish to claim what would become South America and threatened to send an army to stop them. The 1494 Treaty of Tordesillas divided the New World between Spain and Portugal.

THE KINGDOM OF NAVARRE

Navarre was on the Biscay coast between Castile to the west and the Pyrenees to the north, bordering with what is now France. Aragon held the central section of the Pyrenees and Muslim-controlled al-Andalus was to the south.

García Sánchez III received the Kingdom of Navarre and Pamplona when Sancho the Great's kingdom was split in 1035. He was also overlord to his brothers: Fernando ruled Castile, Ramiro controlled most of Aragon and Gonzalo had the rest of Aragon. García helped Fernando defeat King Vermudo at the Battle of Tamarón in 1037 and seized León, expanding Navarre to the Bay of Biscay. But he was defeated by his brother Ramiro at the Battle of Tafalla in 1043 and was killed fighting his brother Fernando at the Battle of Atapuerca in 1054.

Teenage Sancho IV the Noble had his mother as his regent but relations deteriorated between his cousins in Castile and Aragon, resulting in the War of the Three Sanchos in 1067. Castile invaded Navarre, which was defeated despite help from Aragon.

Sancho's brother Ramón and sister Ermesinda were unhappy with his rule so they forced his horse off a cliff during a hunt in 1076. Ramón was nicknamed 'the Fratricide' or 'brother killer'.

Navarre was partitioned between Aragon and Castile until Alfonso the Warrior, King of Aragon died in 1134, when it regained its independence under García the Restorer, grandson of Sancho the Noble's illegitimate brother Sancho Garcés. The following year he made the Pact of Vadoluongo which agreed a relationship 'mutual adoption' between the two kingdoms, with Aragon having supremacy as the 'father' and Navarre being the 'son'. García married French noblewoman Marguerite of L'Aigle, but she had many lovers and he refused to recognise their second son. He later married Urraca, the illegitimate daughter of Alfonso VII of Castile, to seal an alliance.

Sancho VI the Wise, son of Sancho and Marguerite, was crowned in 1150 and was the first to use the title King of Navarre, dropping Pamplona from the title. He clashed with Castile and Aragon during his fifty-four-year reign and his territories were soon reduced by the treaties of Tudejen and Carrión, but he eventually reclaimed some of his lands. Sancho married his daughter Berenguela to Richard I of England in 1191 and his son, Sancho, supported the Angevin Empire against the French.

Sancho VII the Strong was over seven feet tall. He ruined relations with Castile by arriving too late to help Alfonso VIII fight the Almohads at the Battle of Alarcos in 1195. He then campaigned with the Almohads against Castile, so Alfonso VIII of Castile and Pedro II of Aragon retaliated by invading Navarre. Sancho returned to the Crusaders' fold and his leadership was decisive when Navarre joined Aragon, Castile and Portugal to defeat the Almohads at the Battle of Las Navas de Tolosa in 1212.

Sancho suffered from a painful ulcer on his right leg, was unable to walk, became obese and went into retirement, so his sister Blanca administered the kingdom. Her son Thibault (Teobaldo in Spanish) helped when he turned 21, but he had had an affair with Louis VIII's widow, Blanche, which led to him being accused of poisoning the King of France.

Thibault I the Troubadour was crowned in 1234, the first Frenchman to rule Navarre, after bribing his cousin Alix of Cyprus not to make a claim. He went on Crusade in 1239 but made treaties with Damascus and Egypt and returned home after he was defeated near Gaza.

Thibault's teenage son Teobaldo II the Young was crowned in 1253, with his mother and King Jaime I of Aragon as regents. He married Louis IX's daughter, Isabelle, in 1255 and joined him on the Eighth Crusade to North Africa in 1270. Louis died during the Siege of Tunis and Teobaldo died on the return journey.

His brother, Enrique, was crowned when he did not return and planned to marry his young son, also Teobaldo, to Violante of Castile but Teobaldo fell from a castle battlements and died in 1273. Enrique, known as the Fat, died soon afterwards, suffering from obesity, and his widow, Blanca, took their young daughter, Juana, to the French court, fearing for their lives. Juana was soon married to Philippe, the future King of France. But she died during childbirth (some say she was murdered by her husband) in 1305.

Louis X the Quarreller inherited Navarre from his mother in 1305 and became King of France in 1314. He was kept busy with the Tour de Nesle scandal involving his wife Marguerite of Burgundy and two sisters-in-law. Marguerite and Blanche were imprisoned and their lovers were executed while Juana was found innocent. Louis wanted his marriage annulled but Marguerite died soon after, and he married Clémentia of Hungary five days later. Louis died after drinking too much cold wine following a strenuous game of indoor tennis in 1316; his son died the same year.

His daughter Juana married Philippe, Count of Évreux in 1318 but her claim to Navarre was questioned due to the scandal. It would be ten years before she became Queen of Navarre in 1328 and that only after renouncing her claim to the crown of France.

Philippe joined the King of France, Jan of Bohemia and David II of Scotland against the English in 1339 (the start of the Hundred Years War). He then joined Alfonso XI of Castile's Crusade but was mortally wounded during the Siege of Algeciras in 1343, leaving Juana to rule alone until she died six years later.

Son of Philippe and Juana, Carlos II married Joan of Valois, daughter of Jean II of France, in 1352.

He murdered the Constable of France, Charles de La Cerda, because he had seized his mother's territories, and then repeatedly switched between supporting France and England while plotting against his father-in-law, Jean II. He was arrested by Jean in 1356 and his supporters were beheaded. But then Jean was defeated and captured by the English at the Battle of Poitiers. In the chaos that followed, Carlos was rescued, and he then had the audacity to demand Normandy and Champagne from the *Dauphin*. The *Dauphin* was arrested and his advisers murdered but he escaped and beat Carlos to Paris, regaining control of the city.

Carlos then opened negotiations with England, proposing that he and Edward III should divide France between them, but Edward did not trust the Navarrese king. Instead Edward agreed that the King of France, still in captivity, would be ransomed and his son, Louis, would be held hostage while he raised the money. In return Jean would give Edward III French lands – including all of Carlos's territory.

John handed himself over to Edward when Louis escaped, and he would die in England. The *Dauphin* conquered Normandy and defeated Carlos's army at the Battle of Cocherel in 1364 only for Carlos to recapture the area. In a further twist, Carlos poisoned Seguin de Badefol with a crystallised pear when he claimed money for his services in Burgundy in 1365.

Starting in 1365, Carlos tried to exploit the War of the Two Pedros by officially allying with Castile while secretly working with Pedro of Aragon to replace Pedro of Castile. He then defaulted on all agreements when Enrique of Trastámara forced Pedro of Castile to flee.

Carlos's next move was to agree to let Pedro and Edward the Black Prince to pass through Navarre to recapture Castile. He told Enrique he would stop them but he let them through when he was threatened. Carlos was eventually captured in a staged ambush and held prisoner until the war was over to avoid the consequences, making him the laughing stock of Europe. Carlos finally made peace with Castile by marrying his son Carlos to Enrique II's daughter Leonor, in 1375.

England and France went to war in 1369 and Carlos did a secret deal with Edward III after Charles V of France refused his offer of help. The English army was destroyed at the Battle of Pontvallain in 1370 but Carlos later let the English use his territories in Normandy to launch an attack on France. Carlos also became involved in several attempts to assassinate King Charles, but his intrigues unravelled when his son was arrested en route to Normandy in March 1378. French troops captured Normandy, Carlos's son submitted and the rest of his party was executed.

Castile invaded Navarre in 1378 and Carlos eventually signed the Treaty of Briones. Carlos 'the Bad' had kept his crown but his country had been devastated. He fell ill in 1387 and his doctor suggested wrapping him in a linen cloth impregnated with brandy. His maid servant accidentally set light to the shroud one night and ran away as the king was burnt alive.

Carlos III became known as Carlos the Noble because he abandoned his father's claims to Champagne and Brie to make peace with France. He then supported Castile's campaign against Granada.

His daughter, Blanche, was married to Juan, son of Fernando I of Aragon, and she became queen regnant in 1425 while Juan became king. When Blanche died in 1441, Juan prevented their son, Carlos of Viana, becoming king, encouraged by his second wife, Castilian noblewoman Juana Enriquez de Córdoba. The rivalry between father and son resulted in the Navarrese Civil War in which the Catalans and Castile supported Carlos. Carlos was captured in 1452 and released on the condition that he would not claim his father's title.

Alfonso V of Aragon died in 1458 and Juan became took the Aragonese throne. Carlos declined the crowns of Naples and Sicily and returned to Navarre, hoping to marry Isabel of Castile. Instead he was imprisoned by his father until the Catalans rebelled in his favour and recognised him as heir. The Navarrese Civil War ended when Carlos died in 1461, probably poisoned by his stepmother.

Carlos of Viana's sister, Blanche II of Navarre, had been married to Enrique IV of Castile as part of a peace deal in 1440. Thirteen years later, Pope Nicholas V granted a divorce on the grounds that witchcraft prevented them from consummating the marriage, so

Blanche was sent home and imprisoned by her family. Some proclaimed Blanche queen when her brother died in 1461 and her father wanted to marry her to Charles, Louis XI's brother, to ally himself with France. She refused and was poisoned in 1464.

Carlos and Blanche's sister, Leonor of Castile, had recognised her father as Navarre's monarch, signing the Treaty of Olite in 1462, and she became queen regnant when Juan died in 1479. She died three weeks later and her young grandson, Count Francis of Foix, was crowned with his mother, Madeleine, as regent. He died a teenager four years later and his teenage sister Catalina became queen, with Madeleine continuing as regent. Her uncle, Jean of Foix used Salic law (the male claim over female claim) to seize power, which resulted in a nine-year civil war.

THE KINGDOM OF ARAGON

When he died in 1035, the lands of Sancho III of Navarre were divided and his son Ramiro became the first King of Aragon. Aragon occupied the central area of the Pyrenees and lands to the south, bordering with Navarre to the west, al-Andalus to the south and the County of Barcelona to the east.

Ramiro invaded Navarre with the Muslim Emir of Tudela and though he was defeated at the Battle of Tafalla, he gained semi-autonomy for his kingdom. He advanced toward Huesca and Zaragoza in 1043 and was killed trying to capture the town of Graus in 1063. The illegitimate Sancho Ramírez was chosen as Ramiro's successor over his five legitimate children and he became engaged in the War of the Three Sanchos between Aragon, Castile and Navarre in 1067. Castile wanted Navarre's territories and Navarre asked Aragon for help; Castile beat them both. Sancho Ramírez was elected King of Navarre when Sancho IV was murdered in 1076 and gave some territory to Castile to keep the peace. Sancho tried to expand south but he was defeated by El Cid at the Battle of Morella in 1084 and was killed during the Siege of Huesca in 1094.

Pedro I completed the siege and moved his capital to Huesca. He allied with El Cid of Valencia and they seized the Cinca valley and then turned on the Moors at the Battle of Xàtiva and conquered the Valencia region. Although Pedro wanted to join the Crusade to the Holy Land in 1101, Pope Paschal II ordered him to capture Zaragoza instead.

Following Pedro's death, his half-brother Alfonso the Warrior was crowned in 1104 and married Queen Urraca of Castile and León, entitling him to use the title Emperor of Spain. But Urraca refused to be a subservient queen and they quarrelled until he got the pope's permission to declare the marriage void in 1110, using the excuse that they were cousins. She refused to stay out of politics, flirting and seducing nobles to get their support, so Alfonso imprisoned her when he went to war in 1112.

Alfonso conquered Zaragoza in 1118, making it his new capital, and then captured Calatayud and Lleida. He raided the Almoravid-held territories of Andalusia and Granada in 1124 and would fight twenty-nine battles against his cousins and the Moors, gaining the nickname 'the Warrior'. His stepson Alfonso VII seized the Castilian possessions acquired through his marriage in 1127 and they signed the Peace of Tamara. Alfonso the Warrior died childless following his final battle at Fraga in 1134.

Although Alfonso left Aragon to the Knights Templar, the Knights Hospitaller and the Knights of the Holy Sepulchre, the barons chose his brother Ramiro, the Bishop of Barbastro, to be king. Ramiro II suspended his monastic vows to take the crown and to marry Agnes of Aquitaine. They had a daughter, Petronilla. She was betrothed to Ramón Berenguer IV, Count of Barcelona aged only 1, uniting Aragon with the coastal county of Barcelona.

When Ramiro asked an abbot how to deal with a rebellion of nobles, he responded by cutting the heads of the tallest roses in a rose garden. The king understood the message. He beheaded the kingdom's most powerful nobles and hung them like a bell, with the chief noble's head as clapper; it became known as the Bell of Huesca. With peace restored and an heir secured, Ramiro the Monk passed royal authority to Ramón and Petronilla and returned to his abbey in 1137.

Ramón negotiated his way out of Aragon's submission to Castile, aided by his sister Berenguela, wife of Alfonso the emperor. He then helped Castile conquer Almeria before invading Valencia and Murcia, and they signed the 1151 Treaty of Tudilen, defining zones of conquest in Andalusia. Ramón took territories from the Moors to the south before campaigning in Provence, north of the Pyrenees.

Petronilla renounced the crown of Aragon to her young son Alfonso II the Chaste when her husband died in 1162. Alfonso continued the close alliance with Castile, with several treaties and divisions of territory, most notably the Treaty of Cazorla between the two kings in 1179, which defined their respective zones of conquest in the south.

Alfonso's son Pedro II took the throne in 1196 and he went to Rome to be crowned by Pope Innocent III in 1205, becoming known as 'the Catholic'. He married Maria of Montpellier to get control of the port, and then divorced her once she had given him a son. Pedro joined Castile and Portugal in a Crusade and they defeated the Almohads at the Battle of Las Navas de Tolosa in 1212.

But Aragon's lands north of the Pyrenees had come under the influence of the Cathar heretics and Pope Innocent instructed Louis IX of France to suppress them with a new Crusade led by Simon de Montfort. Pedro's young son, Jaime, had been handed over to de Montfort and betrothed to his daughter in 1211, to stop his Crusade across Pedro's lands. But the pope reminded Simon to continue his Crusade, so Pedro crossed the Pyrenees to challenge the Crusaders and was killed at the Battle of Muret in 1213.

Aragon appealed to Pope Innocent III and Jaime I was returned so he could be raised by the Knights Templar. The teenage Jaime married Eleanor, daughter of Alfonso VIII of Castile, in 1221 and conquered Mallorca in 1229. He also negotiated a treaty with Sancho under which he would have inherited Navarre, but the Navarrese nobles crowned Teobaldo instead. Jaime annulled his marriage to Eleanor as soon as she had a son and married Jolanta of Hungary for her dowry. He then captured Valencia and Murcia on behalf of his son-in-law Alfonso X of Castile, gaining the name 'the Conqueror'.

Jaime later married a non-royal called Teresa by a private document which excluded her and their children from his will; he later left her, accusing her of developing leprosy. Jaime died in 1276 after sixty-three years on the throne; he left the mainland possessions to Pedro and Mallorca to Jaime.

The Sicilians offered Pedro their throne in 1282 and the King of Sicily, Carlos of Anjou, fled when he invaded, starting the War of the Sicilian Vespers. Pedro and Carlos were supposed to end the war by personal combat but they turned up at different times and both claimed victory so Pope Martin IV excommunicated Pedro and offered Aragon to Carlos, Count of Valois in 1284. Jaime II of Mallorca joined the French invasion of Sicily but their fleet was destroyed at the Battle of Les Formigues, their army was destroyed at the Battle of the Col de Panissars and Philippe III of France died of dysentery. Pedro died soon after and left Aragon to his son Alfonso and Sicily to his son Jaime.

Alfonso III the Liberal seized the Balearics from his uncle Jaime II of Mallorca but returned it under the Treaty of Anagni when Jaime recognised his nephew under the Treaty of Argilers. But Alfonso was forced to sign over rights to the barons, plunging his kingdom into anarchy, and he eventually became a monk, after refusing to consummate his marriage to Leonor of Castile.

His brother, Alfonso IV the Kind, was crowned in 1327 and married Leonor of Castile. Though he had a son, Pedro, with Leonor, he favoured his second wife.

Alfonso's son, Pedro IV the Ceremonious, was crowned in 1336 and married María, daughter of Philip III of Navarre. He allied with Alfonso XI of Castile against Morocco. Jaime III of Mallorca delayed paying homage to Pedro and allied with the Moroccans instead. Pedro seized Mallorca when Jaime asked for help to defend Montpellier against the French.

Pedro had no son and he mistrusted his brother Jaime so he named his daughter, Costanza, heir. Jaime rebelled and the brothers reconciled, but Pedro probably poisoned Jaime to stop him seizing power. Pedro was then taken prisoner during an uprising by the anti-royalist Union of Valencia movement and was forced to dance with the peasants to show his subservience. He escaped when Valencia was hit by the Black Death and defeated the unionists at the Battle of Épila in 1348. He had the union bell melted down and poured into the mouths of the union leaders so they 'should taste its liquor'.

Jaime of Mallorca tried to retake his kingdom in 1349 but he was defeated by Pedro's troops at the Battle of Llucmajor, bringing his kingdom to an end. Aragon then fought Castile in the War of the Two Pedros, a war over ownership of the Valencia area, starting in 1356. It ended with the Treaty of Almazan in 1375 after the Black Death and various natural disasters had ravaged both kingdoms. Pedro finally conquered Sicily in 1377 and gave it to his youngest son, Martín.

Pedro's son Juan I the Hunter was crowned in 1387 and allied Aragon with Castile and France; he also supported Antipope Clement VII when the Church split. But while Aragon had secured its place on the Iberian Peninsula, its overseas territories were in danger. The Sardinians recaptured their island in the 1380s, Greek territories were lost in 1390 and there was a revolt in Sicily in 1391. Juan died falling from his horse while out hunting in 1396 and he left no sons.

Juan's brother, Martín the Humane, was acting as regent to his young cousin, María of Sicily. His wife, also María, claimed the throne of Aragon on his behalf until he returned to Aragon.

After stopping a challenge by Count Mathieu of Foix, north of the Pyrenees, Martín went on a Crusade to North Africa in 1398.

Martín rescued the Aragonese Antipope Benedict XIII (known as 'Papa Luna', the Moon Pope) in 1403, following a five-year siege of the papal palace. He then instructed his son Martín of Sicily to reconquer Sardinia. Martín of Sicily died of malaria after having defeated the rebels at the Battle of Sanluri in 1409, leaving Sicily to his father. Martín senior thus died childless the following year after laughing uncontrollably at his favourite jester on a full stomach.

Fernando, Juan I's son, had declined the Castilian crown when his brother, Enrique III of Castile had died in 1406. Instead he served as co-regent with Enrique's widow, Katerina, until his nephew Juan II came of age. He was crowned Fernando I the Just of Aragon under the 1412 Compromise of Caspe. He agreed to depose Antipope Benedict XIII, ending the Western Schism, only to die in 1416, leaving the crowns of Aragon and Sicily to his son Alfonso the Magnanimous.

The childless Queen Giovanna II of Naples adopted Alfonso as heir to her kingdom in 1421 and he went to Naples to be crowned. When Pope Martin V announced that he favoured Louis III of Anjou as heir to Naples, Alfonso switched allegiance to Antipope Benedict XIII. He took control of Naples but relations between him and Giovanna deteriorated. In 1423 he arrested Giovanna's lover, but he failed to capture the queen and she named Louis III as her new heir.

Alfonso had to return to Aragon to deal with a war his brothers had started with Castile. Giovanna and Louis seized Sicily in his absence. Both soon died and Sicily was left to Louis's brother, René of Anjou. The new pope, Eugene IV, was against the inheritance, so Alfonso invaded Sicily. He was taken prisoner but persuaded his captors that it was not in their interests to stop his quest and was freed to capture Naples and Sardinia. He also obtained Pope Eugene IV's consent to make his illegitimate and immature son Fernando heir to the Kingdom of Naples.

Alfonso's other son, Juan II the Faithless, was an unscrupulous man who had ruled Navarre since 1425 through his first marriage to Blanche of Navarre. He inherited the crown of Aragon in 1458 but was always envious of his son, Carlos the Prince of Viana. His second wife Juana encouraged his jealousy, which caused the Navarrese Civil War. The Catalans supported Carlos but he was still forced to pawn Roussillon to Louis XI of France to fund his campaign. Carlos died in 1461 (possibly poisoned on Juana's orders) and the Catalan revolt was pacified in 1472, but Juan fought the French king until his death in 1479.

Juan's son Fernando II had been betrothed to Isabel of Castile at an early age. But as relations between the two countries changed the alliance fell out of favour and Enrique IV of Castile offered his sister to several other suitors, all of whom she rejected. Juan II secretly arranged a second betrothal in 1469 and the couple eloped, Fernando entered Castile disguised as a servant and Isabel escaping by pretending to visit her brother's tomb. They had a prenuptial agreement on sharing power, and he became King of Castile by right of his wife when Isabel succeeded her brother Enrique the Impotent in 1474. Fernando then defeated Enrique's daughter, Joana, who was rumoured to be illegitimate. Fernando succeeded his father as King of Aragon in 1479, uniting Aragon and Castile.

Fernando and Isabel conquered the Emirate of Granada, the last Islamic power in the Iberian Peninsula, in 1492 and then forced the Jews to either convert or leave. The Moors would soon have to leave too, and Fernando and Isabel were both called 'the Catholic'. The same year, they sponsored Cristoforo Columbo to set sail for the New World, leading to a huge Spanish empire in the Americas.

The Kingdom of Mallorca

Jaime I of Aragon's will divided his kingdom when he died in 1276: his son Pedro III was given the mainland, and Jaime II inherited the Balearic Islands and lands in southern France. Pedro made his brother a vassal under the 1279 Treaty of Perpignan so Jaime allied with Philip III of France and joined the Aragonese Crusade only to be defeated at the Battle of Les Formigues in 1285. Pedro's son, Alfonso III, annexed the Balearic Islands but they were returned to Aragon by the 1295 Treaty of Anagni.

Jaime II died in 1311 and his eldest son, Jaime, became a monk, so Sancho the Peaceful was crowned. He had no sons so his nephew Jaime III inherited the crown in 1324, but he too refused to submit to Pedro IV of Aragon and was driven out of Mallorca. He tried to retake the island but was killed and his children, including his heir, were taken prisoner at the Battle of Llucmajor in 1349.

Jaime IV escaped captivity in 1362 and Giovanna I of Naples married him hoping for an heir, but they had no children. Jaime's invasion of Aragon was easily defeated so he supported Edward the Black Prince's attack on Castile, in the vain hope that he might help him take back Mallorca. Jaime fell ill and was captured by Enrique of Trastámara, but he hoped to retake his lands when Castile and Aragon fought the War of the Two Pedros. An outbreak of the plague ended the war with the Treaty of Almazan and Jaime fled to Castile, where he died of illness or from poison in 1375.

His wife Isabel had been released around 1358 after promising to renounce her rights to the kingdom, but she was still determined to regain Mallorca. Her four sons did not want to be kings so she adopted two men to fight on her behalf. Her daughter agreed that Isabel's grandson would be the future King of Mallorca, but he never was.

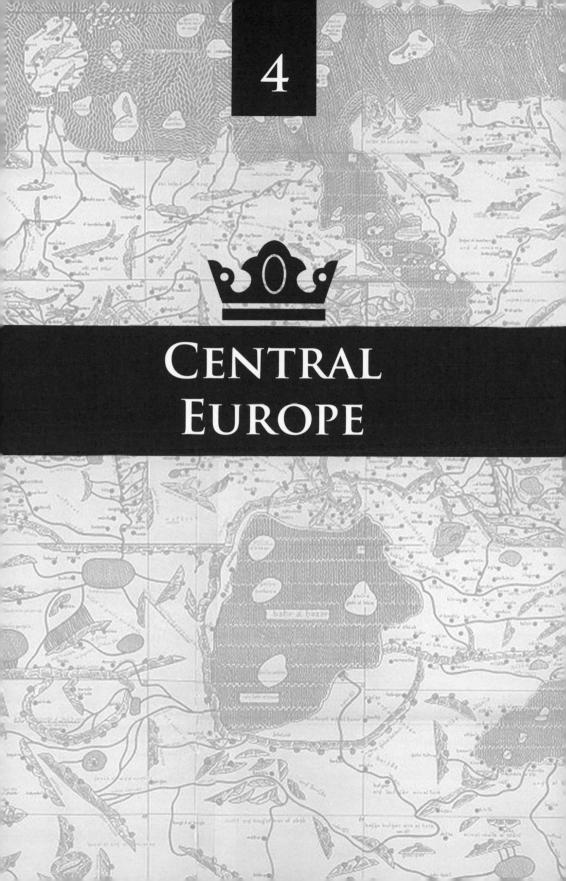

4

CENTRAL EUROPE

CENTRAL EUROPE WAS CONTROLLED BY the King of the Romans, who controlled vast territories from the North Sea and Baltic coasts in the north down into what is now northern Italy. The King of the Romans was entitled to claim the title of Holy Roman Emperor, provided the pope would crown him. The ongoing power struggle between the emperors and popes would influence Europe for many years.

Bohemia was between Germany and Poland and often became embroiled in their plays for power. It became a kingdom in 1198 and Prague became the Holy Roman Empire's capital after the Black Death swept through Germany in the 1340s.

Austria was on the south-eastern side of the Holy Roman Empire, between Bavaria and Hungary. It was promoted from margrave to duchy in 1156 and Rudolf IV declared himself archduke in 1358, to make himself equal with the Holy Roman Empire's prince-electors.

THE HOLY ROMAN EMPEROR AND THE KING OF THE ROMANS

The Empire bordered France to the west, Poland to the north-east and Hungary to the south-east. It also controlled what is now northern Italy, sharing a frontier with the Papal States north of Rome. Heinrich III was crowned in 1039 and visited Rome, where he was granted the decisive vote in papal elections. He would name four German popes who cleaned up and renewed the strength of the papacy. It would lead to the long-running Investiture Controversy, an argument over who appointed popes and kings – the Church or the state.

Heinrich argued with Henri I of France over Lorraine in 1056 and then left quickly when challenged to a personal combat because he knew he faced a seasoned warrior. Heinrich died soon after, leaving his wife as regent of his young son, Heinrich IV. Agnès made poor decisions, so the Archbishop of Cologne kidnapped the young Heinrich in 1062 and took control.

Heinrich IV was declared king and emperor of a rebellious kingdom when he came of age in 1065. He wanted to divorce his wife, Bertha, but gave up following an outcry. He continued to appoint bishops and was excommunicated by Pope Gregory VII, who was adamant that this was the Church's business. Heinrich apologised, atoning by going to Canossa in 1077, where he stood in the snow in a hair shirt and no shoes for three days until he was forgiven.

Rudolf von Rheinfelden disagreed with Heinrich's stance on the Church, so he was crowned anti-king and defeated Heinrich at the Battle of Flarchheim in 1080. Pope Gregory then excommunicated Heinrich for a second time. Rudolf was mortally wounded at the Battle on the Elster the same year and Hermann of Salm was appointed his successor as anti-king. Heinrich invaded Italy and deposed Gregory (whom he called 'the False Monk') and his biggest supporter, Matilde of Tuscany. In 1084, he captured

Rome, installed Antipope Clement III and was crowned King of Italy and Holy Roman Emperor. But this 'Truce of God' only kept the peace for a short time because Hermann of Salm defeated him at the Battle of Bleichfeld in 1086. Hermann then retired, ending the Great Saxon Revolt.

Pope Urban II excommunicated Heinrich and Clement III while Matilde turned Heinrich's son, Konrad, against him so that he crowned himself King of Milan. Heinrich was accused of being a member of the heretical Nicolaitan sect in 1094. His wife Adelaida (called Eupraxia of Kiev before she married) also accused him of forcing her to take part in orgies, holding black masses on her naked body and offering her to his son. Konrad confirmed the accusations and swore loyalty to Pope Urban II in return for a promise of the imperial crown. Henry disowned Konrad and made his second son Heinrich promise not to interfere in his business before he appointed him his heir.

Pope Paschal II excommunicated Heinrich for a third time in 1103 and he promised to go on a Crusade to get it lifted, but his enemies encouraged his son to revolt. Paschal relieved young Heinrich of his oath, so he imprisoned his father and forced him to abdicate. But Heinrich IV soon escaped and defeated his son's army at Vise in 1106, only to die soon after.

On taking the throne, Heinrich V turned his attention east, attacking Könyves of Hungary in support of Prince Álmos in 1108. Bolesław III intervened, so Heinrich invaded Poland, but was defeated at the battles of Glogow and the Hundsfeld. He turned south-east and secured Bohemia on behalf of Ladislaus I, Duke of Bohemia instead.

The Pope Paschal refused to attend a council in Germany to debate the Investiture Controversy, so Heinrich invaded Italy and forced him to discuss the issue. Heinrich agreed to renounce the rite of investiture in return for a promise of coronation but neither the pope nor the emperor kept their promise. So Heinrich V's soldiers arrested Pope Paschal and sixteen cardinals and forced them to crown him emperor in 1111. He was then excommunicated for his heavy-handed methods.

Heinrich returned to Germany, only to be defeated by a citizen army at Andernach in 1114 and by Lothar of Supplinburg at Welfesholz in 1115, leaving the country in the hands of Friedrich II and Konrad of Hohenstaufen. Matilde of Tuscany died the following year so Heinrich crossed the Alps, seized her estates and bribed Rome's cardinals to crown him a second time.

Pope Gelasius II was elected in 1118 and although Heinrich made sure Antipope Gregory VIII was elected, he finally bowed to Rome's requests at the 1122 Concordat of Worms and was allowed back into the Church. Heinrich died three years later and Lothar was elected King of Germany, a departure from the usual hereditary succession. Heinrich's choice, Friedrich II of Swabia, had been placed under a papal ban, but his supporter, Konrad of Hohenstaufen, was elected anti-king in 1127.

While Lothar campaigned in Germany, Konrad crossed the Alps to be crowned King of Italy, where the election of Pope Innocent II made it clear Lothar had everyone's support. Lothar led a small army into Italy to support the pope in his fight against Roger II of Sicily and was crowned emperor as a reward. Meanwhile, Konrad relinquished his title as King of Italy and acknowledged Lothar as his emperor in 1135.

Lothar allied with Heinrich the Proud of Bavaria, at the pope's insistence, and together they invaded Sicily. Roger offered them the Apulia area of Italy and a son as a hostage, hoping they would withdraw, but Innocent wanted to conquer his kingdom. Unfortunately, the German troops refused to fight because of the summer heat so Lothar instead gave Capua and Apulia to Roger's enemies, against Innocent's wishes. Lothar died while returning over the Alps during the winter of 1137.

Although Konrad of Hohenstaufen was elected emperor, he was unsuccessfully challenged first by Lothar's heir, Heinrich the Proud, and then by Heinrich the Lion. In 1142, Konrad invaded Bohemia to put his brother-in-law, Vladislav II, on the throne and then attempted to reinstate another brother-in-law, the Polish prince, Ladislaus the Exile.

Konrad crowned his son Heinrich Berengar co-king in 1147 before he left to join Louis VII on the Second Crusade. The Crusaders caused disruption in the Byzantine Empire only to be defeated by the Seljuk Turks at the Battle of Dorylaeum. A sick Konrad remained in Constantinople during the Siege of Damascus and then returned home to find Heinrich Berengar had defeated the Welfs' rebellion at the Battle of Flochberg in 1150. Both father and son died soon after.

Friedrich I Barbarossa ('red beard' in Italian) was elected King of Germany in 1152 and immediately upset Pope Eugene III by forgetting to ask him to confirm his appointment. He promised to capture Rome to make amends and led an army into Italy, where he received the Iron Crown and the title King of Italy at Pavia. Friedrich then seized control of Rome and was crowned emperor. He intended to attack Wilhelm I of Sicily but once again the hot summer troubled his troops, and a rebellion in Germany forced him to head home.

Pope Adrian IV upset Friedrich by implying that the empire was a fief of the papacy, so Friedrich took an army to Italy for a second time in 1158. Adrian died and although Pope Alexander III and Antipope Victor IV both asked Friedrich for support, only Victor would meet the emperor. Alexander III excommunicated both Friedrich and Victor and then allied with Sicily. An angry Friedrich returned to Germany in 1162 to discover that the power-mad Heinrich the Lion was out of control in Bavaria; he intervened to prevent conflict escalating between Heinrich the Lion and the rulers of neighbouring countries.

Friedrich invaded Italy when Alexander III returned to Rome in 1166 and defeated the Romans at the Battle of Monte Porzio. The new antipope, Paschal III, crowned him for a second time but an epidemic forced him to withdraw his army north of the Alps. He was defeated by the pro-papal Lombard League at Alessandria in 1175 and Legnano in 1176 when he tried to return. Friedrich finally agreed the Peace of Anagni with Alexander III and the Lombard League.

Pope Gregory VIII wanted to secure the Holy Land so Friedrich joined Richard the Lionheart of England and King Philippe II of France on the Third Crusade in 1189. They reached Constantinople only to learn that Emperor Isaac II had warned Saladin and the Ayyubids they were coming. The Crusaders continued on their journey beyond Byzantine territory, and were crossing the Saleph River when Friedrich walked his horse into the water to avoid the congested bridge. The fast current swept the animal off its feet, Friedrich drowned and the Crusade ended in panic. Friedrich's body was preserved in vinegar to take it home but it disintegrated, so his flesh was interred in Antioch, his bones in Tyre and his organs in Tarsus.

Heinrich VI succeeded his father as King of the Romans and had to suppress a revolt by the outlawed Heinrich the Lion before he could be crowned emperor by Pope Celestine III. Heinrich VI was married to Costanza of Sicily, but Tancred, Roger II's illegitimate grandson, was chosen to rule the kingdom instead of Costanza. Heinrich led his army through Italy declaring that he wanted what was rightfully Costanza's, but an epidemic forced him to break off his siege of Naples. Costanza was kidnapped and only released after Pope Celestine III had recognised Tancred as King of Sicily.

Heinrich's luck took a turn for the better when Leopold V, Duke of Austria handed Richard I of England over to him. Richard was suspected of murdering Konrad of Jerusalem, and while Heinrich was excommunicated for imprisoning a Crusader, he received a huge ransom for freeing him. The money would pay for another attack on Sicily. Tancred died as the imperial army approached so the emperor was crowned King of Sicily on Christmas Day 1194. Henry had Tancred's young son, Wilhelm, blinded, castrated and imprisoned and many Sicilian nobles were executed. He was putting down a revolt against his tyrannical rule when he died (possibly poisoned) in 1197.

Heinrich's 40-year-old wife Costanza had become pregnant; she knew that people would doubt that the child was really hers because of her age, so she gave birth to her son in a marquee erected in a market square so no one could question the birth. On the emperor's death, 2-year-old Friedrich II was elected King of the Germans and Holy Roman Emperor with Costanza as regent. Pope Innocent III became Friedrich's guardian when Costanza died in 1198, but Markward of Annweiler, Wilhelm of Capparone and Walter of Palearia each kidnapped the child in quick succession because they wanted to be his regent.

The princes were against crowning the young Friedrich II. Some elected Heinrich's brother, Philipp of Swabia, others Otto IV of Brunswick. Otto was crowned in fake regalia with Innocent's support and he was joined by Otakar of Bohemia during a campaign to drive Philipp from the north of Germany. But many of Otto's allies, including his brother Heinrich, later switched to Philipp's side and Otto was defeated and wounded in the Battle of Wassenberg in 1206. The pope also switched sides, and Philipp offered Otto his daughter Beatrix in marriage with a huge dowry to restore the peace. The issue was resolved in 1208, when Philipp was killed by Count Otto VIII of Wittelsbach and Philipp's wife miscarried and died soon afterwards. Otto murdered Philipp because he had refused to marry any of his four daughters to him after hearing he was a cruel man. Henryk I the Bearded of Lower Silesia also prevented his own daughter Gertrud from marrying Otto after hearing the same rumour. Otto of Wittelsbach was himself murdered a few months later.

Otto of Brunswick still married Beatrix to get everyone's support. He then travelled to Milan and received the Iron Crown of Lombardy and the title of King of Italy in 1208. The following year he was crowned emperor by Pope Innocent only to be excommunicated because he failed to carry out his promises. Otto had to abandon his attempt to capture Sicily because the German barons were causing trouble at home and Valdemar II of Denmark had captured his northern provinces.

Friedrich II was elected king in 1211, and while Otto returned to Germany, Friedrich was elected king for a second time in 1212. His election divided Western Europe: Philippe II of France allied with Friedrich and John of England supported Otto. John invaded France after he had destroyed the French fleet, but Philippe won the Battle of Bouvines in 1214 after Otto was carried off the field by his injured horse. Friedrich soon forced Otto to abdicate and he was crowned emperor when Otto died. He would help Philippe II of France end the French War of Succession by capturing Thiébaud I of Lorraine in 1218.

Friedrich II had promised Pope Innocent III that he would go on a Crusade. The papal legate in the Holy Land rejected an offer to restore the Kingdom of Jerusalem to the Crusaders in exchange for their withdrawal from Egypt because he thought Friedrich was on his way. But Friedrich stayed at home and had to agree to a new Crusade after hearing about the Fifth Crusade's failure. Instead he restored imperial power in northern Italy and the Lombard League reformed to challenge him. He also gave the East Prussian territories to the Teutonic Order, marking the start of the Northern Crusade.

Friedrich married Isabella II of Jerusalem by proxy, hoping to inherit the holy city, and set out to claim the kingdom when he heard that his new father-in-law, Jean of Brienne, had been disposed. But his army was struck by an epidemic so he turned back in 1227.

A disappointed Pope Gregory IX excommunicated Friedrich, so he organised another attempt the following year and was excommunicated a second time for crusading while excommunicated. Gregory even went as far as to call the emperor 'the Antichrist'.

Friedrich negotiated the return of Jerusalem, Nazareth and Bethlehem in 1229 but the Dome of the Rock and the al-Aqsa Mosque stayed under Muslim control, a deal condemned by the Templars and Hospitallers. He was then crowned King of Jerusalem only for his wife to die soon afterwards, leaving their baby son Konrad the rightful king.

Friedrich II had left his armies fighting the Lombard League while Jean of Brienne invaded southern Italy on behalf of Pope Gregory IX. The emperor returned in 1229 and recovered his lost territories before agreeing the Treaty of San Germano. Friedrich also discovered that his son, Heinrich, had annoyed the German barons in his absence and had handed over powers to appease them. Gregory had excommunicated Friedrich for the problems this caused the Church. Friedrich imprisoned his son because he was suffering from leprosy and made his young son Konrad, King of the Romans. Heinrich would die following a riding accident in 1242.

After dealing with a rebellion by Friedrich II, Duke of Austria, Emperor Friedrich invaded Italy and defeated the Lombard League at the Battle of Cortenuova. He twice tried to take Rome. Gregory died in 1241 and Pope Innocent IV declared the emperor deposed in 1245, referring to him as a 'friend of Babylon's sultan'. Innocent also sent money to Germany to undermine Friedrich's power and his plot to murder the emperor resulted in many being blinded, mutilated, burnt or hanged.

The archbishops elected Heinrich Raspe emperor in 1246 and used Rome's money to depose Friedrich and defeat his son, Konrad. Heinrich died soon after and was replaced by a new anti-king, Wilhelm II.

Friedrich thought he had control of Italy until Parma expelled all the imperial officials. He put the city under siege in 1247, but his fortified camp was captured and his army routed, encouraging resistance in other cities. He then had to blind and imprison his chief adviser for plotting against him. To make matters worse, his son Enzo was captured at the Battle of Fossalta and was never released. A distraught Friedrich died soon afterwards, in 1250.

Wilhelm of Holland succeeded Heinrich Raspe as anti-king but he first had to capture Aachen in 1248 in order to be crowned. While Konrad took Sicily, Germany and Jerusalem, Wilhelm fought the Flemish, upsetting Louis IX of France. When Wilhelm defeated Konrad in 1251, Konrad retaliated by conquering most of Italy; he was excommunicated and died of malaria soon after. Meanwhile, Wilhelm became lost during the Battle of Hoogwoud (in what is now Holland) in 1256 and his horse fell through a frozen lake, and then he was killed and buried in secret by the Frisians.

Richard of Cornwall turned down Pope Alexander IV's offer of Sicily and instead bribed enough German princes to elect him their king in 1256. He was opposed by a dissident faction, who had chosen Alfonso X of Castile, León and Galicia. The title cost Richard a lot of money but meant little to him as he only visited Germany four times over the next twelve years. He instead fought alongside his brother King Henry III of England in the Second Barons' War and was captured at the Battle of Lewes in 1264. Richard's imprisonment resulted in a power struggle in Germany and he died in England in 1273.

Rudolf of Habsburg was elected emperor, the first of many Habsburgs who would hold the position. His claim was helped by marrying two daughters to supporters, but he had to renounce his rights in Rome, the papal territory and Sicily. He also promised to lead a new Crusade so that Pope Gregory X would recognise him and persuade the anti-king Alfonso to renounce his claim. But Otakar II, King of Bohemia and Duke of Austria refused to recognise Rudolf despite the fact he had married one of his daughters to the Bohemian heir, Václav. Otakar allied with Poland, while Rudolf allied with Ladislaus IV of Hungary. The war between them ended when Otakar was killed at the battle on the Marchfeld in 1278. Rudolf could thus take control of Austria.

Despite Rudolf's efforts to have his son Albrecht elected as his successor, when he died in 1292 Adolf of Nassau was elected after making a lot of promises he could not (or did not wish to) keep. He also allied with Edward I of England against France in exchange for money, but failed to carry out his obligations. Adolf declared war on the French in 1294, alleging that they had seized imperial estates. King Philippe IV mocked him and Pope Boniface VIII threatened to excommunicate him and refused to crown him emperor.

Adolf extended his kingdom by buying Thuringian lands. But his days were numbered when angry electors brought a lawsuit against him for breach of peace and breaking the promises made to the Archbishop of Mainz. Adolf was deposed and Albrecht of Habsburg defeated and killed him at the Battle of Göllheim in 1298 to become Albrecht I.

In 1303, Pope Boniface VIII recognised Albrecht as the German king and future emperor while Albrecht recognised the authority of the pope alone to bestow the imperial crown. But things did not go well: his claim on Thuringia ended in defeat at the Battle of Lucka in 1307. His son Rudolf died the same year and Albrecht was then murdered by his nephew, Johann the Parricide, who had been deprived of his inheritance.

Heinrich VII was elected in 1308, ahead of the two main contenders, Friedrich of Austria and Charles of Valois. Two years later he accepted Elisabeth of Bohemia's offer to marry his son, Johann of Luxembourg, and acquired her kingdom. Heinrich also wanted to make Italy a source of imperial power, a move welcomed by Pope Clement V, so he was crowned King of the Lombards and anointed emperor. He then allied with King Friedrich II of Sicily but died as he prepared to attack Roberto of Naples.

Popes Clement V and John XXII declared that the imperial throne was vacant and the empire was therefore under papal rule. Friedrich the Fair was Rome's choice for King of Germany, but Louis IV the Bavarian was chosen as a rival king and defeated and captured Friedrich at the Battle of Mühldorf in 1322, for which he was excommunicated. Louis agreed to release Friedrich if he recognised Louis as emperor and made his brothers submit to Louis as well. When Friedrich failed he stuck to his oath and returned back to prison. His honourable actions impressed Louis so much he offered to share Germany. When the pope and the electors objected to the sharing of the position, a new treaty was agreed making Louis emperor and Friedrich King of Germany; Friedrich soon withdrew to rule Austria.

In 1328, Louis visited Italy, where the people crowned him emperor, and though he replaced John XXII with Antipope Nicholas V, they later reconciled. In 1342, Louis acquired the Tyrol by voiding the Countess Margarethe's first marriage so that she could marry his son.

Four years later he gave Holland, Zeeland and Friesland to his wife, Margarethe of Hainaut, upsetting the princes. Pope Clement VI deposed the king and Karel IV of Luxembourg was elected in his place.

Karel had escaped from the Battle of Crécy in 1346, where his father was killed, and returned home to be crowned King of Germany. He was elected emperor after making so many promises to the pope that he became known as 'the Priest's King'. A civil war with Louis was averted when he died of a stroke during a bear-hunt, but the empire was then hit by the Black Death and Karel moved his capital to Bohemia to avoid the plague.

Günther XXI von Schwarzburg was offered the German throne after Edward III of England refused it and was elected king in 1349 by Karel's opponents. But Karel quickly won over Günther's supporters and defeated him at the Battle of Eltville the same year; Günther died of illness soon afterwards.

Karel crossed the Alps without an army in 1354, to show he came in peace, and received the Lombard crown. He then issued a Golden Bull regulating the election of the king. The announcement encouraged Kazimierz III of Poland, Louis I of Hungary and Otto V of Bavaria to conspire against him. Karel went a step too far when he revoked privileges of imperial cities to secure the election of his teenage son, Václav, as King of the Romans in 1376.

Karel IV's division of his lands amongst his sons and relatives left Václav the Idle with no resources when he succeeded his father. The imperial cities, angered by Karel's interference with their affairs, came together to form the Swabian League and went to war with Václav. Fortunately for Václav the League was weakened by internal squabbles and he was able to defeat the cities. However, he was captured and imprisoned by Bohemian nobles for two years from 1394.

Václav supported the religious reformer Jan Hus and his heretic followers at a time when the Church was split by the Western Schism, and he failed to visit his German lands. He was deposed in 1402, accused of 'futility, idleness, negligence and ignobility'.

Supporters had declared Ruprecht of the Palatinate king in 1400 but he had no power in Germany and his plans to capture Milan and get the imperial crown failed. Zikmund of Luxemburg was briefly elected king in 1410 and again three months later, when his rival, Karel IV's brother Jobst of Moravia, died. He was present when three popes were forced to abdicate at the 1414 Council of Constance to end the Western Schism.

Zikmund of Luxemburg promised the Bohemian religious reformer Jan Hus safe conduct and protested when the Council of Constance had him burned at the stake for heresy in 1415. He became titular King of Bohemia in 1419 but entrusted government to the dead king's widow Žofie after he was accused of betraying Hus. He would be forced to fight three unsuccessful campaigns against the Hussites.

The German princes refused to help when the Ottomans invaded Hungary and Zikmund could achieve little without their support.

Zikmund received the Iron Crown of Italy in 1431 and was crowned emperor in Rome in 1433 by Pope Eugenius IV. He then returned to Bohemia, where he was finally recognised as king in 1436.

Zikmund had no sons so he married his daughter Elisabeth to Albrecht V of Austria, whom he named his successor. Albrecht turned the offer down so Friedrich III the Peaceful was elected King of Germany in 1440 and crowned Holy Roman Emperor by Pope Nicholas V in 1452. He also married young Leonor, daughter of Duarte I of Portugal, and paid off his debts with the dowry. But Friedrich's brother Albrecht challenged his rule and imprisoned the young Ladislaus the Posthumous, who was under Friedrich's protection, to take control of his Lower Austria.

Friedrich tried to gain control over Hungary and Bohemia, starting in 1468, but gave up after ten years. He then fought in the ten-year Austrian–Hungarian War only to be defeated by the Hungarian general Mátyás Hunyadi (Matthias Corvinus) in 1485. Friedrich would outlive all his opponents and eventually inherited both Upper and Lower Austria.

During the Siege of Neuss in 1475, Friedrich had forced Charles the Bold of Burgundy to marry his daughter Marie to his son, Maximilian, so he would inherit Burgundy.

Maximilian would be elected and crowned King of the Romans in 1486. Friedrich also agreed to marry his daughter Kunigunde to Albrecht IV of Bavaria, but withdrew his consent when he heard that Albrecht had been seizing imperial fiefs. Unfortunately, Kunigunde was married before the news reached her. Friedrich died in 1493, bleeding to death as his leg was amputated.

THE KINGDOM OF BOHEMIA

Bohemia was the east side of the Holy Roman Empire, with Poland to the north-east, Hungary to the south-east and Austria to the south.

Brětislav I, Duke of Bohemia captured Silesia from Poland but Heinrich III of Germany drove him out in 1040 and then negotiated a peace whereby Bohemia paid an annual fee so the Poles would not retaliate.

Brětislav's son Spytihněv II came to the Bohemian throne in 1055 and immediately expelled all Germans from his lands. He also stripped his brothers of their rights and one brother, Vratislav, fled to Hungary until Spytihněv died in 1061, when he inherited the dukedom.

Emperor Heinrich IV helped Vratislav II stop a rebellion at the Battle of Langensalza in 1075. Vratislav in turn helped Heinrich defeat anti-king Rudolf of Swabia at the Battle of Flarchheim in 1080. He also supported the emperor's campaign in Italy and entered Rome alongside him in 1083. Heinrich crowned Vratislav King of Bohemia, but it was not a hereditary title. In the latter part of Vratislav's reign, his son Brětislav turned on his father and forced him into exile, where he died while out hunting.

Vratislav's brother Konrád ruled briefly in 1092 but Brětislav seized control when Konrád died and began stamping out paganism, hoping to win Rome's favour. He made his half-brother, Bořivoj, a duke in 1097 and in doing so disinherited Konrád's son, Oldrich. Oldrich promptly assassinated Brětislav and made his challenge. Bořivoj called on Emperor Heinrich IV for support and they forced Oldrich to flee.

When a dispute broke out about the Polish succession, Bořivoj and his cousin Svatopluk supported Zbigniew of Poland until his rival Bolesław III paid them off and they withdrew from the war for the Polish throne.

Svatopluk 'the Lion' had promised Heinrich IV that he would support Bořivoj but forgot about his pledge when Heinrich V usurped his father in 1105. He captured Bořivoj with the help of the king's brother, Vladislav.

The Hungarian succession in 1108 was the next problem, and while Svatopluk helped Emperor Heinrich V to support Álmos, Duke of Croatia, Bořivoj and Bolesław III of Poland helped Álmos's brother Könyves to counter-attack Bohemia. Emperor Heinrich and Svatopluk invaded Poland on behalf of Bolesław's brother Zbigniew the following year. Svatopluk executed the head of the Bosnian Vršovice family at the Battle of Głogów, because he had supported Bořivoj, only to be murdered by a relative of the dead man in the emperor's tent.

Vladislav and Bořivoj tried to rule jointly but an argument forced Bořivoj to escape to Hungary.

Soběslav I, Bořivoj's younger brother, returned from exile to rule after Vladislav died in 1125, but he was challenged by Svatopluk's brother, Otto II of Olomouc, who attacked with German support. Soběslav exiled Otto II, so Holy Roman Emperor Lothar III used the imperial investiture as an excuse to invade Bohemia. Otto was killed at the Battle of Chlumec in 1126 and Lothar, who had been captured, was released after promising to support the investiture. Soběslav's nephew Brětislav was not so lucky when he too conspired against his uncle: he was blinded and his supporters were executed.

Soběslav died in 1140 and Emperor Lothar II recognised the right of Soběslav's son, Vladislav, but the Bohemian nobles rejected him. Konrad III of Germany helped them appoint his own nephew, also called Vladislav, as Vladislav II, Duke of Bohemia. Vladislav of Bohemia captured Prague with Konrad's help, and Vladislav returned the favour by accompanying his uncle on the Second Crusade.

Vladislav II was crowned King of Bohemia in 1158 for supporting the Crusade but he abdicated in favour of his son Bedřich in 1172 without asking permission. Emperor Friedrich deposed Bedřich and nominated Oldrich, Soběslav's son, instead. Oldrich stepped down in favour of the imprisoned Soběslav II, who would become known as 'the King of the Peasants'. Pope Alexander III excommunicated Soběslav, and Emperor Friedrich and Bedřich counter-attacked after he attacked Austria. The emperor then exiled Soběslav and reappointed Bedřich after winning the battles of Loděnice and Prague.

Konrad I's son, Konrad II, seized control in 1182 and helped the emperor's son, Heinrich, capture Sicily on behalf of Heinrich's wife, Costanza. Konrad died of the plague in Naples and Soběslav II's brother, Václav II, returned from exile to claim the throne, only to be deposed three months later by Friedrich's half-brother Otakar. Václav went to the emperor looking for help but was imprisoned instead. Otakar could not pay Bohemia's debts to the Holy Roman Empire so Heinrich VI took his chief supporter, Brětislav, hostage while he was on a pilgrimage. Heinrich then invaded Bohemia, deposed Otakar and appointed Brětislav III in 1193, leaving Václav II to die in prison.

Vladislav III, Otakar's brother, was elected in 1197 and when he blinded his opponent Spytihněv, the emperor decided he wanted Otakar back on the throne. So Vladislav abdicated and Otakar was formally acknowledged as King of Bohemia by Philipp of Swabia, King of the Romans.

Otakar immediately became involved in the German civil war. Philipp of Swabia invaded Bohemia after Otakar switched his support to Emperor Otto IV in 1200, only to withdraw when Bohemia paid him off. Otakar then supported the emperor's invasion of Austria in 1226, an attack caused by Friedrich II of Austria revoking the betrothal of his daughter to the emperor's son. Emperor Friedrich then stopped Austrian Friedrich marrying his daughter to Henry III of England and she chose to enter a convent to avoid further offers.

Otakar was overthrown for joining a German conspiracy to bring down the Hohenstaufen monarchy.

His successor, his son Václav the One-Eyed, had to provide troops for Emperor Friedrich II's attack on the north Italian Lombard League and then saw an imperial ban placed on Austria, which forced Friedrich II to flee. This meant the empire had control right up to Bohemia's border. Václav the One-Eyed responded by allying with Friedrich of Austria and Bavaria in 1237. The emperor lifted the Austrian ban and then everyone abandoned him when he was excommunicated in 1239.

Central European politics changed when the Mongols invaded Eastern Europe in 1241. The hordes were soon riding across Bohemian lands, forcing Václav to regroup following a defeat at Legnica. The Mongols then turned around and headed home to elect a new grand khan, leaving everyone to think they had been defeated.

Otakar II the Iron of Austria was elected King of Bohemia in 1253 but he was more interested in hunting and drinking than in his wife, and he became known as 'the Golden King'. He defeated a Hungarian army at the Battle of Kressenbrunn in 1260 so Béla IV offered his granddaughter to make peace. Otakar immediately divorced the elderly Margarete and married young Kunigunda.

Otakar II led two Crusades against the pagan Old Prussians, hoping to be elected emperor for his troubles. But Rudolf of Germany besieged Vienna in 1276 and forced him to give up all his territories except Bohemia and Moravia. Otakar also had to betroth his son, Václav, to Rudolf's daughter Guta (Judith) to make the peace. Infuriated, Otakar counter-attacked, only to be killed at the Battle on the Marchfeld in 1278.

Otto of Brandenburg was regent for young Václav II but his mother, Kunigunda, and her new husband, Zavis, interfered with the running of the state. Václav would behead his stepfather for treason as soon as he came of age. Przemysł II of Poland ceded Kraków to Václav in 1291 and he became overlord of Poland, after the high duke died in 1296, and then became king in 1300. His situation was helped by the discovery of the Bohemian Kutná Hora silver mines, which produced 20 tons a year.

Václav II's young son, also named Václav, was betrothed to András III's daughter, Elizabeth of Töss, in 1298 and he became King of Hungary under the name Ladislaus V in 1301. Many Hungarian nobles preferred Károly Róbert of Anjou, so the younger Václav asked his father for help. Father rescued son, and they returned to Bohemia with the Hungarian crown, leaving Ivan of Gussing behind to represent them.

Václav II died in 1305 and his son, now Václav III of Bohemia, immediately broke off his engagement to Elizabeth, renounced the Hungarian throne and relinquished the crown. He wanted to claim his hereditary right to Poland instead but he upset many by making Jindřich of Carinthia regent of Bohemia in his absence; he caused even more offence when he married Jindřich to his sister Anna. Nevertheless, when Václav was assassinated in 1306, Jindřich was elected King of Bohemia and titular King of Poland. Albrecht of Germany wanted control of Bohemia, so he captured Prague and crowned his son Rudolf, who died soon after. Jindřich was duly re-elected. Albrecht's second attack failed and the Habsburg dynasty fell apart when he was assassinated in 1308.

Heinrich VII of Germany also wanted Bohemia so he married his son, Jan, to the late Václav's sister, Elizabeth of Bohemia, in 1310. Jan deposed Jindřich for a second time but the Bohemian nobility hated the new king, so he left his wife and went travelling. He fought with the Teutonic Knights against Poland until its king, Kazimierz III the Great, paid him to renounce his tenuous claim to the Polish throne. Jan's eyesight was failing but he still fought alongside Philippe VI of France at the Battle of Crécy in 1346. He had his reins tied to his supporters' horses and said, 'Let it never be the case that a Bohemian king runs!' Jan the Blind was found dead with his men.

Jan's injured son, Karel, escaped from the battlefield and returned home to be crowned king. He was also elected Holy Roman Emperor after making huge concessions to Rome and became known as 'the Priest's King'. A civil war was only averted because his rival, Louis the Bavarian, was killed during a bear hunt. Karel IV then had to administer the empire during the Black Death, moving his capital to Prague because it had not been affected by the plague.

Karel was re-elected in 1349 and five years later crossed the Alps without an army, to show he came in peace, receiving the Lombard crown as a reward.

In 1356 he issued the Golden Bull, which was designed to regulate the election of the King of the Romans, and Kazimierz III of Poland, Louis I of Hungary and Otto V of Bavaria conspired against him. Karel then revoked the privileges of the imperial cities, to make sure his teenage son Václav the Idle would be elected King of the Romans in 1376.

Václav was indeed idle after inheriting the Bohemian throne because his father had split his lands between his sons and relatives, leaving him with none of his own. He had to defeat an alliance of imperial cities, known as the Swabian League, and was then arrested by the Bohemian nobles in 1394 while his cousin Jobst of Moravia was named regent.

Václav's brother Zikmund of Hungary made peace with Bohemia in 1396 in return for recognition as heir to the Bohemian throne. Václav was accused of protecting the religious reformer Jan Hus and his heretic followers. He also failed to visit his German lands and was consequently deposed in 1402.

Emperor Zikmund was King of Hungary, Croatia, Germany and Bohemia when he opened the Council of Constance in Germany in 1414 to discuss the Schism. He asked Jan Hus to attend, offering him safe conduct, but the religious reformer was arrested and burnt at the stake; the two-decade Hussite Wars would follow. Václav died during a hunt in 1419 so Zikmund entrusted the running of the kingdom to Václav's widow, Žofie. The Bohemians thought Zikmund had betrayed Jan Hus. It was seventeen years before they acknowledged him as their king, and he had little power.

Albrecht the Magnanimous of Austria was elected King of Bohemia in 1438 but he was unable to defeat the Bohemians and their Polish allies. He would be killed defending Hungary from the Ottomans in 1439. His son, Ladislaus the Posthumous, was born four months later but Jiří of Poděbrad's Hussites had already seized Prague. Emperor Friedrich III was young Ladislaus's guardian and he entrusted the administration of Bohemia to Jiří until Ladislaus was crowned in 1453. The teenage king died mysteriously in 1458 and some thought Jiří had poisoned him, but he was suffering from leukaemia, an unknown disease at the time.

Despite opposition from Pope Pius II, Bohemia chose Jiří of Poděbrad to be their king and he declared that all the Christian kingdoms should settle their differences through a parliament, and prepare to fight the 'abominable Turk', who had conquered Constantinople in 1453. Pope Pius II opposed the treaty but his successor, Pope Paul II, went further: he excommunicated Jiří and gave Hungary permission to invade Bohemia. Mátyás Hunyadi, King of Hungary and Croatia, had captured large parts of the country by the time a truce was made in 1470. George died soon after and his followers supported teenage Vladislav II, son of Kazimierz IV of Poland, because they wanted a young king they could control.

The 1479 Peace of Olomouc let Mátyás Hunyadi rule Moravia, Silesia and the Lusatias while Vladislav ruled Bohemia. Mátyás died in 1490 and the Hungarian nobility forced his illegitimate son János into exile. In his place they crowned Vladislav, because he was the nephew of the long-dead King Ladislaus the Posthumous, and he lived in Hungary for the rest of his life. He became depressed after the death of his third wife and left the barons to make most of the decisions. His nickname would be 'Bene' because he answered most requests with the word *bene*, Latin for 'fine'.

THE DUCHY OF AUSTRIA

Austria was at the south-east corner of the Holy Roman Empire, with Hungary to the south-east. Until 1156 the title given to the ruler of Austria was not duke but the slightly lower rank of 'margrave'.

Margrave Albrecht the Victorious supported Emperor Heinrich III in his prolonged wars with Hungary and Bohemia. His son and successor Ernst the Brave appropriated the Bohemian and Hungarian marches to form Austria and then sided with Emperor Heinrich IV against the Saxons, only to be killed at the Battle of Langensalza in 1075. Ernst's son Luitpold II the Fair initially supported Heinrich IV in the Investiture Dispute but switched his support to Pope Gregory VII in 1081. The emperor gave Luitpold's lands to Vratislav II of Bohemia and then defeated Luitpold at the Battle of Mailberg in 1095. Luitpold III the Good married Heinrich V's sister, Agnes, and would be granted royal right. He would also become Austria's patron saint.

Luitpold IV the Generous was appointed margrave ahead of his two older brothers in 1137. He supported Emperor Konrad III in his dispute against the Welfen family and was given Bavaria as a reward. His brother Heinrich II Jasomirgott was appointed margrave in 1141 and he moved Austria's capital to Vienna. He served as regent of Bavaria until Heinrich the Proud came of age and Emperor Friedrich I then upgraded him to duke and Austria to an independent duchy in 1156.

Luitpold V the Virtuous succeeded his father as duke in 1177 and immediately helped Friedrich in his struggle for Bohemia against Soběslav II. He also negotiated the 1186 Georgenberg Pact, which incorporated Styria into Austria. Luitpold joined the Third Crusade and took command of the Siege of Acre following the death of Friedrich VI, Duke of Swabia, in 1191. It was noted that his blood-soaked tunic had a white stripe when he removed his belt and the colours were adopted as Austria's new flag.

Acre surrendered but Luitpold abandoned the Crusade and returned to Austria after his colours were removed from the city walls by Richard of England. A vengeful Luitpold arrested Richard as he passed through Austria on his way home and accused him of murdering Konrad of Jerusalem. Luitpold was excommunicated by Pope Celestine III for imprisoning a Crusader but Emperor Heinrich VI paid Luitpold the huge ransom. He used it to build Vienna's new walls and found the city mint. A horse crushed Luitpold's foot during a tournament and he died of gangrene in 1194.

The Georgenberg Pact also called for the division of the realm into two and Friedrich I was given Austria while Luitpold VI was given Styria. Friedrich the Catholic joined Emperor Heinrich VI's Crusade in 1197 but died on his return, leaving Luitpold VI the Glorious to take control of all Austria. Luitpold was also a Crusader and he joined the fight against the Almohads in the Iberian Peninsula and the Albigensians in southern France in 1212 before joining the Fifth Crusade in 1217.

Friedrich II the Quarrelsome succeeded his father Luitpold in 1230 but refused to appear at the Imperial Diets (meeting of the imperial estates) and supported Heinrich of Germany's rebellion against his father Emperor Freidrich. In response the emperor gave Václav I of Bohemia permission to invade Austria in 1235. The emperor's son, Konrad, was given most of the duchy and Vienna was made an imperial free city, leaving only a rump state. So Friedrich changed his mind, became the emperor's ally and was given his territories back.

In 1245 Friedrich married his niece Gertrud to Konrad IV to ally himself with Germany. But the teenager refused to consummate her marriage with the 50-year-old emperor, thwarting the alliance. Friedrich the Quarrelsome was killed fighting Béla IV of Hungary along the Leitha River in 1246.

Although Vladislav of Moravia and Herman VI of Baden made claims for Austria, Otakar II of Bohemia seized it in 1253. Otakar II refused to recognise Rudolf I when he was elected King of Germany, so Rudolf allied with Ladislaus IV of Hungary while Otakar allied with Poland and a few rebellious German princes. Otakar was killed at the Battle on the Marchfeld in 1278, so Rudolf took control of Austria and gave his sons control of the Austrian and Styrian duchies. Teenage Rudolf the Debonair was forced to hand over his share to Albrecht under the 1283 Treaty of Rheinfelden and then died suddenly, just after his son Johann was born.

Rudolf I tried to secure Albrecht's election before he died but Count Adolf of Nassau was elected in 1292 instead. Adolf tried to ally with Václav II of Poland but was replaced by King Albrecht of Germany in 1298 and was killed at the Battle of Göllheim. Pope Boniface VIII recognised Albrecht's appointment in 1303 and he in turn recognised the authority of the pope and was bestowed with an imperial crown.

Albrecht invaded Bohemia and besieged Prague after Václav III, King of Hungary, Bohemia and Poland was assassinated in 1306. He expelled the unpopular Henry of Carinthia and married his son, Rudolf III the Good, to Václav II's widow, Elizabeth. But King Porridge, as he was known, died a few months later and Heinrich was restored. Meanwhile, Albrecht was murdered by his nephew, Johann the Parricide. He had been seeking revenge even since he learnt that his father had been forced to hand over his inheritance to Adolf under the Treaty of Rheinfelden.

Adolf's son, Friedrich the Handsome, was forced to give up his claim to the German crown. He invaded Bavaria when Heinrich VII was crowned emperor in 1312 but was beaten by Ludwig of Bavaria (who was soon to be Germany's anti-king) at the Battle of Gammelsdorf in 1313. Friedrich's co-ruler, Luitpold I the Glorious, would accompany Heinrich when he invaded Italy, but Heinrich died before the campaign ended.

Friedrich was successful in the first imperial vote but Ludwig IV of Wittelsbach won the second vote, so Friedrich was crowned anti-king. He was defeated by the Swiss Confederacy at the Battle of Morgarten in 1315 and then defeated and captured by Ludwig, along with 1,300 nobles, at the Battle of Mühldorf in 1322. Luitpold handed over the imperial regalia to Ludwig IV but the nobles remained in prison and the fighting continued until the 1325 Treaty of Trausnitz.

Luitpold recognised Ludwig as his emperor and Friedrich was released but their brother, Heinrich, refused to submit. So a defeated Luitpold voluntarily returned to prison and an impressed Ludwig agreed to share rule of the empire. Pope John XXII and the prince-electors rejected the idea, so Ludwig was crowned Holy Roman Emperor and Friedrich was made regent of Germany as a compromise. Friedrich withdrew from the regency of Germany to rule Austria when Luitpold died.

In 1330, Albrecht II the Wise became joint ruler with his brother Otto the Merry, so called because he enjoyed a lively court life. Albrecht was asked to mediate in the conflict between Pope Benedict XII and Emperor Ludwig in 1335 while Otto founded the *Societas Templois* to organise Crusades against the pagan Prussians and Lithuanians. But Otto died in 1339, and his teenage sons Luitpold and Friedrich died only five years later, leaving their uncle Albrecht under suspicion of poisoning them.

Rudolf IV became Duke of Austria, Styria and Carinthia when his father Albrecht died in 1358. Austria had not been given an electoral vote in Emperor Karl IV's Golden Bull so Rudolf forged the *Privilegium Maius*, giving him equal powers with the Holy Roman Empire's seven prince-electors. He also called himself archduke while others called him the founder of Austria.

Rudolf had married Katharina of Luxembourg, Emperor Karl's daughter, creating a mutual assured inheritance between the Habsburg and Luxembourg dynasties. He also made an inheritance contract with the widowed Countess of Gorizia-Tyrol, expecting to bring Tyrol under his rule when she died; unfortunately, he died before she did.

Rudolf's brothers, Luitpold III and Albrecht III, ruled jointly until they divided Austria under the 1379 Treaty of Neuberg, which decreed that Leopold's descendants would receive Further Austria (west) and Tyrol while Albrecht's descendants would receive Lower (north-east) Austria.

The Luitpold Line, Further Austria

Duke Luitpold the Just campaigned in Switzerland and Swabia until he was killed at the Battle of Sempach in 1386, leaving his four sons to argue over his lands. His eldest, Wilhelm the Courteous, had wanted to marry Hedwig of Hungary, so he could take control of her kingdom, but she became queen regnant of Poland instead. He married Giovanna of Naples instead, hoping to secure her inheritance, but he died in 1406 before she succeeded her brother. Wilhelm left no sons, so his brother Luitpold IV the Fat became head of the family and argued with the third brother Ernst the Iron over the guardianship of their young cousin Albrecht V, heir to the Albrecht line. Luitpold failed to take control of Lower Austria before he died in 1411, leaving no heir. Ernst the Iron became head of the family, calling himself archduke, the first Habsburg to do so.

Meanwhile, Friedrich, the fourth brother, had trouble controlling the nobles in his part of Austria and was called 'Empty Pockets'. Friedrich sided with Antipope John XXIII at the 1417 Council of Constance so Emperor Zikmund placed him under an imperial ban. Ernst failed to capture Tyrol and Friedrich succeeded him when he died in 1424. Friedrich IV's rule was secured when silver was found in the Tyrol the following year.

Zikmund came to his father's throne in 1439 and was crowned Duke of Austria and ruler of Tyrol when he came of age seven years later. Pope Pius II excommunicated him when he imprisoned Bishop Nikolaus of Cusa over a territorial dispute, but he was made an archduke by Friedrich III in 1477. Zikmund became known as 'the Rich' when new technology allowed the Tyrol silver mines to reopen. He became even richer when he seized the Venetian silver mines in the War of Rovereto in 1487. However, the people of Tyrol forced Zikmund to hand power to Maximilian I in 1490.

The Albrecht Line, Lower Austria

Albrecht with the Pigtail concentrated on crusading against Lithuanian pagans and was briefly succeeded by his son Albrecht IV the Patient.

His son, Albrecht V, was looked after by his uncles from the Luitpold line, Luitpold and Ernst, who tried in vain to appropriate his lands until he came of age. Albrecht V the Magnanimous supported his father-in-law Zikmund of Hungary in the Hussite Wars and was present when the Hussites defeated the imperial army at Domažlice in 1431. Zikmund died in 1437 and Albrecht moved to Budapest to be crowned King of Hungary. He was also crowned King of Bohemia six months later, but the Bohemians and their Polish allies refused to accept him so he refused to be King of the Romans. Albrecht was killed at the Battle of Neszmély in 1439, defending Hungary from the Ottomans.

Albrecht's son, Ladislaus the Posthumous, was born four months later and his mother, Elizabeth, took him and Hungary's crown to Austria. Unfortunately, Friedrich IV of Germany (and V of Austria) imprisoned her baby and took the crown for himself. Hungary chose Ladislaus to be their king when Vladislav I was killed fighting the Ottomans at the Battle of Varna in 1444 but Friedrich still refused to surrender the child and the crown.

Friedrich signed the 1448 Vienna Concordat, which regulated the relationship between the Habsburgs and the Holy See, and Pope Nicholas V crowned him Emperor Friedrich III in 1452; he would be the last emperor crowned in Rome. The Austrians joined the Mailberg Confederation and young Ladislaus the Posthumous of Austria, Hungary and Bohemia was finally released.

The teenage Ladislaus did nothing when the Ottomans attacked Hungary. After Ladislaus Hunyadi of Hungary was executed, Ladislaus the Posthumous fled to Prague and died suddenly in 1457. Poisoning was suspected, but he had actually died of leukaemia.

Friedrich the Peaceful invaded Bohemia in 1468 but had failed to conquer it by 1478 because Hungary joined the Bohemian War. Friedrich forced Charles the Bold of Burgundy to marry his daughter to Friedrich's son, Maximilian, to end the Siege of Neuss in 1475. Marriage had won where military action had not and the motto of Friedrich's dynasty became 'Let others wage wars, but you, happy Austria, shall marry'. Friedrich was defeated by Mátyás Hunyadi in the 1485 Austrian–Hungarian War. He had only just had Vienna restored to him when he bled to death in 1493 after the amputation of his leg went wrong. He was succeeded by his son, Maximilian I, the Last Knight, with whom he had shared rule for ten years.

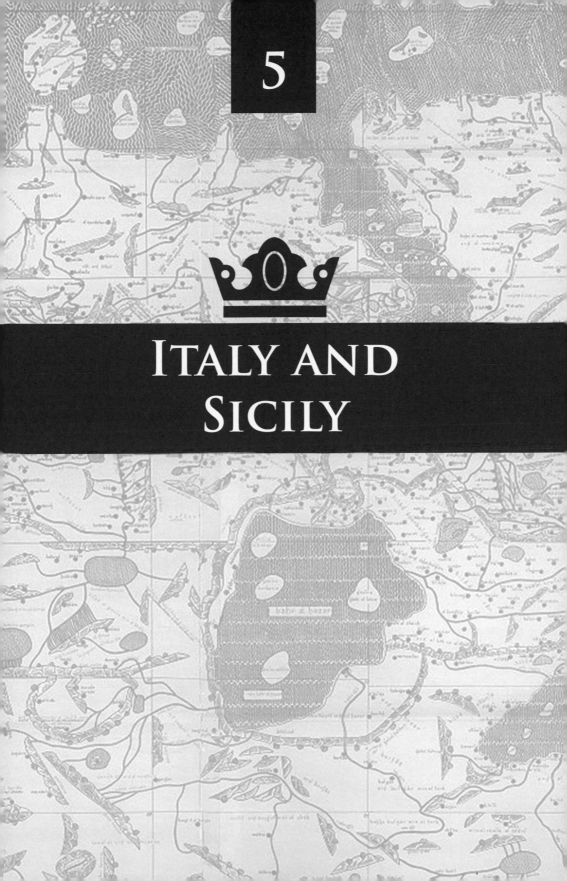

5

ITALY AND SICILY

WHILE THE HOLY ROMAN EMPIRE included what we know as northern Italy today, the central area of the peninsula was ruled from Rome. The two thrones argued over who ruled over whom, and a long line of elderly popes and antipopes either fought or allied with the emperor. Rome would influence most of the countries across Europe at some point, appointing crowns, excommunicating kings, calling for Crusades and approving (or annulling) marriages.

The Kingdom of Sicily was formed in 1160 and the Kingdom of Naples emerged following the War of the Sicilian Vespers in 1282. Rome was always anxious to stop the emperor ruling southern Italy because it would undermine its power.

THE PAPAL STATES AND THE ROMAN CATHOLIC CHURCH

The Papal States were a small area around Rome, with the mighty Holy Roman Empire to the north and the Kingdom of Sicily to the south.

Emperor Heinrich III appointed his relative Bruno of Egisheim-Dagsburg as pope Leo IX in 1049, and Leo travelled Europe, trying to stop the clergy selling privileges and having concubines. In 1053 Leo organised an army to fight the Normans in southern Italy, but was taken prisoner and had to make many concessions before he was released.

Leo IX's legates and the Patriarch of Constantinople, Mikhaël Keroularios, fell out and excommunicated each other in 1054, marking the final separation of the Greek and Roman Churches.

Pope Victor II continued cleaning up the Church despite resistance and tried to limit the emperor's influence in Church affairs. He also introduced papal elections before he died in 1057. Pope Stephen IX stopped any more clergymen marrying and tried to stop Heinrich IV selling Church honours and posts. Pope Nicholas II prohibited the selling of favours and banned all priests from marrying, forcing those already wed to leave their wives or be defrocked. There was an outcry over his decree that the pope could only be elected by cardinals, in particular in Germany, so he employed Roberto of Sicily to fight on his behalf.

Pope Alexander II was elected with Sicily's support in 1061 so Emperor Heinrich IV elected Antipope Honorius II.

Pope Gregory VII threatened to excommunicate anyone who opposed him when he was elected in 1073, so Heinrich provoked an uprising in Rome and Gregory was imprisoned. Heinrich ignored a summons to Rome, so Gregory retaliated by declaring the pope above the emperor and excommunicating Heinrich. Heinrich repented and visited the pope's castle, waiting outside in a cassock for three days and nights before he was pardoned and his excommunication was lifted.

But Heinrich fought back once back in Germany and he was excommunicated again. In response, he appointed Antipope Clement III and besieged Rome for three years. Gregory eventually hid in the city's Castel Sant'Angelo until Robert Guiscard took him to Salerno, to keep him safe.

Gregory sent crowns to Iziaslav of Rus' and Bolesław of Poland in 1076; Luitpold II of Austria and Dmitar of Croatia also pledged allegiance to Gregory; but Géza of Hungary rejected an offer to join the Roman Church and accepted a crown from the Byzantine Church instead. Ladislao of Hungary then seized Croatia and refused to acknowledge Rome's supremacy over his new territory. In Germany, Rudolf of Rheinfelden was crowned anti-king of Germany and defeated Heinrich at Flarchheim in 1080. Gregory added insult to injury, excommunicating Heinrich again. Heinrich retaliated by invading Italy and replaced Gregory with Antipope Clement III in 1084, so he could be crowned King of Italy and emperor.

Pope Victor III was elected in 1086 but was already suffering ill health and retired almost immediately to Monte Cassino. He died a few months later. Antipope Clement III refused to let Victor's successor Pope Urban II into Rome until 1093.

During Urban's reign, Emperor Heinrich IV was accused by his wife Adelaide of being a member of the heretical Nicolaitan sect. His son Konrad backed up his stepmother and swore loyalty to Pope Urban II in return for a promise of the imperial crown.

Byzantine Emperor Alexios asked for help to capture Jerusalem and Pope Urban II declared the First Crusade. He had denied Philippe I of France's request for a divorce, so the latter refused to support the Crusade and was excommunicated until he promised to leave his mistress. Pierre the Hermit organised the Crusade but it was a chaotic affair and, after pillaging the Balkans, the rabble of Crusaders were massacred in Asia Minor in 1096. Urban died before hearing about the capture of Jerusalem in 1099.

Pope Paschal II was elected but Antipope Clement III again returned to Rome and had to be driven out by Roger of Sicily. In 1100 Clement died and Heinrich IV appointed Antipope Theoderic as his successor, but Paschal captured him and he died in captivity. Paschal excommunicated Heinrich IV for a third time and he promised to go on a Crusade. His enemies encouraged his son, Heinrich (later Heinrich V), to revolt, despite the fact that he had sworn to take no part in the business of the empire during his father's lifetime. Pope Paschal II relieved young Heinrich of his oath so that he could imprison his father and force him to abdicate.

Pope Paschal II refused to attend a council in Germany to debate the Investiture Controversy so Heinrich V seized Rome, exiled Paschal and appointed Antipope Silvester IV. Heinrich forced a discussion and agreed to renounce the rite of investiture in return for a promise of coronation. Neither pope nor emperor kept his promise, so Heinrich arrested Paschal and forced sixteen cardinals to crown him emperor in 1111; he was then excommunicated for resorting to such heavy-handed methods. The religious warriors, the Knights Templar, the Teutonic Knights and the Knights Hospitaller, were formed to protect pilgrims to the Holy Land during Paschal's reign.

Pope Gelasius II was elected in 1118 but was captured and imprisoned by Heinrich V's supporters when he entered Rome. They freed Gelasius and he fled when Heinrich arrived and elected Antipope Gregory VIII. Gelasius was exiled to France, where he excommunicated both Heinrich and Gregory before he died in 1119.

At the 1122 Treaty of Worms, his successor Callixtus II and Heinrich agreed that the clergy would elect bishops and imperial legates would approve them. Meanwhile, the Normans were advancing north from Sicily, driving Antipope Gregory VIII from Rome. It made no difference to Callixtus and Heinrich because they both died soon afterwards.

Both Honorius II and Celestine II were chosen for pope in 1124; both were willing to cede and Honorius was chosen. He worked for papal supremacy and a Christian alliance for a holy war but supported Lothar of Saxony against Konrad of Swabia. Roger of Sicily continued to extend his control over southern Italy and a sick Honorius was forced to confirm his investiture before he retired and died in 1130.

Pope Innocent II fled to France when Anacletus II became lord of Rome but Lothar of Saxony led him back into the city on a mule and kissed his foot as a sign of submission. Lothar was crowned emperor in return for acknowledging his subservience to the pope. Antipope Victor IV resigned when Anacletus died, and Innocent declared war on Sicily and excommunicated Roger of Sicily before he was taken prisoner.

Innocent excommunicated Louis VII of France for following Peter Abelard's heretical doctrines, but Celestine II withdrew the excommunication when he was appointed. Celestine had to escape to a fortified monastery when Rome was seized and died there.

Pope Lucius II was pope for only a year. He fought Giordano Pierleoni's government when it abolished the popes' temporal power, only to be mortally injured during a riot.

Although Pope Eugene III was elected in 1145, he had no say in Rome's administration and concentrated on recruiting Louis VII of France and Konrad III of Germany for a Second Crusade instead; this would end in disaster at Damascus. Eugene also called for a Crusade against the Almoravids, and Portugal, Castile and Aragon signed the 1151 Treaty of Tudilén, defining their zones of conquest.

Friedrich Barbarossa succeeded Konrad III in 1152 and immediately upset Rome by forgetting to ask Pope Eugene III for confirmation of his appointment. He had to promise to defend the 'honour of the Church' by capturing Rome and refused to ally with Roger II of Sicily to make amends. Now able to return to Rome, Eugene in turn promised him a coronation and the 'honour of the empire'. He built a new palace, which became the basis for the Vatican palaces, and approved the formation of the Knights of Malta before he died in 1153. A new but elderly pope, Anastasius IV, died only a few months later.

Pope Adrian IV was elected in 1154, the only English pope in history. He immediately had the anti-papist Arnaldo da Brescia hanged and his corpse burned at the stake for calling on the Church to renounce its properties.

From 1155 he allied the Vatican states with the Byzantines against Sicily, and negotiations towards a union between the western and eastern Churches began. He encouraged Byzantine Emperor Manuel I to attack Sicily, but confirmed Guglielmo's title after he defeated the Byzantines.

Pope Adrian then upset Friedrich Barbarossa by implying that the empire was a fief of the papacy. Friedrich invaded Italy in 1158, refusing to hold the stirrups of the pope's horse when they met, so Adrian refused to give him the kiss of pardon. Friedrich would eventually be crowned emperor and then laid claim to the exclusive rights of the 'Roman' emperors to Rome; Adrian died before he could excommunicate him.

Pope Alexander III was elected in 1159 and he too opposed Friedrich Barbarossa, so the emperor appointed Antipope Victor IV. He then invited Alexander and Victor to Rome but since only Victor showed up, he was proclaimed pope. All Alexander could do was excommunicate Friedrich and Victor while he searched for allies. Friedrich appointed Antipope Paschal III in 1164 and then invaded Italy when Alexander returned to Rome, defeating the Romans at the Battle of Monte Porzio. Antipope Callixtus III subjected himself to Pope Alexander ten years later.

The Lombard League would finally defeat Friedrich at the Battle of Legnano in 1176. The emperor visited Rome, prostrated himself and renounced all imperial claims but Alexander put his foot on Friedrich's bowed head and raged, 'Thou shalt crush the asp and the basilisk under foot.' An insulted Friedrich switched his support to Antipope Innocent III, who died only a year later.

Pope Lucius III was elected and then forced to leave Rome, never to return. Friedrich refused to help him because he would not crown his son Heinrich VI. In absentia, Lucius declared a war on heresies across Roman Catholic Europe, a process which would grow into the Inquisition.

Pope Urban III did not want the Holy Roman Empire and Sicily to join forces so he opposed the marriage between Emperor Friedrich's son and Roger of Sicily's daughter. He was en route to Venice to excommunicate Friedrich when he heard that Saladin had captured Jerusalem; he died soon afterwards. Pope Gregory VIII failed to get the emperor or the north Italian states to join the Third Crusade before he died, but Pope Clement III got Philippe of France and Richard of England to join the emperor, Venice, Pisa and Genoa. The Third Crusade collapsed when Friedrich Barbarossa was drowned in Anatolia in 1191.

When Pope Celestine III crowned Tancredi's young son Guglielmo III of Sicily, Emperor Heinrich VI invaded Italy because he believed the Sicilian throne was his wife Costanza's inheritance. An epidemic forced him to break his siege of Naples; Costanza, who had been kidnapped, was released before she could be delivered to Rome. Heinrich died unexpectedly in 1197, possibly poisoned; Celestine died in 1198.

Pope Innocent III's first move was to urge King Imre of Hungary to stamp out the Balkan-based Bogomilism, a Christian religion which worshipped in the open and shunned Roman Catholic trappings. Innocent proclaimed Friedrich II King of Sicily and gave the emperor's crown to Otto of Brunswick in order to divide power between them. He then wielded his own power to prove the Church all-powerful: Otto was excommunicated for not keeping the faith; England's King John was excommunicated for rejecting the pope's choice for the Archbishop of Canterbury; Philippe II of France was excommunicated for refusing to reinstate his wife (whom he had sought to divorce); and Alfonso IX was excommunicated for being married to his cousin. Innocent also proposed the Fourth Crusade, which ended in disaster in 1202, and the Albigensian Crusade, which stamped out the Cathar heresy in southern France.

Pope Innocent's envoys visited Galicia–Volhynia in 1204 but when they promised to place its prince, Roman the Great, 'under the protection of St Peter's sword', he replied, 'Is the pope's sword similar to mine? So long as I carry mine, I need no other.' But Innocent was no doubt pleased to hear that Leszek of Poland had pledged himself to Rome.

Innocent organised the Fifth Crusade but was disappointed to hear that Leszek refused to participate because there was no beer for the Polish knights in Palestine. He was also frustrated to hear that Bosnia was still a Bogomil stronghold. He brokered peace between the Byzantines and Bulgaria, offering to crown Kaloyan of Bulgaria in the hope it would unite the Bulgarian Church with Rome.

Innocent died from malaria before the Fifth Crusade began in 1216.

Pope Honorius III crowned Friedrich II on the promise that he would cede the Kingdom of Sicily to a relative and lead the Fifth Crusade. An offer to restore the Kingdom of Jerusalem if the Crusaders left Egypt was rejected because it was believed Friedrich was on his way. But the emperor neglected to keep his pledge and the Crusade failed.

Young Heinrich VII was elected King of Germany in 1220 but Honorius refused to recognise the election and deprived him of his Sicilian rights, to stop Germany and Sicily uniting. Jaime II of Aragon seized the Kingdom of Sicily, despite promising he would not, and the war only ended because a plague decimated Charles de Valois's army.

Honorius gave the Teutonic Knights equal status with the Knights Templar and Knights Hospitaller because their grand master, Hermann von Salza, helped in the discussions with the emperor.

Friedrich's Crusade eventually began in 1227, but it did not have Hungarian support because András was embroiled in a civil war. The Crusaders were turned back after they were struck by an epidemic, so a disappointed Pope Gregory X excommunicated Friedrich. The emperor organised another attempt the following year, only to be excommunicated again for crusading while excommunicated. A third excommunication followed in 1239 because Friedrich did not leave Sicily when he had promised.

Pope Gregory IX was almost 100 years old when he died in 1241. The next election took so long that the cardinals were locked in (conclave means 'with key') for several weeks. One died and many fell ill, including the winner, Celestine IV, who died only seventeen days later. It took two years to elect Pope Innocent IV and he immediately fled to France and excommunicated the emperor. Meanwhile, the Mongols were riding across Europe and Innocent was unable to help Poland or Hungary because of Rome's war with Friedrich.

Pope Innocent IV appointed Heinrich Raspe as anti-king and declared a deposed Friedrich a 'friend of Babylon's sultan' in 1245. The dispute only ended when Friedrich died in 1250 and Innocent returned to Italy. Meanwhile, Innocent was looking to spread Christianity by whatever means necessary. He tried to ally with the new grand khan Möngke in order to foster Christianity among the Mongols (they would adopt Islam fifty years later). He also sanctioned the Seventh Crusade, on which Louis IX of France was captured in Egypt and forced to hand over all his money to pay the ransom.

In 1253 Daniel of Galicia became first King of Rus' and captured Galicia after it had been ravaged by the Mongols. But Innocent only sent a representative crown, meaning Daniel had no support from the rest of Europe. He had no option but to pay tribute to the Mongols to stop them returning.

Innocent sold Sicily to Edmund Crouchback, son of Henry III of England, but the English barons refused to pay for the crown and Manfredi of Sicily refused to stand down. Manfredi was excommunicated; he handed over Apulia to Rome but it was not enough, so he raised Islamic support from North Africa and defeated a papal army at Foggia in 1254. News of the defeat reached Innocent on his deathbed.

Pope Alexander IV crowned Manfredi only to excommunicate him when he failed to pay for the privilege. Alexander put the Sicilian crown up for offer. Richard of Cornwall turned it down, replying, 'You might as well say, "I make you a present of the moon; step up to the sky and take it down."' Charles of Anjou, Louis IX of France's brother, bought the crown from Pope Urban IV in 1262 on the condition that he would not unite with the emperor. Charles defeated and killed Manfredi at Benevento, and then captured young Corradino, the heir to the Sicilian throne, and beheaded him in 1266, despite the pope's protests. He subsequently took control of Apulia and Sicily, paying the Church to seal his authority over his new kingdom.

Pope Clement IV would inspire the Eighth Crusade, this time against North Africa. Louis IX died of plague in Tunis, Edward I of England arrived too late to make a difference and Charles of Anjou's fleet was ravaged by a storm.

The conclave that elected Pope Gregory X's had dragged on for three years when the people lost patience and took the roof off the election hall in 1272 and forced a decision. Two years later, Gregory convened the Council of Lyon to liberate the Holy Land but Emperor Mikhaël VIII asked for help against the Mongol invasion of the Byzantine Empire. He also suggested uniting the western and eastern Churches in return for help, only to change his mind when the hordes withdrew. Gregory believed that Charles of Anjou had too much power, so he restored the German empire and did not crown anyone until he offered it to Rudolf of Habsburg twenty years later.

Innocent V was briefly pope in 1276 and sought a settlement with Charles of Anjou while stopping Rudolf of Habsburg entering Italy, avoiding a war. Adrian V was pope for even less time, and his successor, John XXI also failed to get an agreement between Charles of Anjou and Rudolf of Habsburg. John too was frail and elderly by the time he was elected and he retired to Viterbo, where a roof collapse killed him rather than old age.

Pope Nicholas III discussed splitting the Holy Roman Empire into four kingdoms, Lombardy, Burgundy, Tuscia and Germany, with Rudolf taking the hereditary emperor's title. He spent a fortune on buildings while promoting his relatives and Charles of Anjou rigged the next election. Pope Martin IV excommunicated Pedro of Aragon for seizing Sicily and offered Aragon to Charles de Valois, providing he could capture it. He also excommunicated Emperor Mikhaël VIII for opposing Charles's attempt to take over the Latin Empire. Martin died in 1285 and Pope Honorius IV also refused to recognise Pedro of Aragon was King of Sicily, excommunicating his wife Costanza and his son Jaime as extra punishment.

Pope Nicholas IV was elected in 1288 and, while he failed to drum up support for a new Crusade to the Holy Land, he promoted missionary work amongst the Mongols. He also crowned Charles de Valois King of Sicily in 1289 and excommunicated Alfonso III of Aragon, giving Charles a reason to revive the Aragonese Crusade.

Pope Celestine V was elected in 1294 but became a hermit after failing to get his reforms through and was then imprisoned and died in Fumone Castle. Boniface VIII drew up the 1295 Treaty of Anagni but Friedrich refused to agree to it and was crowned King Friedrich III of Sicily two years later.

The pope excommunicated Friedrich Barbarossa for supporting Antipope Victor IV and Heinrich IV for imprisoning the Crusader Richard the Lionheart of England. He would excommunicate Friedrich II four times.

King Adolf of Germany declared war on the French in 1294, alleging they had seized imperial estates, but he was mocked by Philippe IV and threatened with excommunication by Pope Boniface VIII. The pope then refused to crown Adolf emperor. Boniface recognised Albrecht as King of Germany so Albrecht recognised the pope's authority to grant the imperial crown. Philippe IV of France's emissaries, Philippe de Nogaret and Sciarra Colonna, retaliated by arresting the elderly pope in 1303 and beating him; he died just three days after he was released.

His successor Benedict XI made peace with Philippe but refused to pardon Boniface's two captors and died after eating a plate of dried figs soon afterwards, possibly poisoned.

The cardinals and Philippe IV chose Pope Clement V as a compromise and he moved to Avignon, where he was under the French king's control. He was forced to abolish the Knights Templar in 1307 because Philippe wanted to cancel his debts to them and its French members were accused, tortured and executed. Their leader, Jacques de Molay, was burned at the stake in 1314 and cursed the king and pope from the flames. Clement died a month later and Philippe died in a hunting accident, seven months later. Having seen the brutal demise of the Templars, the Teutonic Knights moved their headquarters outside the Holy Roman Empire and the pope's influence.

Both popes Clement V and John XXII claimed the imperial throne to be vacant and the empire under papal rule. But when Ludwig IV the Bavarian and Friedrich the Fair decided to share Germany between them, John XXII appointed Ludwig emperor and Friedrich King of Germany. Ludwig visited Italy in 1328, where the people crowned him emperor. He also replaced John XXII with Antipope Nicholas V but the two reconciled, ruining his plans to undermine the Church.

Pope John XXII called for a Crusade in 1320 but the recruitment drive turned into a violent anti-Semitic uprising across France. He built a new papal palace in Avignon and his successor, Pope Benedict XII, remained there, accumulating a large amount of money. Pope Clement VI spent that fortune. He also deposed Ludwig of Germany and made sure that Karl IV of Luxembourg was elected in his place.

Pope Clement VI concerned himself with Valdemar of Denmark's Crusade in Lithuania. Valdemar failed and was then censured for going on a pilgrimage to Jerusalem without Rome's approval. Kęstutis of Lithuania finally accepted Christianity and a royal crown was promised to Lithuania until the negotiator, Kazimierz III of Poland, invaded Lithuania and progress was halted.

Pope Innocent VI was elected in 1352. He wanted to return to Rome, but it was his successor, Pope Urban V, who did so in 1367. Byzantine Emperor John V promised to end the schism with Rome in exchange for help against the Ottomans. But John was told he had to convert to Roman Catholicism or recognise the pope's supremacy before the Hungarians would help. He refused and had to roam Europe looking for help; he found none. Urban failed to bring order or discipline to the clergy and returned to Avignon, where he died in 1370.

Pope Gregory XI finally returned the papacy to Rome and established himself in the Vatican in 1377, only to die shortly afterwards.

Gregory was succeeded by Urban VI, nicknamed 'Inurbano' (meaning rude), whose lack of diplomacy led to a new schism and the election of Antipope Clement VII. Giovanna of Naples allied with France and Clement, so Urban declared her a heretic. He gave her kingdom to her cousin Carlo the Short in 1380, and Giovanna was suffocated or strangled. Pope Urban VI soon suspected Carlo of plotting and uncovered the conspiracy after torturing six cardinals. He excommunicated Carlo and raised an interdict over Naples, so Carlo besieged the pope in Nocera for six months. Urban was rescued by two Neapolitan barons, while Carlo left for Hungary. Although Urban's troops forced Antipope Clement to flee to Avignon, Urban died in 1389, hated by everyone.

His successor, Boniface IX, recognised Carlo's son Ladislao as King of Naples but Louis II, son of Giovanna's nominated heir, captured it the following year and was crowned by Antipope Clement. Boniface was courteous, but while he could negotiate with Clement VII, he struggled to talk to the hostile Antipope Benedict XIII.

Pope Innocent VII had vowed that he would refuse to accept if he were voted pope but changed his mind the moment he was nominated. He too refused to negotiate with Antipope Benedict XIII and had eleven of his supporters murdered and their bodies thrown into the street. He then had to flee Rome as riots broke out.

Ladislao had retaken Naples but Pope Innocent VII deposed him when he accepted lordship of Rome. Ladislao retaliated by invading the Papal States when Pope Gregory XII was elected. Antipope Alexander V excommunicated Ladislao and wanted Louis II of Anjou to retake Naples, but Ladislao captured Louis's war chest, forcing him to withdraw. Antipope John XXIII authorised a Crusade against Ladislao but Louis was again beaten. A peace was signed in June 1412 and Ladislao promised to abandon Gregory XII when John was crowned pope.

Popes Gregory XII and Benedict XIII then both reneged on their promises to renounce their post. So the Sacred College deposed them and elected Alexander V in 1409 instead. Alexander died soon after, so John XXIII took his place. All three popes were deposed at the 1417 Council of Constance; Gregory accepted, Benedict refused and John was imprisoned. This brought the Western Schism to an end and Pope Martin V was greeted enthusiastically when he entered Rome in 1420.

Giovanna II of Naples refused to rebuild the papal army so Pope Martin gave Ladislao's son, Luigi III, permission to invade in 1420. Giovanna adopted Alfonso of Aragon as her heir, only for him to arrest her in order to seize power immediately. She named Luigi as her heir when she was arrested. Alfonso retaliated by getting permission from Pope Eugene IV to make his illegitimate son Fernando heir to the Kingdom of Naples.

Byzantine Emperor John VIII approached Eugene IV, asking for help to fight the Ottomans invading the Byzantine Empire. The Council of Basle opposed the idea of reuniting the western and eastern Churches and Eugene was deposed in 1440 for saying he ruled over them. Antipope Felix V was elected because he agreed that the council was higher than the pope.

Pope Nicholas V was elected in 1447 and things started well when Felix submitted to him. They got better when the 1448 Vienna Concordat with Friedrich III of Austria regulated the rights and privileges of the Church and empire and he was crowned emperor. Pope Nicholas then issued two bulls granting Afonso V of Portugal the right to reduce 'Saracens, pagans and any other unbelievers' to slavery; the bulls would be used as justification for future colonialism and the slave trade. Pope Nicholas's reign ended on a sour note when the Ottomans captured Constantinople and killed Constantine XII in 1453.

Pope Callixtus III was elected in 1455. He was obsessed with recapturing Constantinople and the Holy Land but not many took any notice. He also declared Naples a Church fief because Fernando was illegitimate but his successor Pope Pius II recognised Fernando. However, Naples's nobility refused to accept Fernando and offered the crown to René of Anjou's son Jean instead.

Bohemia chose Jiří of Poděbrad to be their king, who declared that all the Christian powers should settle their differences through a parliament and fight the 'abominable Turk', but Pope Pius II opposed such a treaty. (His successor, Pope Paul II, was later to excommunicate Jiří and give Hungary permission to invade Bohemia.) The Ottomans advanced across mainland Europe until they were stopped by János Hunyadi's Hungarians at Belgrade in 1456 and Pius II called him 'Christ's Champion'.

Pius II wanted to strike back but France, Hungary and Venice refused to help. King Stjepan Tomaš asked for help to defend Bosnia against the Ottomans, but Rome was more concerned with crushing the Bogomils. Pius had sent money to Mátyás Hunyadi (Matthias Corvinus) so that Hungary would fight the Ottomans in 1459 but he spent it on himself instead. He then forged a letter saying that Vlad of Wallachia had offered Mehmed support before imprisoning the Wallachian prince to cover his tracks.

Pope Paul II was powerless to stop the Ottomans advancing deep into Christian territory. Although he approved the marriage of Grand Prince Ivan III of Russia and Sophia Palaiologina, sister of the last Byzantine emperor, he did not approve of her introducing Byzantine etiquette to Moscow, or his efforts to make his capital a worthy successor to Constantinople. Pope Sixtus IV also missed an opportunity to negotiate a deal with the Ottomans when Mátyás of Hungary took Sultan Cem hostage. Instead, he concentrated on favouring his friends, making enemies all across Italy.

The Ottomans continued to hold south-east Europe but Pope Innocent VIII was pleased to hear that Granada, the last Islamic fortress in Europe, had been captured by Fernando and Isabel of Spain. He was also open to scientific ideas and convinced the royal couple to fund Cristoforo Columbo's voyage to discover the New World. Innocent died shortly after the discovery of the Americas in 1492. He was succeeded by Pope Alexander VI, who authorised Fernando and Isabel to reign over the newly discovered islands and lands still to be discovered in America.

When João II of Portugal publicised the claims granted to him by Pope Eugene IV, Alexander divided the New World into two parts, one for Spain and one to Portugal. Pope Alexander would become a symbol of the corruption, intrigue, lack of scruples and lack of morality linked with the name Borgia. He died in 1503, possibly murdered by poison meant for someone else.

THE KINGDOM OF SICILY

Roger I captured Sicily around 1055 and then captured southern Italy from the Moors, becoming Count of Sicily in 1071. Although he was called 'the Great Count', his eldest son was a bastard and his second son was a leper. His young third son, Simon de Hauteville, succeeded him in 1101 only to die four years later. Roger's remaining young son would rule for forty-nine years.

Roger II supported Antipope Anacletus II against Pope Innocent II in 1130. Anacletus proclaimed him King of Sicily but he faced a ten-year battle against Innocent's supporters.

Roger II's half-sister Matilda claimed her husband Rainolfo of Alife was abusing her, so Roger annexed her husband's lands. Roberto of Capua joined Rainolfo, and although they defeated Roger at the Battle of Nocera in 1132, Roger's troops forced Rainolfo to submit and exiled Roberto. They joined forces again when they heard Roger was dead in 1135 but they soon learnt the news was untrue when Roger landed in Salerno and captured Rainolfo's base.

After Emperor Lothar withdrew from Italy, Rainolfo stopped Roger occupying the mainland at the Battle of Rignano in 1137, only to die of fever two years later. Innocent II refused to confirm Roger's title, so Roger's son captured the pope and he was forced to proclaim Roger king to secure his freedom. Roger then rampaged across Greece while the Second Crusade drew everyone's attention away from the area. He had also conquered Tunisia by 1153, spreading Sicily's influence to North Africa.

Roger II's fourth son, Guglielmo I, was crowned in 1154, after outliving his three brothers. The new Pope Adrian IV encouraged Byzantine Emperor Manuel I to attack Sicily, only to confirm Guglielmo's title when he defeated the Byzantines. Tunisia was soon lost as the fanatical Almohads swept across North Africa and the nobles were losing patience with Guglielmo the Bad, as he became known. They even murdered the power behind the throne, Chancellor Maio, planning to put his son Roger on the throne. Guglielmo's illegitimate brother Simon, with the help of his bastard nephew Tancredi Fitzroger, eventually imprisoned Guglielmo and his family in the royal palace, but the uprising which freed William killed Roger. Guglielmo blinded Maio's assassin, only to die a few years later.

After her husband's death, Guglielmo II's mother, Margaret of Navarre, stopped him leaving the palace so she could keep rule. But as soon as he came of age he made pacts with Genoa and Venice, he married Joan, daughter of Henry II of England, and signed the Treaty of Venice with Emperor Friedrich I. He also agreed to marry his Aunt Constance to the emperor's son Heinrich, making him potential successor to Sicily. With his home position secure, Guglielmo the Good invaded Egypt in 1174 but he failed to reduce Saladin's threat on Jerusalem. He then invaded the Byzantine Empire and although he captured Thessalonica in 1185, he was stopped at the gates of Constantinople and made peace with the Emperor Isaac.

Guglielmo died in 1189 leaving no heir so he was succeeded by Roger II's illegitimate grandson, Tancredi Fitzroger. He was nicknamed 'Tancrediulus', due to his small size. Richard I of England stopped at Sicily, en route to the Holy Land, and demanded the release of Tancredi's stepmother, Giovanna and his sister along with her dowry and inheritance. He also asked Tancredi to support his Crusade, as William II had promised. Philippe II's French army arrived next and Richard decided to stay the winter, forcing Tancredi to agree to his demands.

Tancredi's problems increased when Emperor Heinrich invaded and claimed Sicily in the name of his wife, Costanza. While many towns welcomed the imperial soldiers, they soon changed their minds because the emperor withdrew when his army was struck down by an epidemic. Tancredi captured the pregnant Costanza but Heinrich's soldiers recaptured her as he was taking her to Rome, hoping for a reward. The 40-year-old Costanza gave birth in a tent in a market square in 1194, while all the town matrons watched, and then breast-fed the infant in public to dispel doubts about her child.

Father and eldest son died in 1194 so Pope Celestine III crowned Tancredi's young son, Guglielmo III, with his mother Sibilla as regent. Emperor Heinrich VI used ransom money paid by Richard I of England to invade again, and this time he captured most of Sicily's territories. Heinrich was crowned on Christmas Day but a plot to remove him was soon uncovered, and while the Sicilian conspirators were imprisoned in Germany, young Guglielmo disappeared; he was probably blinded, castrated and imprisoned.

Emperor Heinrich VI had promised to recognise Costanza's succession when he married her but neither Rome nor Sicily wanted him to rule. Tancredi was dead, Guglielmo had disappeared and Heinrich died three years later, so Costanza saw her infant son Friedrich declared King of Sicily, just before she died.

Friedrich reasserted his power over Sicily when he came of age in 1208 and then appointed his son, Heinrich VII, King of Sicily in 1212. Heinrich was also elected King of Germany in 1220, so Friedrich II could redeem his Crusade promises, but Pope Honorius III refused to recognise the election to stop Germany and Sicily uniting.

Friedrich outlawed Heinrich when he intervened in Italian affairs and then dethroned him after he allied with the north Italian Lombards in 1235. His brother Corrado was elected king while a leprous Heinrich was imprisoned; he died soon after in a riding accident. Their father, Friedrich II, died the same year, and while Corrado took the Sicily, Germany and Jerusalem titles, he was defeated by the German anti-king, Wilhelm of Holland.

Manfredi was the son of Emperor Friedrich II and Bianca, the mistress he had married on her deathbed. Friedrich II considered him to be legitimate and made him Sicily's administrator only for Pope Innocent IV to incite riots in the kingdom. Corrado also thought Sicily was his and he conquered most of Italy and stripped Manfredi of all his lands in 1252.

Meanwhile, Corrado was excommunicated just before he died in 1254 and Pope Innocent IV offered Sicily to Edmund Crouchback, son of Henry III of England, but the English barons refused to pay for the title. Manfredi declared himself regent to Corrado's young son (known as Corradino) and refused to stand down; he was excommunicated for his disobedience. Manfredi handed Apulia over to Rome but it was not enough so he raised Islamic support in North Africa and defeated a papal army at Foggia in 1254. News of the defeat reached Pope Innocent on his deathbed and his successor, Alexander IV, excommunicated Manfredi for a second time.

Manfredi defeated another papal army in 1257 and then crowned himself king when he heard young Corradino had died. The rumour was false but Manfredi refused to abdicate, and while Alexander voided the coronation, his successor, Pope Urban IV, excommunicated him a third time.

The pope offered to sell Sicily to Richard of Cornwall as he returned from the Holy Land but he refused it. His brother, Henry III of England, planned to buy the kingdom for his son Edmund but he did not have enough money.

Charles of Anjou, Louis IX of France's brother, bought the crown from Pope Urban IV in 1262 on condition Sicily could not be united with the empire. Enrique of Castile had lent Charles a huge amount of gold to buy the title but he never repaid it and instead defeated and killed Manfredi at the Battle of Benevento in 1266. He also captured Corradino at the Battle of Tagliacozzo in 1268 and beheaded the teenager. Charles was then able to buy the rest of the kingdom, executing anyone who objected to consolidate his power.

The 1267 Treaty of Viterbo with King Baudouin II and Guillaume de Villehardouin transferred the defunct Latin Empire title to Charles. Baudouin's son and Guillaume's daughter married Charles's children and he was preparing a Crusade to Constantinople when Emperor Mikhaël VIII proposed joining the Roman and Latin Churches to Louis IX of France. Charles suggested crusading to North Africa instead but Louis died of dysentery before Charles arrived in Tunis in 1270. The Caliph agreed to pay tribute to Charles but an epidemic struck his army and a storm devastated his fleet. The only good news was Charles's troops had captured the Adriatic coast and Albania.

Pope Gregory X had called the Council of Lyon in 1272, hoping to unify the Greek and Latin Churches, but Pope Martin IV soon called off the union and authorised Sicily to restore the Latin Empire. Charles had also bought Maria of Antioch's claim on the title of King of Jerusalem in 1277 but nothing came of it. As a Byzantine army invaded Albania's interior, Charles counter-attacked Constantinople in 1282.

Pedro III of Aragon had married Manfredi's heir, Constaza, and he invaded Sicily in 1282, on behalf of his wife while Charles was focused on the Byzantines. The War of the Sicilian Vespers began in Palermo, followed by a massacre of French citizens across Sicily. Pedro then sailed to Tunis, and when the Sicilians appealed to Pope Martin for help, he excommunicated Pedro and Emperor Michael for interfering in Sicilian matters. Charles returned to Sicily but Pedro followed and was declared king so Charles had to withdraw to the mainland to rally support from Philippe III of France and Pope Martin.

Pedro and Charles arranged to decide who would rule Sicily by pitting their best knights against each other. But both turned up at the jousting arena at different times and declared a victory over their absent opponent before leaving. Eventually Pope Martin decided the matter by excommunicating Pedro and declaring war on the Sicilians. He then gave the title to Charles de Valois and told him to capture the kingdom. But Charles was defeated by Roger of Lauria and his son was taken prisoner. Charles died soon afterwards, as did Pedro.

Aragon was left to Alfonso while Sicily was left to his second son, Jaime, but Jaime's position was compromised by French attacks. Alfonso died in 1291 and Jaime became King of Aragon. He left his brother Federico II as regent for Sicily. The 1295 Treaty of Anagni promised him possession of Sardinia and Corsica while the Church handed Sicily to the Angevins. But the Sicilians ignored the treaty and Federico was crowned in 1296 even though Pope Boniface VIII offered him money to refuse.

Jaime II of Aragon declared war on Federico in 1298 so he made trouble in his homeland. He also seized Sicily and the mainland despite promising Pope Honorius III he would not and peace only came after the plague decimated Charles de Valois's army. The 1302 Treaty of Caltabellotta finally recognised Federico as King of Trinacria (another name for Sicily) on condition it would revert to the Angevins when he died.

Emperor Heinrich VII entered Italy in 1313 and while Federico attacked the Angevins, Heinrich died; Charles's son Roberto eventually called a truce in 1317. Federico had used Church money to pay his soldiers so Pope John XXII excommunicated him and placed his kingdom under an interdict in 1321 resulting in new Angevin raids on Sicily. Pietro II was crowned in 1337 only to die suddenly, leaving his infant son Ludovico as king.

The Black Death struck in 1347 as the Italian and Catalan nobles fought for control. Ludovico's sister Costanza became regent when his mother died in 1352. Sadly, he and his entourage couldn't escape the plague, and young Ludovico died in 1355.

Four families took control when the teenage Federico III the Simple was crowned and they continued to rule when he reached his majority, making peace with Pope Gregory XI and Naples in 1372.

The teenage Maria was crowned queen in 1377 but the four families continued to govern. In 1379 she was taken to Aragon to stop her marrying the Duke of Milan and she married King Martín the Humane instead ten years later. Their son, Martín the Younger, defeated the barons but died young, so Martín and Maria ruled jointly until Maria's death in 1401; Martín then ruled alone, ignoring the Treaty of Villeneuve of 1372. His two sons had died young so he tried in vain to make his illegitimate son Fadrique his successor. His death in 1409 ended the Kingdom of Sicily.

THE KINGDOM OF NAPLES

Charles I had conquered Sicily and Naples in the 1260s. The War of the Sicilian Vespers broke out in Sicily in 1282 and Charles's son was captured by the Sicilians during the naval battle for Naples. When the king died in 1285 and although his son, Charles II 'the Lame', was freed in 1288, there were conditions attached. Pope Martín IV had taken Aragon from Pedro for starting the Sicilian Vespers conflict and had given it to Charles de Valois. Charles II's task was to bribe his Valois cousin to return Aragon to its rulers in return for 9 tons of silver. Sicily was then to be given to Aragon as well. Charles II left his three sons as hostages while he carried out this task and promised to return to prison if he failed.

Pope Nicholas IV absolved Charles from the conditions and crowned him King of Sicily in 1289. He also excommunicated Alfonso III of Aragon, giving Charles de Valois a reason to revive the Aragonese Crusade. While Alfonso agreed to the Treaty of Tarascon, he died before it took effect and Jamie II took possession of Aragon, leaving Sicily to his brother, Federico.

Another new pope, Pope Boniface VIII, drew up the Treaty of Anagni in 1295 but Federico refused to agree to it and he was crowned King of Sicily two years later. Charles of Naples even married his son, Roberto, to Jaime's sister Violante, so he would renounce his claim. As neither Charles of Naples nor Charles de Valois could take Sicily from Federico by force, a compromise called the Peace of Caltabellotta was agreed which handed the island to Federico and the mainland to Charles of Naples in 1302.

Roberto the Wise was crowned King of Naples and titular King of Jerusalem in 1309. He opposed Emperor Heinrich VII's invasion of Italy and occupation of Rome. The Emperor died in 1313 and no replacement was elected, so Pope John XXII named Roberto the Senator of Rome and vicar general of all Italy. Ludwig IV of Bavaria invaded Italy in 1328 with the support of Peter of Sicily and he replaced Pope John with Antipope Nicholas V before leaving, thus diminishing Roberto's power.

Roberto died in 1343, leaving his teenage granddaughter, Giovanna I, Queen of Naples and claimant to the crowns of Jerusalem and Sicily. She had been betrothed at an early age to Prince András of Hungary, and while Roberto tried to exclude him from rule, András's mother Elżbieta bribed Pope Clement VI to allow him to do so. She gave a ring to András to protect him from death by blade or poison but conspirators strangled him, tied a rope to his genitals and hung his body from a window when Giovanna fell pregnant in 1345. Her baby died a week later.

Giovanna refused to marry András's brother, Stephen, and married Luigi of Taranto instead. They had to flee to France when Lajos I of Hungary invaded seeking to avenge his brother's murder. The Black Death forced Lajos to withdraw but he soon returned to remove all Giovanna's supporters. He also executed her favourite, Enrico Caracciolo, accusing him of adultery.

Meanwhile, Giovanna was having a tough time and Pope Clement reprimanded Luigi of Taranto for 'treating the queen as a prisoner and servant'. He was crowned King of Naples in 1352 but their child died the same day and Giovanna would have no more children. Luigi and Giovanna were crowned rulers of Sicily in 1356 but they failed to capture the island from Federico the Simple. Pope Innocent VI even excommunicated the couple for failing to pay him the money they owed.

Giovanna resumed authority when Luigi died from the plague in 1362, and while she became infatuated with Carlo the Short of Hungary (Károly in Hungarian), he spurned her advances, even though she adopted him. She was even more annoyed when he married her niece, Margherita, widow of the murdered András. Instead Giovanna married Jaime IV of Mallorca but she adopted Louis I of Anjou, Jean II of France's son, when they had no children. Unfortunately Louis's brother, Charles V, died and her adopted heir had to remain in France as king. She had allied with France, and Pope Urban VI declared her a heretic and gave her kingdom to Carlo III the Short in 1380 when she supported Antipope Clement VII.

Giovanna's fourth and final husband Otto, Duke of Brunswick-Grubenhagen, was defeated in battle near Anagni and she was imprisoned. Carlo the Short had Giovanna murdered in July 1382 when he heard Louis I of Anjou was heading to Naples and her body was displayed in Naples before it was tossed down a well. Louis died in 1384, still fighting for his kingdom.

Pope Urban VI suspected Carlo of plotting in 1385 and he tortured six cardinals to uncover the conspiracy. He excommunicated Carlo and raised an interdict over Naples, so Carlo besieged the pope in Nocera for six months. Urban was eventually rescued and Carlo turned his attention to Hungary.

However, Urban VI refused to recognise Carlo's young son Ladislao when Carlo died the following year and appointed Louis II of Anjou to take Naples from him. A riot forced Ladislao and his mother to hide in Gaeta castle while his stepfather, Otto of Brunswick, occupied Naples on his behalf. The new Pope Boniface IX eventually recognised Ladislao in 1389 but the Archbishop of Arles refused to and attempted to poison the teenager, leaving him with a stutter.

Louis II captured Naples in 1390 and was crowned by Antipope Clement VII but Ladislao retook the throne in 1399 and then married Marie de Lusignan, daughter of the King of Cyprus. He also tried to restore Angevin rule in Hungary and claim the crown of Croatia. Both ideas failed. Pope Innocent VII deposed Ladislao when he accepted lordship of Rome in 1405 and he invaded the Papal States when Pope Gregory XII was elected. Antipope Alexander V excommunicated Ladislao and wanted Louis II de Anjou to invade Naples but Ladislao captured Louis's war chest and he had to withdraw.

Antipope John XXIII authorised a Crusade against Ladislao but Louis was again defeated and he returned to Rome and died. A peace was signed in June 1412 and Ladislao promised to abandon Gregory XII when John was crowned. Ladislao the

Magnanimous then sacked Rome and conquered the Papal States the following summer. He died soon after, leaving Naples to his sister Giovanna.

Giovanna II married Jacques de Bourbon, expecting to get the French support, but he imprisoned her, murdered her lover and held the throne until a riot forced him to renounce his title. He left for France, so Giovanna took a new lover, seized Rome and was crowned Queen of Sicily and Naples. Giovanna refused to rebuild the papal army so Pope Martin V gave her brother Luigi III permission to invade in 1420.

Giovanna of Naples adopted Alfonso of Aragon as her heir and he went to Naples to be crowned only to hear Pope Martin V had announced his support for Luigi III. Relations between Alfonso and Giovanna deteriorated, however, and he arrested Giovanna. When he released her she named Luigi as her heir instead.

Alfonso returned to Aragon to deal with a war with Castile, allowing Giovanna and Luigi to seize Sicily. Luigi died in 1434 followed by Giovanna a year later, leaving Sicily to his brother, René de Anjou. The new Pope Eugene IV was against him inheriting the kingdom so Alfonso invaded, only to be taken prisoner. He persuaded his captors it was not in their interest to stop him so he was freed to capture Naples in 1443. He also obtained Pope Eugene IV's consent to make his illegitimate son, Fernando, heir to the Kingdom of Naples.

When Fernando I was crowned in 1458, Pope Callixtus III declared Naples was a Church fief because the Aragon line was extinct. After he died, his successor Pope Pius II recognised Fernando, but the nobility rejected him and offered the crown to René's son Jean instead. Fernando would defeat Jean's invasion at the battles of Troia in 1462 and Ischia in 1465. Fernando was known for keeping his enemies close to him, either alive in prison or embalmed as costume dummies. His oppressive rule led to the Conspiracy of the Barons in 1485.

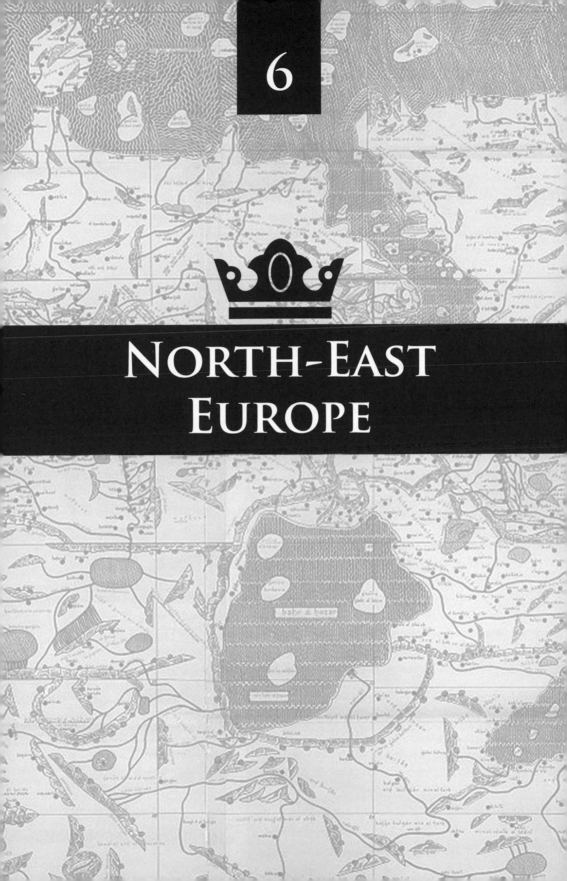

6

NORTH-EAST
EUROPE

POLAND WAS SANDWICHED BETWEEN THE Holy Roman Empire to the west, Russia to the east and Hungary to the south. The Teutonic Knights expanded into the area starting in 1199, ending up with two areas north-west and north-east of Lithuania. Meanwhile, the Lithuania Order forced the pagan Lithuanians to move inland as they advanced along the Baltic coast. Around the same time, Galicia–Volhynia was formed after Roman the Great united Galicia (Halych) and Volhynia between Poland and the Principality of Kiev, in what is now the Ukraine. What we know as Russia today was split into several principalities, including Kiev, Chernigov, Novgorod and Vladimir. There would be many changes in the wake of the Mongol invasions in the 1240s as the princes and kings came to terms with the Golden Horde's demands.

THE KINGDOM OF POLAND

Poland had been recognised as a state by the Holy Roman Empire and the pope since 1000 and Bolesław was crowned the first king in 1025. But rulers of Poland were known as dukes and any of their sons had the right to inheritance, so the strongest usually ruled after beating his siblings.

Kazimierz drove Bretislaus of Bohemia out of Poland, with Emperor Henry III's support, and then signed an alliance with Yaroslav the Wise of Rus'. After securing his territory, Kazimierz the Restorer moved his capital to Kraków because it had escaped the ravages of war.

Bolesław II inherited Poland in 1058, and while he refused to pay for Silesia, he did marry his sister to Vratislaus II to secure an alliance with Bohemia. His alliance to Hungary ended when his uncle Béla I died in 1063 and Emperor Henry IV installed Solomon. Bolesław helped Iziaslav regain Kiev's throne in 1069 and he allied with Vladimir II of Kiev when his alliance with Vratislaus II of Bohemia fell through.

Emperor Heinrich IV planned to invade Poland in 1073 but Bolesław encouraged a Saxon rebellion to keep the imperial army busy. Bolesław then retaliated by supporting Pope Gregory VII during the Investiture Controversy and he received a crown in 1076. Bishop Stanislaus of Kraków had hoped to place his brother on the throne so he excommunicated the king for infidelity and was executed soon afterwards. Bolesław the Generous then helped two pretenders assume the throne, Ladislaus in Hungary, and Iziaslav in Kiev. But he was becoming too powerful and was exiled to Hungary in 1079 where he was assassinated as a result of his appalling behaviour in Ladislaus I's court.

Bolesław's successor was his brother Władysław I. He refused to bow to Rome so Pope Gregory VIII declined to acknowledge his marriage to the Bohemian princess Judith and declared their son, Zbigniew, illegitimate. An incompetent Władysław handed

Kraków over to Bohemia, lost lands to Germany and Galicia and was unable to retake Pomerania. He then married the emperor's sister Sophia and joined the anti-papal camp in 1089.

Sophia had her stepson Zbigniew exiled as a monk and Mieszko, son of Bolesław II, poisoned when her son Bolesław was born. But the tyrannical Count Palatine Sieciech was the real ruler of Poland until the nobles kidnapped him and Bolesław. They then recalled Zbigniew and forced Władysław to recognise him as his heir in 1093. Sieciech and Bolesław escaped three years later and they captured Zbigniew at the Battle of Goplo. But the half-brothers later joined forces after discovering Sieciech and Queen Sophia planned to take over the country. Władysław divided rule of Poland between them, but kept control of Mazovia and its capital at Płock. However, Sieciech began to intrigue against the half-brothers and Władysław joined him; Bolesław and Zbigniew defeated their combined army at the Battle of Plock, and the treacherous Sieciech was exiled in 1101.

The half-brothers initially succeeded their father as joint rulers, but Bolesław attacked Zbigniew with Kievan and Hungarian support in 1106. Zbigniew was forced to surrender Greater Poland, recognise Bolesław III the Wry-mouthed as high duke and eventually had to flee to Germany; the Holy Roman Emperor counter-attacked to support Zbigniew. Bolesław married Princess Zbyslava of Kiev to get her family's support and they defeated the emperor at the Battle of Hundsfeld in 1109. Zbigniew escaped to Bohemia but he continued to raid Poland until a treaty was signed with the Holy Roman Empire in 1111 under which Zbigniew returned to Poland; but he continued to defy his brother and was eventually blinded and excommunicated on Bolesław's orders in 1112.

Bolesław III established the 'senioral principle', which meant the high duke ruled over the other dukes, and added central Poland and Pomerania to his lands. His eldest son, Władysław II, became high duke following his death in 1138. He gave territories to Władysław's half-brothers Bolesław and Mieszko; their mother, Salomea, intended to marry her daughter into the Kiev family to support her sons' cause, but her plans were thwarted when Władysław II married his own daughter into the family.

Civil war soon broke out between Władysław II and his brother. The high duke was backed by Rus', Bohemia and the Holy Roman Empire, but he was still defeated at the battle on the Pilica River in 1145. It required troops from his Kievan in-laws to turn the war in his favour and force his half-brothers to back down.

Count Palatine (military leader) Piotr Włostowic was one of Poland's most senior nobles, and his power and ambition caused problems for Władysław; the high duke had him blinded and muted in 1146. The Archbishop of Gniezno excommunicated the high duke for this action. Meanwhile, Włostowic fled to Rus' and convinced the Kievans to break their alliance with the evil Władysław, forcing him to flee to Emperor Friedrich Barbarossa.

Władysław's half-brother, Bolesław IV the Curly, became high duke and Władysław's attempt to reconquer Poland was stopped when the Oder River flooded. With King Konrad III of Germany absent on the Second Crusade, Władysław had to wait until 1157, when Emperor Friedrich Barbarossa agreed to undertake and expedition to Poland. But Władysław was disappointed once more; Emperor Friedrich Barbarossa accepted Bolesław's oath to become his vassal – and his brother Kazimierz as a hostage. However, Friedrich did compell Bolesław to promise to return Silesia to Władysław's sons. Władysław stayed in exile, dying two years later.

Bolesław IV and his brothers Mieszko and Henryk divided Poland between themselves, leaving their youngest brother, Kazimierz (still Emperor Friedrich's hostage), with nothing. Bolesław gave Silesia to his nephews Bolesław and Mieszko as promised when Władysław died in exile in 1163, but they still tried to usurp him. Bolesław received no support from his brothers when he crusaded against the Prussian pagans in 1166. When Henryk died, Kazimierz demanded his brother's lands, but Bolesław tried to absorb them into his own territory. Henryk rebelled, supported by his brother Mieszko. Bolesław was deposed, Mieszko III the Old was proclaimed the new high duke and Kazimierz received the lands he wanted. Things went from bad to worse for Bolesław when his teenage son died in 1172; he died a year later.

Mieszko III the Old married for a second time in 1177 and made his son Odon from his first marriage a priest, to remove him from the succession. But Odon rebelled and Kazimierz II the Just became the high duke. Mieszko had soon seized part of Greater Poland and Kazimierz the Just could do nothing because he was too involved in the battle for the Galician succession.

Mieszko convinced the sickly Duke Leszek of Masovia, son of his brother Bolesław IV, to leave Greater Poland to him but he gave them to Kazimierz instead on his death-bed in 1186. An outraged Mieszko seized the lands and Kazimierz again did nothing. Instead he led a successful expedition against the Baltic tribes in 1194 only to die (probably poisoned) at the celebration banquet.

The barons put Kazimierz's young son Leszek the White on the throne to avoid a conflict, but Mieszko and his son Władysław Spindle Shanks (so called because he had long, thin legs) still argued over the regency. Mieszko tried to seize Lower Poland only to be defeated by Leszek's supporters at the Battle of Mozgawa in 1195. Mieszko died in 1202 and Władysław III became high duke. But when Władysław's chief supporter died, he was deposed.

Leszek was crowned in 1206 and he pledged Poland to Pope Innocent III, angering Emperor Friedrich. Pope Innocent III then mysteriously excommunicated all the Polish rulers and declared them deposed in 1210, throwing the country into turmoil. It would later transpire that Henryk the Bearded had anonymously asked the pope to do it.

As Leszek the White, Henryk the Bearded, Konrad of Masovia and Władysław Odonic attended a synod to discuss the problem, Mieszko IV Tanglefoot, son of Władysław II, seized Kraków and declared himself high duke. He died a year later and Leszek the White's excommunication was lifted so he could return to Kraków.

Pope Innocent III asked Leszek to participate in the 1217 Fifth Crusade but he refused, arguing that Polish knights would not participate because there was no beer for them in Palestine. Instead Poland was busy fighting Hungary for control of Galicia and Rus'. Leszek married the Grand Prince of Kiev's daughter Grzymisława to secure the peace after his troops were defeated.

Leszek the White and his cousin Władysław III Spindle Shanks secretly agreed the other would be their successor if they died without an heir, to cut Władysław Odonic, Spindle Shanks's nephew, out of their wills. Władysław Spindle Shanks also signed a similar agreement with Henryk the Bearded (who was his cousin's son). Leszek then invited dukes, bishops and nobles to attend a congress in Gasąwa to make the peace in 1227, and while Konrad and Henryk attended, Władysław Spindle Shanks missed the meeting. It saved his life. Swietopelk II of Pomerania was furious because they refused him his independence and he murdered Leszek and injured Henryk. There were suspicions that Władysław Odonic arranged the attack; whatever the truth, it sparked a new power struggle for the Polish throne.

Spindle Shanks captured Odonic in battle in 1228, but Odonic escaped to Plock and the following year he captured Greater Poland, with the support of Konrad of Masovia, who was himself locked in a conflict with Henryk the Bearded. Spindle Shanks had appointed Henryk to govern Kraków and he had defeated Konrad three times. So Konrad invited Henryk to discuss a truce and imprisoned him at the meeting, leaving him free to seize Lesser Poland and Sandomierz. The elderly Spindle Shanks fled and was murdered by a German girl he tried to rape in 1229, leaving Henryk as his heir.

Konrad I seized power, unaware Spindle Shanks had made Henryk the Bearded his heir. Henryk had been released and was given Greater and Lesser Poland, only to be defeated by Odonic at Gniezno in 1231. But Henryk captured Kraków and became high duke in 1233; he then captured Greater Poland and installed his son, Henryk II the Pious, as the area's ruler in 1238. But he would regret switching Poland's allegiance from the Emperor Friedrich II to Pope Gregory IX when the Mongols rode through Lesser Poland in 1241. Friederich ignored his calls for help and, though Wenceslaus I of Bohemia sent troops, most of Lesser Poland's nobility were killed in the battles of Tursko,

Tarczek and Chmielnik. Henryk was defeated and killed at the Battle of Legnica and his wife was only able to identify his decapitated body because of the six toes on his left foot.

Bolesław II the Horned, son of Henryk the Pious, was appointed Duke of Kraków but he did nothing when Konrad of Masovia seized his lands, so he had to hand over power to his nephew two years later. Bolesław V rebuilt Kraków but the Mongols returned to destroy it again in 1259. He became known as 'the Chaste' because his pious wife, Kinga, a daughter of Béla IV of Hungary, refused to consummate their marriage and his own religious convictions prevented him from taking a mistress. Instead he nominated his nephew Leszek as his heir, but his stepmother tried to cut him out of the inheritance to support her own son's claim (she may also have tried to poison him).

She failed and Leszek II the Black (so called because of his hair colour) was appointed high duke in 1279. But he too had no heir and his wife Gryfina publicly blamed her husband for not consummating their marriage. They were forced to escape to Hungary when the Mongols returned in 1287 and Leszek never returned.

Bolesław II of Masovia defeated Henryk IV the Righteous, Henry II the Pious's grandson, at the Battle of Siewierz in 1289 and then seized Kraków. But the barons supported Henryk, so Bolesław was forced to retire to his duchy, where he founded the city which would become Warsaw.

Henryk was another one who had problems producing an heir. He divorced his first wife, Constance of Opole, after seven years, declaring she was unable to have children. But the real reason was he had been having an affair with Matilda of Brandenburg, who would become his second wife. Henryk IV sent money to Rome to get approval for his coronation but some was stolen en route to Rome and Pope Nicholas IV cancelled his promise. The robbers employed a court doctor to poison Henryk IV but another doctor saved Henryk by inducing vomiting; a second poisoning attempt in 1290 succeeded.

Przemysł II of Bohemia was the most powerful Polish duke. On succeeding Henryk he gave Kraków to Wenceslaus II and kept the rest. Przemysł obtained the hereditary title of King of Poland in 1295, but his first wife Ludgarda could not have children, so he strangled her. He was later kidnapped and murdered by nobles in 1296.

Wenceslaus II Přemyslid of Bohemia was appointed King of Poland in 1300 and his situation was helped enormously by the newly discovered Bohemian Kutná Hora mine, which produced 20 tons of silver a year. Wenceslaus died in 1305 and although his son Wenceslaus III intended to claim his hereditary right to the Polish throne, he was assassinated after appointing his brother-in-law Henry of Carinthia as his regent.

Władysław the Short (or Elbow High) had occupied Lesser Poland and Pomerania in 1304 and Greater Poland came under his rule ten years later. When John of Bohemia claimed the Polish crown and attacked with the Teutonic Knights, Władysław drove them off. He was eventually crowned king in 1320, having succeeded in uniting the country, but a war with the Teutonic Order occupied his final years.

Kazimierz III the Great reigned from 1333 but he had to give privileges to the nobility and pay large amounts of tribute to the Mongols, leaving a ruined economy and a depopulated country. He had five daughters but three were of dubious legitimacy because of his bigamy, so Louis I of Hungary succeeded his uncle in 1370.

Louis sent his mother Elżbieta to rule Poland on his behalf, to get her out of his court. The Poles hated her tax rises and killed all her Hungarian bodyguards, forcing her to flee in 1375, so Louis appointed Władysław of Opole regent of Poland instead.

The Hungarian throne passed to Louis's young daughter, Mary, in 1382. But when her fiancé, Sigismund of Luxembourg, tried to seize the throne of Poland, the Poles rejected him and chose Mary's little sister Jadwiga instead. She was crowned King of Poland rather than queen because she was a sovereign in her own right.

Grand Duke Jogaila of Lithuania agreed the 1385 Union of Krėva, making peace between the two countries, and he was betrothed to Jadwiga. He was also adopted by Jadwiga's mother, Elżbieta, so he would retain the throne if Jadwiga died. He was baptised Władysław II, crowned King of Poland and made Lithuania convert to Christianity in mass baptisms in 1387. But the Teutonic Knights claimed his conversion was a sham, and his cousin Alexander (previously Vytautas) started a civil war in Lithuania in 1389. Although Władysław allowed him to rule Lithuania as a Polish vassal under the 1392 Treaty of Ostrow, Alexander wanted Lithuania's independence and he seized Novgorod in 1398. He also allied with the White Horde, only to be defeated by the rest of the Mongols along the Vorskla River in 1399. Alexander finally submitted to Władysław to get his support.

Jadwiga and their daughter died in childbirth in 1399. Greater Poland was against the widowed Władysław keeping the throne, so in 1402 he married Anna, Kazimierz III the Great's granddaughter, to get their support.

At the same time Władysław's brother, Švitrigaila, appointed himself Grand Duke of Lithuania and declared war with the Teutonic Knights' support. The war ended with the 1404 Peace of Raciąż but Władysław and Vytautas organised an uprising in the Teutonic territories, so the knights retaliated by attacking Poland in 1409.

Władysław claimed the Teutonic Order was trying to conquer the world when it called for a Crusade. Although he agreed a mutual defensive treaty with Wenceslaus IV of Bohemia, Sigismund of Hungary chose to ally with the knights. They clashed at the Battle of Grunwald (or Tannenberg) in 1410 and the Teutonic Order's army was virtually annihilated. The 1411 Peace of Thorn called for the knights to pay huge ransoms and fines, while the 1413 Union of Horodło brought Lithuania and Poland closer together.

The Teutonic Knights used scorched earth tactics against the Poles in the Hunger War of 1414 but the Council of Constance was a turning point in the Teutonic Crusades. The Poles wanted an end to the forced conversions, because they wanted people to be 'baptised in water and not with blood'. The Bohemians offered their throne to Władysław after the Bohemian Hussites revolted against Sigismund but he disagreed with their terms, so Władysław's nephew, Sigismund Korybut, tried in vain to rule Bohemia. Vytautas accepted a crown from Rome in 1429 but the coronation was cancelled because the Poles intercepted it.

Meanwhile, Władysław had defeated the Teutonic Order in the short Gollub War in 1422 and the Treaty of Melno settled the border between Prussia and Lithuania. Władysław then supported his brother, Švitrigaila, when he claimed Lithuania, but he rebelled against Polish overlordship and Vytautas's brother, Sigismund, was elected grand duke instead in 1432.

Władysław died in 1434 and young Władysław III, the son of Władysław II and his fourth wife Sophia of Halshany, was crowned. A challenge by Frederick of Brandenburg was stopped by betrothing him to his half-sister Hedwig, but she was poisoned, possibly by Władysław's mother. Władysław chose not to marry and had no children, leaving him open to allegations about his sexuality. Nonetheless he was offered the crown of Hungary after Albert the Magnanimous was killed by the Ottomans in 1440. Cardinal Olesnicki ran the country while Władysław concentrated on fighting the Ottomans but he died at the Battle of Varna in 1444 and Murad II displayed his head on a pole as his army fled.

Władysław's brother, Kazimierz IV, was crowned in 1447 and he assisted the Prussian Confederation against the Teutonic Order in 1454, eventually establishing Polish overlordship over the Teutonic State. In 1466 he agreed the Second Peace of Thorn at the end of the Thirteen Years War, securing Polish sovereignty over the western Prussian regions. Kazimierz would die in 1492.

THE STATE OF THE TEUTONIC ORDER

Heinrich Walpot von Bassenheim decided to create a new Germanic religious order as part of the Hospitallers. He received a copy of the Knights Templar's rules in 1199, on which he based his new order. His successor, Otto von Kerpen, tried to make the order independent.

The fourth grand master, Hermann von Salza, transformed the Teutonic Knights into a military order and expanded their control into Prussia. He accompanied Emperor Friedrich II on the Fifth Crusade in 1219 and then convinced him to make the Sixth Crusade before returning to Europe to help lift Friedrich's excommunication. Hermann proved to be a useful mediator between the emperor and Rome, and Pope Honorius III rewarded the Teutonic Knights a status equal with the Knights Templar and Knights Hospitaller.

Andras II of Hungary asked Hermann to relocate to Transylvania to protect his southern border from Cumans but the Hungarian nobles made them leave in 1225 when the knights started creating their own state. Konrad I of Masovia asked Hermann to fight the pagan Prussians in 1230 and the Livonian Order was incorporated into the Teutonic Order in 1237. But the knights became tired of Hermann's politicking so he retired in 1238, and Pope Gregory IX excommunicated Emperor Friedrich.

The fifth grand master, Konrad von Thüringen, died during a visit to Rome and Pope Innocent IV gave his successor, Gerhard von Malberg, a ring which represented Prussia as a papal fief in 1243. It left the knights' strength divided between the Baltic coast and the Crusader states and a demand for Malberg's resignation resulted in a papal investigation which exposed his poor leadership. He transferred to the Knights Templar in 1244.

There was an uproar when Heinrich von Hohenlohe supported Friedrich II in his war with Pope Innocent IV, so he rushed to Prussia to start a Crusade only to die in 1249. Günther von Wüllersleben was appointed, even though he was in Acre, and he too wasted his time trying to reconcile the pope and the emperor.

The knights were then divided into the pro-emperor majority, who chose Poppo von Osterna, and the pro-papal minority, who chose Wilhelm von Urenbach. They all soon submitted to Osterna and crusaded across north Prussia with Bohemian support, a Crusade continued by Anno von Sangerhausen. Hartmann von Heldrungen would negotiate the amalgamation of the Livonian Order with the Teutonic Order, receiving more lands in Pomerania.

Burchard von Schwanden was appointed grand master in 1282 and he kept himself occupied in northern Europe while the situation in Jerusalem deteriorated. A Lithuanian invasion devastated Livonia in 1287 and Pope Nicholas IV agreed the order's new Baltic borders to make the peace. Schwanden was forced to help the Crusaders under siege in Acre in 1290, but he transferred to the Knights Hospitaller as soon as he arrived in the Holy Land.

Konrad von Feuchtwangen was grand master when the Muslims captured Acre, the last fortress in the Kingdom of Jerusalem, so he moved the order's headquarters to Venice. Gottfried von Hohenlohe did little before he resigned but his successor, Siegfried von Feuchtwangen, seized the Danzig region by 1308, making the Teutonic Knights Poland's strongest opponent. Pope Clement V denounced the Knights Templar in 1307, so the Teutonic Knights moved their headquarters to Marienburg Castle to get away from the Holy Roman Empire and the Pope's influence.

Karl Bessart von Trier was forced to resign as grand master after he limited the amount of trade the knights were allowed to do and he did not return to Prussia even though Pope John XXII reappointed him in 1318. Werner von Orseln failed to negotiate with Poland over Danzig so the Teutonic Order formed an anti-Polish coalition and Władysław I invaded in 1327. Orseln died following an assassination attempt by a mad knight called Johann von Endorf.

Luther von Braunschweig conquered lands on the knights' southern border and then invaded Greater Poland. Dietrich von Altenburg negotiated peace between Poland, Hungary and Bohemia at the Congress of Visegrád but Pope Benedict VIII instructed the order to surrender all Polish lands in 1339. Ludolf König von Wattzau agreed the Treaty of Kalisz with Poland and the Teutonic Knights invaded Lithuania in 1343 instead, hoping to open a corridor to Livonia and connect their territories. Wattzau resigned, suffering from a mental illness, leaving Heinrich Dusemer von Arfberg and Winrich von Kniprode to spend the next forty years battling with Lithuania and he finally succeeded after the Battle of Rudau in 1370.

Konrad Zollner von Rothenstein kept himself busy colonising the knights' lands while Konrad von Wallenrode fought the Lithuanians. Jogaila would rule Lithuania from 1387 and Christianised the state, removing the knights' reason to attack in 1387. But Rothenstein stirred up trouble between the two Lithuanian dukes, Vytautas and Jogaila, while Konrad invaded Lithuania when he became head of the order in 1392. Wallenrode relieved Wildstein at the gates of Vilnius, because he was jealous, so the rest of the knights headed home in disgust. Konrad rejected the offer of part of Poland in 1392 and invaded Lithuania with guest Crusaders instead. Vytautas of Lithuania called a peace conference at Thorn the following year but Konrad died before it ended.

Grand Master Konrad von Jungingen conquered the island of Gotland, in the middle of the Baltic Sea, in 1398. But he suffered from gallstones and ignored his doctor's suggested cure of sexual intercourse; he died in 1407. Konrad's brother Ulrich allied with Hungary and invaded Poland in 1409. But Vytautas of Lithuania supported Poland and Sigismund failed to support Ulrich so the Teutonic Order was defeated, and many senior knights were killed or captured at the Battle of Grunwald (also known as Tannenberg) in July 1410.

Heinrich von Plauen the Elder missed the battle but he managed to prevent the invaders from taking the order's headquarters, Marienburg Castle, because Jogaila moved too slowly. Heinrich also rallied support from the Livonian Order and Germany to stop the invaders. Heinrich blamed the Lizard Union for the defeat at Grunwald, accusing Nicholas von Renys of lowering his banner, triggering a retreat. Nicholas was executed and the Union was declared illegal.

The Peace of Thorn in 1411 required the order to pay a huge amount to release its prisoners but it was soon in financial difficulties so Heinrich asked Emperor Sigismund to mediate. The amount was reduced, Heinrich paid up and borders were agreed. Heinrich still wanted to attack Poland but the knights ignored him and he was deposed by Michael Küchmeister von Sternberg in 1413. Jogaila wanted Heinrich reinstated so he could defeat him again, so he was eventually arrested but Michael failed to make peace with Poland and resigned in 1422. Poland and Lithuania invaded anyway but the Gollob War ended quickly with Paul von Rusdorf renouncing the order's claims to Lithuania under the Treaty of Melno.

Paul signed the Treaty of Christmemel with Sigismund of Hungary and Bohemia, sparking another war, and while the knights invaded Poland, they were beaten at the Battle of Dąbki in 1431. Poland then allied with the Hussite heretics and counter-attacked, resulting in the Treaty of Łęczyca. Jogaila died in 1434 and the fighting resumed, ending in victory for the Lithuanian–Polish alliance at the Battle of Wilkomierz in 1435.

Paul von Rusdorf, Konrad von Erlichshausen and Ludwig von Erlichshausen as successive grand masters enjoyed twenty-one years of peace. It was broken when the Prussian Confederation asked Kazimierz IV of Poland to support their claim for independence in 1454, resulting in the Thirteen Years War. The knights were defeated on land at the Battle of Świecino in 1462 and on water at the Battle of Vistula Lagoon in 1463. Donations from the Holy Roman Empire ended, forcing Ludwig to sell the Neumark region to Brandenburg to pay for mercenaries. He even had to sell the knights' headquarters to Kazimierz and moved the order to Königsberg. The Teutonic Order finally surrendered western Prussia and became Polish vassals under the Second Peace of Thorn of 1466.

Ludwig died in 1467 and Heinrich von Plauen the Younger became grand master. He delayed paying Poland until 1470 and was then paralysed by a stroke, as he returned from a visit to Kazimierz IV. Heinrich Reffle von Richtenberg maintained an uneasy truce with Poland but Martin Truchsess von Wetzhausen said he would 'rather drown in his blood than pay homage to the King of Poland'. Instead he invaded Poland, was defeated and was forced to pay homage. Johann von Tiefen responded to Poland's call for help against the Ottomans but his small army of knights was struck down by illness and had to return home.

THE GRAND DUCHY OF LITHUANIA

Mindaugas and his pagan followers had to move inland as the Lithuanian Order advanced along the Baltic coast. They stopped their advance at the Battle of Saule in 1236 and Mindaugas was appointed Lithuania's first grand duke. He would be baptised a Roman Catholic and crowned king in 1251 to appease the Crusaders. The peace did not last long because the Mongol hordes attacked Lithuania around 1258. Treniota convinced Mindaugas to return to paganism after the Battle of Durbe in 1260 and he married his sister-in-law when his wife Morta died, even though she was already married to Daumantas. Daumantas and Treniota then joined forces to assassinate Mindaugas and two of his sons in 1263. Treniota only ruled for a year before he was murdered but he had succeeded in turning the nation back to paganism.

Meanwhile, Mindaugas's surviving son, Vaišvilkas, had become a monk, founded a monastery and gone on a pilgrimage to Mount Athos in Greece. He turned back due to a war in the Balkans and stayed with the Teutonic Knights and the Livonian Order after learning his father and brothers had been murdered. He returned after Treniota's death and conquered Black Ruthenia and Lithuania with his brother-in-law, Shvarn of Halych-Volhynia, in 1265. Vaišvilkas then gave Lithuania to Shvarn and returned to his monastery.

Shvarn defeated his own brother Mstislav at the Battle of the Yaselda River and then beat the Tatars at the Battle of Kojdanow in 1267. But another brother, Leo, was angry Vaišvilkas had given him nothing so he murdered Shvarn. Traidenis re-established a pagan state and he expanded west, defeating the Livonian Order on the frozen Baltic Sea at the Battle of Karuse in 1270. He had regained control of Black Ruthenia by 1276, beat the order at the Battle of Aizkraukle and then killed its master. Traidenis died in 1282; the first Lithuanian duke to have died a natural death.

Daumantas was captured by the united forces of Tver, Moscow, Novgorod and Torzhok in 1285 and was soon dead. Butigeidis and then Butvydas faced attacks from the Livonian Order and the Teutonic Knights, as they continued their conquest of the Baltic tribes. But the Lithuanians were forced to withdraw to the Neman River and Butigeidis gave the Vawkavysk area to Galicia to make peace.

Vytenis was crowned in 1295 and he supported Bolesław II against Władysław I in Poland, gaining a powerful ally. Although he was able to recapture many lost territories, the Teutonic Knights and the Livonian Order conquered the Prussians and other Baltic tribes. Vytenis allied with Riga and invaded Teutonic territory eleven times after defeating the Livonian Order at the Battle of Turaida. He finally allied with the Teutonic Knights and they captured Pomerania from Poland in 1308.

Gediminas murdered Vytenis around 1315 and then chose to ally with the Tatars against the Teutonic Knights. Legend says he dreamt of an armour-clad wolf howling on a hill and built a fortification where his priests advised him to, it would become Vilnius, capital of Lithuania. Pope John XXII agreed to baptise Gediminas but he told the papal legate he was under threat so Rome banned anyone from attacking Lithuania for four years to allow him to embrace Catholicism. The Teutonic Order did not believe his promise and they murdered the Lithuanian delegate sent to welcome the grand master to prove their point.

Gediminas defeated Stanislav of Kiev on the Irpin River in 1321 and installed his brother Theodor as Prince. He avoided fighting the Mongols and claimed parts of Galicia–Volhynia after they killed its co-rulers, brothers Kev II and Andrey, in 1323. The same year he agreed a treaty with the Livonians on his northern border and invited monks to build churches. But Gediminas remained a pagan and was hated by Orthodox worshippers and pagans alike and he was probably killed in 1341 during a coup d'état. Jaunutis embraced Christianity and was baptised Ioann, annoying his brothers. Narimantas formed an alliance with the Golden Horde while Algirdas and Keştutis imprisoned him and seized power in 1345. Ioann escaped and fled to his brother-in-law Simeon in Moscow.

Keştutis ruled the west side of Lithuania while his brother Algirdas advanced into western Russia. Pope Clement VI in 1349 promised a royal crown until the negotiator, Kazimierz III of Poland, attacked and ruined the plan. Keştutis accepted Christianity and promised Louis I of Hungary support during the war for Volhynia in exchange for the crown only to default on the deal. He defeated the Tatars at the Battle of Blue Waters in 1362, forced the Kipchak horde to head south towards the Crimea and then tried to capture Moscow.

While Keştutis was busy fighting the Tartars, Algirdas had converted to Roman Catholicism and made peace with the Livonian Order. Jogaila was crowned Grand Duke of Lithuania in 1377 and he ruled the Ruthenian territories while his uncle Keştutis ruled north-west Lithuania. Andrei and Dmitry of Polotsk joined Dmitri of Moscow when Jogaila allied with the Mongols but Dmitri of Moscow failed to support the brothers and they were defeated at the Battle of Kulikovo in 1380.

While Jogaila had negotiated a ten-year truce with Keştutis, he had also signed the secret Treaty of Dovydiškės, which said he would not to interfere if the Teutonic Knights attacked Keştutis. Keştutis heard about the treaty and imprisoned Jogaila until he pledged his loyalty. Jogaila then needed Teutonic help to recapture his throne.

The armies of Keṣtutis and Jogaila met near Trakai in 1382, and while Keṣtutis and Vytautas expected to negotiate, Jogaila imprisoned them and disbanded their army. Keṣtutis was murdered a few days later but Vytautas escaped to the Teutonic Knights and was baptised and renamed Wigand.

Jogaila's next move was the Treaty of Dubysa which promised to hand over the land dividing the knights' territories and convert Lithuania to Christianity in 1383. The knights invaded Lithuania when he refused to ratify it and Jogaila allied Wigand to fight them off. Wigand the Great was rebaptised in 1386 and changed his name again, this time to Alexander.

Jogaila signed the 1385 Union of Krèva, under which he could marry young Jadwiga of Poland, while his brother Skirgaila would become regent of Lithuania. But Jogaila, now called Władysław II, proved to be unpopular with the Polish nobility because he spent all his time in Lithuania. In 1392 it was agreed Vytautas would rule Lithuania on behalf of Władysław, on condition it would return to the King of Poland on his death.

Vytautas agreed to intervene during a civil war in the Golden Horde in 1395 and his armies swept as far south as the Crimea. He finally gave the Teutonic Knights the area they needed to merge with the Livonian Order in return for support against the Tartars. He was rewarded with a large expanse of land which meant Lithuania stretched from the Baltic Sea to the Black Sea. The enraged Tartars soon retaliated and defeated his army on the Vorskla River in 1399.

The strained relationship between Poland and Lithuania was restored in 1399 after Jadwiga died in childbirth, undermining Jogaila's position in Poland. It also helped that Vytautas went to war against his son-in-law, Vasily of Moscow. Jogaila's brother, Švitrigaila. Jogaila and Vytautas would finally unite to defeat the Teutonic Knights at the Battle of Grunwald (Battle of Tannenberg) in 1410 but there would be disputes over the 1411 Peace of Thorn and more campaigns with the Teutonic Knights.

Although Lithuania remained separate and was allowed to elect its grand duke, it was still tied to Poland under the 1413 Union of Horodło. Vytautas was appointed King of Lithuania in 1429, with Emperor Sigismund's support, but his first crown was stolen by Polish barons and he died before the second arrived.

Jogaila's brother, Švitrigaila, had defected to Moscow only to return to Lithuania when the Mongols invaded. He was imprisoned as a traitor but escaped to Hungary and was eventually allowed to return to Lithuania and succeeded Vytautas in 1430. Švitrigaila immediately ignored the Union of Horodło, declared Lithuania independent and refused to submit to Jogaila. He allied with the Teutonic Knights but the knights betrayed him and seized the west side of Lithuania in 1432 while Emperor Sigismund usurped him.

Švitrigaila returned with Mongol support but the Teutonic Knights defeated him at the Battle of Pabaiskas in 1435 and he fled and tried to rally support in Poland before heading into Wallachia. Sigismund was assassinated by Švitrigaila's supporters in 1440 but he was too old to take the throne so Władysław III of Poland's brother, Kazimierz, was crowned king. It was the start of over a century of rule over Lithuania by the House of Jagiełłon.

THE PRINCIPALITY OF GALICIA–VOLHYNIA

Yaroslav of Galicia (or Halych) died in 1187 and Prince Roman of Vladimir urged the Galicians to poison his son, Oleg, and exile his other son, Vladimir. Roman had been invited to rule Halych but he gave it to his brother, Vsevolod. The exiled Vladimir acquired support from Hungary but Béla III made his own son, Andrew, ruler, once they had taken Galicia. Roman was turned away by Vsevolod but his father-in-law helped him recapture Galicia.

Ryurik gave Roman territories in 1195 but he was unhappy with his share. Roman then convinced Yaroslav II of Chernigov to capture Kiev, only for Ryurik to tell Vsevolod. Roman went to Poland for help but only to be attacked and wounded in battle. So he was forced to ask his father-in-law for mercy.

Vladimir II died in 1198 and Leszek of Poland helped Roman defeat all other claimants so he could seize Galicia, merging the two principalities by 1199. Roman, Ryurik and Leszek united to attack the Cuman hordes coming from the east, but they soon quarrelled. Roman imprisoned his father-in-law in a monastery, sent his wife and daughter to a convent and placed his two sons in his dungeons.

Pope Innocent III's envoys visited Galicia in 1204, but when they promised to place Roman under the protection of St Peter's sword, he replied, 'Is the pope's sword similar to mine? So long as I carry mine, I need no other.'

Relations with Leszek deteriorated and Roman the Great was killed fighting the Poles at the Battle of Zawichost in 1205. The barons forced Roman's wife and her infant son, Daniel, into exile and proclaimed one of their own as prince in 1213. Leszek's Poles and Andrew's Hungarians invaded, pretending to support the heir, but instead divided Galicia and forced young Daniel to renounce his claim to the throne in favour of his father-in-law, Mstislav the Bold.

Daniel would establish rule over Volhynia in 1221 but it was 1238 before he defeated the Dobrzyń Knights and recaptured most of Galicia. He captured Kiev the following year but the Mongols razed it to the ground. They then rampaged across Galicia before campaigning against the Poles and Hungarians before heading back to elect a new grand khan. As soon as the hordes left, Daniel captured the rest of the principality and established relations with Poland and Hungary, bringing an end to the Principality of Galicia–Volhynia.

The Kingdom of Ruthenia

Daniel was summoned to the capital of the Golden Horde so he called for a Crusade to help him keep the Mongols at bay. But Pope Innocent IV only sent a representative crown, leaving him no option but to pledge allegiance to Batu Khan. Daniel was accepted and crowned as the first King of Rus' in 1253 but he divided his lands between his sons when he died in 1264. Shvarn received the north-west and Leo the south, where he established his new capital which was called Lviv after him. Shvarn invaded Lesser Poland but was defeated by Bolesław V the Chaste at the Battle of Brańsk in 1264 and Wrota in 1266.

Shvarn had also supported Vaišvilkas when Mindaugas was murdered in Lithuania in 1263. Vaišvilkas wanted to return to monastic life so he gave Lithuania to Shvarn and an outraged Leo murdered Vaišvilkas in 1268. Shvarn defeated another brother, Mstislav, at the Battle of the Yaselda River and then beat the Mongols at the Battle of Kojdanow in 1267.

Control of Lithuania went to a noble called Traidenis when Shvarn died in 1269. Leo had plans to extend his territories to the south and allied with Wenceslaus II of Bohemia so they could invade Poland and annex part of Hungary in 1279. Leo would take Ruthenia to the height of its power, when it defeated Poland in 1292, and he seized the Lublin area.

Leo died in 1301 and his sons, Yuri and George, spent the next twenty years struggling to maintain their huge empire. George was killed fighting the Lithuanians in 1321 and Leo II and Andrew died defending their territories two years later, bringing their family line to an end. The boyars took control and they initially allied with Poland and the Teutonic Knights to fight the Golden Horde. But they soon became worried Władysław I the Elbow-high wanted to take over and asked the Mongols for support.

The throne was eventually given to the Mazovian Duke Bolesław in 1323 because he was related through marriage to the Ruthenian line. He was renamed Jerzy but became unpopular after introducing Magdeburg law and town privileges. He became even more unpopular when he offered to make Kazimierz III of Poland his heir in 1338. Two years later the boyars poisoned him and Poland had annexed Ruthenia by 1349, ending a century of vassalage to the Mongols.

Kazimierz III the Great ruled until he died in 1370 and then his grandson, Louis I the Great of Hungary, became King of Poland. After the rule of Louis I's daughter, Mary, from 1382, and her sister Hedwig from 1387, Ruthenia became part of the Kingdom of Poland in 1399.

THE PRINCIPALITIES OF RUSSIA

The land of the Rus' (or Kievan Rus') was the first senior principality and it was next to Galicia–Volhynia in the west. The title of Grand Prince of Russia passed to Vladimir, to the north-east, in 1169 and to Moscow in 1283. The Principality of Polotsk bordered Lithuania and Teutonic territory to the north-west and Novgorod was to the north, next to Swedish lands (now Finland). Smolensk was to the east and Chernigov was to the south-east.

The Grand Princes of Kiev

Kiev was the senior principality when Yaroslav died in 1054. He had divided his realm between his three sons, Iziaslav, Sviatoslav and Vsevolod, and they formed a triumvirate. The Cuman hordes routed Iziaslav and Vsevolod on the Alta River in 1061 but Sviatoslav defeated them at Snovsk in 1068. The brothers had defeated their cousin, Vseslav, on the Nemiga River in 1067 and Iziaslav took him prisoner during peace talks. The Kievans deposed Iziaslav, in favour of Vseslav the Sorcerer, but Iziaslav retook the throne with help from his son-in-law, Bolesław the Bold. It was then Sviatoslav's turn to take the throne but he fell ill and retired in 1076.

Iziaslav returned with support from Emperor Henry IV and Bolesław of Poland while Pope Gregory VII sent him a crown, making him the first King of Rus'. He seized Kiev and gave Sviatoslav's lands to Vsevolod but Sviatoslav's sons enlisted the Cumans' help to retake them. Iziaslav was murdered in battle in 1078 and Vsevolod held the Kievan throne until he died.

Sviatopolk's illegitimate son, Iziaslav, became ruler and he allied with Vladimir against the Kipchak hordes, only to be defeated along the Stugna River in 1093. The Kievans invited Vladimir to be their ruler when Sviatopolk died in 1113 and he was succeeded by his son in 1125. Mstislav faced many attacks from the Cumans, the Estonians, the Lithuanians and even the Principality of Polotsk. He also defeated his uncle Oleg of Chernigov on the Koloksha River in 1096, creating a long-term enemy in Oleg's descendants. Mstislav the Great died in 1132, the last ruler of a united kingdom before 'the land of Rus' was torn apart'.

Vsevolod of Chernigov and the Cumans crossed the Dnieper in the south to loot Kiev and they defeated Yaropolk along the Supoy River in 1135. Sviatoslav continued the fight against Yaropolk, again with Cuman help, but he made peace when Yaropolk acquired Hungarian support. Meanwhile, Novgorod had deposed Vsevolod in the north and he was killed trying to recapture it.

Viacheslav succeeded his brother Yaropolk in 1139 but was soon driven out by Oleg's son, Vsevolod II, and he jointly ruled Kiev with his nephew Iziaslav II. Vsevolod died in

1146, leaving the throne to his brother Igor rather than his two sons. But the Kievans accused him of being dishonest, greedy and violent and they invited his cousin Iziaslav, to be their prince in 1149. Igor captured him and held him in a pit until he fell ill and then imprisoned him as a monk. But the people rioted, tore down Igor's balcony, murdered him and displayed his body in their market place.

Yuri I recaptured Kiev and he became known as 'Long Arms' because his activities stretched so far south. He would also become known as the founder of Moscow, but his nephew Iziaslav returned in 1151 and drove him out. Rostislav headed south from Novgorod to take the Kievan throne when Iziaslav died, leaving his son to rule Novgorod. But Iziaslav III chased him out after only a week, while Novgorod rebelled against his son. The title of Grand Prince of Russia then passed between Iziaslav, Yuri and Rostislav between 1154 and 1167. Mstislav II took the title in 1167 but Andrey of Vladimir sacked Kiev in 1169 and exiled the last Grand Prince of Kiev to Byzantine Emperor, Manuel I.

The Grand Princes of Vladimir

Andrey I the God-loving became grand prince in 1157 and he tried to get Novgorod and Kiev under his control. The Scythian Caesar, as he was known in the west, plundered Kiev in 1169 and he moved his capital to Vladimir. He increased the princes' authority, upsetting many, and twenty angry retainers murdered him in his bed in 1174. His half-brother Mikhail returned from exile and took over Vladimir but the Kievan boyars soon became jealous of Vladimir's rise to power. He planned to meet them but had to return to Vladimir to fight off his nephew, Yaropolk in 1175; he died the following year.

Vsevolod III allied with his brother Mikhail against the boyars and then succeeded him in 1176. He placed a puppet ruler on Novgorod's throne to control the north and married his daughters to Chernigov and Kiev princes to get approval in the south. With the boyars' support, Vsevolod headed south-east to raid the Volga area, to raze Ryazan and Belgorod to the ground and seize huge tracts of land. He had at least fourteen children with Maria by the time he died in 1212 and became known as 'Big Nest'.

Vsevolod had intended Konstantin to rule the west from Vladimir and Yuri to rule the east from Rostov but Konstantin wanted it all. So Vsevolod gave everything to Yuri so Konstantin allied with Mstislav the Bold and they defeated his brothers along the Lipitsa River. Yuri was sent to rule Rostov but he returned to Vladimir when Konstantin died only two years later and he let his younger brother, Yaroslav, rule the north from Novgorod.

Family differences were forgotten when the Mongols approached in 1223 but Yuri's army missed a disastrous battle along the Kalka River. While Yuri breathed a sigh of relief when the Mongols withdrew, Yaroslav invaded Estonia and Finland and then defeated the Lithuanians and Teutonic Knights in 1234. Yuri refused to ask for help when the Mongols returned in 1237 and dismissed their envoys. So the hordes rode west, defeating Yuri's sons near Kolomna and then torched Vladimir. Yuri's family were trapped and died in a burning church, and while Yuri escaped the city, he was killed at the Battle of the Sit River in 1238.

Yaroslav was appointed grand prince as the Mongols withdrew to elect a new grand khan. He rebuilt Vladimir and then visited the Blue Horde's capital, Sarai, in 1243, to get Batu Khan's approval. He also visited Karakorum with Sviatoslav, Andrey and Alexander in 1247 when they could not pay and Grand Khan Guyuk refused to believe Alexander's lie that Andrey had stolen part of the gold. He made Andrey grand duke instead of Sviatoslav and gave Yaroslav a slow poison so he died on the return journey. But Andrey returned to find his brother Mikhail the Brave had seized Vladimir in his absence and he was killed fighting the Lithuanians at the Battle of Protva in 1248.

Alexander signed a peace treaty with Norway in 1251 and then invaded Finland and routed the Swedes after they blockaded the Baltic Sea. But the attack angered the Mongols and Batu Khan defeated Alexander near Pereslavl in 1256 and forced him to flee to Sweden. Alexander visited the Blue Horde for a pardon, giving them his eastern lands, and promised to pay tribute. But Batu died and Alexander returned to get Sartaq Khan's approval, only to die on the way home.

Yaroslav III argued with his brother Andrey and although the Golden Horde arbitrated in Yaroslav's favour, an alliance of princes forced Yaroslav to surrender Novgorod to his nephew in 1270. They then escorted Yaroslav to Sarai to get the khan's approval but he too died on the return journey and his son Vasily was appointed grand prince.

Alexander's son Dmitri was his successor, crowned grand prince in 1276, so his offended brother Andrey visited the Golden Horde and joined the Mongols. He returned in 1281 and drove Dmitri from Vladimir, ravaged his lands and then went to the Black Sea and allied with Nogai Khan. Andrey renounced his claims to Vladimir and Novgorod and then led the Mongol horsemen across Russia three more times, forcing Dmitri to abdicate and retire to a monastery in 1293.

Andrey ruled from Novgorod but the fighting was far from over because he had to fight an alliance of princes led by Daniel of Moscow for over a decade. Daniel defeated Constantine of Ryazan and his Mongol allies and then tricked Constantine into prison and Kolomna fortress, which controlled the Moskva River, was the ransom. Daniel was then given Pereslavl when his nephew, Ivan, died childless.

Yuri of Moscow seized Vladimir while Tokhta Khan appointed Mikhail grand prince in 1304. So Mikhail returned with the Blue Horde and recaptured it in 1316. A stubborn Yuri went to the Golden Horde where he married the khan's sister, Konchaka, to confirm his appointment and returned with Uzbeg Khan to depose Mikhail. But as soon as the Mongols left, Mikhail defeated Yuri and captured his wife at the Battle of Bortenevo in 1317. Unfortunately, Konchaka died in custody and Mikhail was summoned to the Horde where he was accused of poisoning her and was executed.

Yuri returned home in 1319 and Mikhail's son, Dmitri the Terrible Eyes, was selected to collect the Horde's tribute. While Dmitri was gathering the money, he convinced the Uzbeg Khan that Yuri was stealing part of the tribute so they were both summoned in 1326. Dmitri murdered Yuri before he could be questioned, so Uzbeg Khan executed him to stop him finding out the truth.

Alexander succeeded his brother Dmitri, only to see a large retinue of Mongols, led by Uzbeg's cousin, Baskaki Shevkal, arrive in the city and squat in the palace. They terrorised the people and there were rumours he wanted to assassinate Alexander and seize the throne so the mob retaliated and trapped and burnt the leaders alive in a house.

The Grand Princes of Moscow

Yuri's brother, Ivan, visited the Golden Horde and was appointed grand prince. He returned with a huge army and forced Alexander into exile while the Mongols made sure their money was collected. Ivan based himself in Moscow because it was on the east–west caravan trade route and he invited people to pay him ransoms so he could free hostages held by the Mongols. Ivan also lent money to neighbours and annexed them when they got into debt, so he was also called the 'gatherer of the Russian lands'. It made him rich, powerful and loyal to the Horde, earning him another name: Ivan the Money Bag.

Meanwhile, Alexander had been drumming up support in Lithuania and he sent his son, Fyodor, to the Horde to ask for forgiveness and then went himself in 1337. But Alexander and Fyodor were summoned to the Blue Horde, executed and their bodies quartered, after they started new conflicts. Ivan would convince the khan that his son, Simeon the Proud, should succeed him before he died in 1341. Ivan was the last of the Grand Princes of Vladimir to rule Russia.

Three contenders went to the Blue Horde in 1340 and Simeon the Proud bribed his way to be appointed. He had to return when Uzbeg Khan died and met Jani, who had murdered his two brothers to get control. Simeon's position was confirmed but he had to leave Bishop Theognostus as a hostage until the tribute was paid. Simeon divorced his second wife, Eupraxia, claiming he had been cursed since the wedding and complained she 'appears to be dead each night'. A third marriage to Maria was definitely cursed because his four sons all died young. When the Black Death reached Moscow in March 1353, Simeon, his two baby sons and his brother Andrey all died.

Simeon's apathetic brother, Ivan II the Fair, did not intervene when Lithuania captured Bryansk or when Oleg of Ryazan ravaged his lands. Ivan died in 1359 and the khan's next choice, Dmitri the One-Eyed, was deposed in 1363. Young Dmitri Donsky became Grand Prince when he came of age. He stopped the Lithuanian invasion with the Treaty of Lyubutsk and was acknowledged by the northern princes, doubling the size of Moscow's territory.

Dmitri then ravaged the Bulgarian Volga to challenge the Mongols and Mamai Khan's punitive invasion was beaten along the Vozha River in 1378 and at Kulikovo in 1380. But Tokhtamysh dethroned Mamai, overran Moscow and made Dmitri pledge his loyalty. Dmitri of the Don died in 1389 and he was the first grand duke to bequeath his titles to his son without consulting the Horde.

Vasily I allied with Lithuania by marrying Vytautas the Great's daughter, Sophia, offending the Mongols. Their raid in 1395 resulted in twelve years of anarchy for the Golden Horde and Vasily used the tribute he collected to raise his own army. But many Moscow lands were razed to the ground in another Mongol raid in 1408 and Vasily eventually made the long-deferred journey to submit to the Horde.

A young Vasily II was crowned grand duke in 1425 but his uncle Yuri contested his appointment under the House of Rurik Law which passed the title between brothers rather than from father to son. The grand khan decided in Vasily's favour but Yuri maintained his challenge and started the Muscovite Civil War. The Golden Horde had promised to support Yuri but their army turned back when a Muscovite boyar called Ivan Vsevolozhsky betrayed him. Vasily was also betrayed by Ivan, allowing Yuri to defeat him on the Klyazma River in 1432. He retaliated by exiling Yuri and blinding Ivan. Many Muscovite boyars joined Vasily and he returned to Moscow after Yuri resigned. Yuri's sons would defeat Vasily along the Kus River and again near Rostov in 1433.

Although Yuri seized Moscow, he died soon afterwards and his son, Vasily the Cross-Eyed, was proclaimed the new grand duke. His brother Dmitri visited Moscow with a wedding invitation but Vasily was justifiably suspicious and imprisoned him, accusing him of allying with their cousin. Dmitri was then sent to fight Olug of Kazan but Vasily only gave him a small army, in the hope he would be defeated. Dmitri allied with Vasily II in 1435, captured Moscow, proclaimed himself grand prince and blinded his brother, Vasily the Cross-Eyed. But the Muscovites rose up and helped Vasily regain the capital. He was forced to flee when Olug besieged the city in 1439 and six years later he was captured and ransomed for a huge amount.

Dmitri retook Moscow in Olug's absence and blinded Vasily as soon as he returned but the Muscovites again rejected him and forced him into exile. He was plotting his return when Vasily had him poisoned with a chicken dinner in 1453 and showed 'indecent joy' at his cousin's death.

The civil war was finally over and Vasily the Blind was again grand duke with his son Ivan helping him rule until he died in 1462. Ivan III became known as the 'gatherer of the Russian lands' because he tripled his territories, taking them from his brothers through conquest, purchase or marriage. By uniting such a vast area he ended the dominance of the Golden Horde over the Rus'. He would also be remembered as Ivan the Great.

Two Novgorodian envoys accidentally addressed Ivan as Gosudar (sovereign) instead of Gospodin (sir) in 1477 and then disagreed when he said they had accepted his sovereignty. He executed one and sent the other back with the bad news. He seized his brother Iurii's lands when he died childless and he took Boris's lands when his sons died young. His brother Andrei the Younger left his lands to him but he imprisoned Andrei and took his lands when he refused to help against the Golden Horde.

Pope Paul II had suggested Ivan marry Sophia, daughter of Thomas, despot of Morea and sister of the last Byzantine emperor, Constantine XI. He did, and while the princess endorsed Orthodoxy, she made the court of Moscow adopt Constantinople's etiquette. Ivan pleased his wife by building cathedrals, palaces and the Kremlin walls, making his capital a worthy successor to Constantinople. It was not what the pope had had in mind.

7

SOUTH-EAST
EUROPE

THE HUNGARIAN AND BYZANTINE EMPIRES shared south-east Europe in the eleventh century until the Bulgarians declared their independence in 1185, after sixty-seven years under Byzantine rule. Following the Mongol invasions in 1240s, two Hungarian warlords broke away to form their own principalities, Wallachia in 1330 and Moldavia in 1345 (today they form part of Romania).

THE KINGDOM OF HUNGARY

Hungary was the dominant kingdom in the area but it faced threats from all sides. It had the Holy Roman Empire to the west, Poland to the north and the Grand Principality of Kiev to the north-east. The Pecheneg hordes were to the east and the Byzantines were never far away to the south.

Hungary was struggling between Christianity and paganism and the pagan Duke Vazul had his eyes gouged out and molten lead poured in his ears after trying to assassinate the Christian King István. Vazul's sons were exiled, and while András and Levente settled in Kiev, Béla married into the Polish royal family.

István named his nephew, Peter, his successor after his son was killed during a boar hunt but András and Levente returned from exile when István died in 1038. They captured and blinded Peter and the brothers agreed András would rule. András refused to be a vassal of Henry III and he defeated the emperor in the Vértes Hills in 1051 with Béla's help. András made peace with the new Emperor Henry IV by betrothing his young son, Salaman, to Henry's sister, Judith.

But András offered Béla the choice of a crown or a sword to test his allegiance and although he selected the sword, the challenge angered him. So Béla returned with an army from his Polish in-laws and he captured András after he fell from his horse in the Theben Pass, en route to Austria; he died in captivity.

Béla was crowned in 1060 and was named the Champion for putting down pagan revolts across the kingdom. Three years later Béla was discussing how to repel an invasion by Emperor Henry IV when his wooden throne collapsed under suspicious circumstances, mortally injuring him. Henry took the opportunity to seize control of Hungary by marrying young Salaman to his widowed sister Judith. Béla's sons, Géza, László and Lampert returned with a Polish army after Henry returned to his empire. They accepted Salaman's rule in return for their father's lands but the compromise ended when Pécs Cathedral burnt down during the coronation and both sides accused each other of arson. The arguments ended when the Pecheneg hordes invaded Transylvania in 1068 but they stopped them at the Battle of Chirales.

Salaman and the three brothers then joined forces to invade the troubled Byzantine Empire and they besieged Belgrade in 1071. The Byzantines refused to surrender to Salaman but they agreed to surrender to the brothers, hoping to stir up resentment.

The plan worked better than they hoped because Géza used the king's share of the booty to buy Polish and Bohemian help so he could defeat Salaman at the Battle of Mogyoród in 1074 and seize the throne. Salaman planned to counter-attack with imperial troops but he had to wait until Henry had put down an uprising in the empire. They defeated Géza in 1076 but the sick king abdicated and proclaimed his brother, László, king, thwarting Salaman's attempt to seize the crown.

Géza had rejected Pope Gregory VII's offer to join the Roman Church in favour of the Byzantine Church because Emperor Michael VII offered him a crown. Pope Gregory also tried to get László interested in joining the Roman Church, playing on the fact they had a common enemy: Emperor Henry IV. But László rejected the offer and married Adelaide, the daughter of Rudolf I of Swabia, anti-king of Germany.

Salaman continued to control Hungary's western territories, with Henry IV's support, until László offered him lands so he would abdicate in 1081. But Salaman continued to plot and turned to the Pechenegs after the emperor refused to help. He married Kuteshk's daughter and promised them territories but was defeated in 1085. Instead Salaman joined the Pecheneg campaign against the Byzantine Empire and was killed in the Battle of Adrianople in 1087.

László turned his attention to Croatia when King Dmitar died in 1089, leaving his sister, Ilona, a widow. But Hungary's plans to capture Croatia were thwarted when Emperor Alexios I encouraged the Cumans to invade. László struck back and defeated the Cumans along the Temes River, seized Croatia and then refused to acknowledge Rome's rule over his new territory.

László appointed Álmos heir ahead of his physically disabled older brother, so Könyves went to Poland looking for support. László dropped dead after hearing his nephew was invading in 1095 and Álmos acknowledged Könyves the Learned as his king in return for lands.

Walter the Penniless led the People's Crusade peacefully through Hungary in 1096 but Peter the Hermit's unruly Crusaders had to be driven out. Könyves took Baudouin hostage until his brother Godfrey had led their army out of his kingdom. He also took sides with the pope in his struggle with the emperor, marrying Roger I of Sicily's daughter, Felicia, in 1097.

King Petar of the Croatians rose up against Hungarian rule only to be beaten at the Battle of Gvozd Mountain. Álmos staged an uprising while Könyves was in Croatia but the Hungarian boyars forced him to back down. Instead Álmos asked Henry IV for support when Könyves crowned his son, István, only to be told the emperor was too busy fighting his own son. Álmos was about to get Polish support when Könyves convinced Bolesław III to join his attack on Henry IV. Álmos eventually conceded, acquired the king's pardon and went on a Crusade.

Despite the pardon, Könyves seized his brother's lands while he was away, so Álmos convinced Henry IV's son, Henry, to attack Pozsony on his return. Könyves and Bolesław counter-attacked Bohemia until the emperor sued for peace and although Álmos was allowed to return to Hungary, he did not get his lands back.

An elderly Könyves had married into the Kievan family in 1112 to make an alliance but Eufemia was sent back to her father, Vladimir II, after committing adultery. Könyves refused to acknowledge their son Boris while his mother was sent to a monastery. A dying Könyves had Álmos and his infant son, Béla, blinded in 1116 to make sure his own son became King of Hungary and Croatia.

István II met Vladislav I of Bohemia at Lucko Field hoping to improve relations but had to defeat the Bohemian army instead. Prince Yaroslav of Volhynia asked Hungary for help to get his throne back in 1123 so István invaded and besieged Vladimir, even after the prince was killed, until the Hungarian boyars threatened to dethrone him.

István spent his teenage years with his concubines until the boyars forced him to marry. He also gave the Pechenegs shelter from the Byzantines. István employed the Pechenegs as his bodyguards, leading to a conspiracy to put his blinded uncle Álmos on the throne. Álmos fled to Constantinople and Emperor John II refused to hand him back so István invaded. He was defeated by the Byzantines at the Battle of Haram in 1128, so István returned with Sobéslav I of Bohemia and defeated Emperor John II. The childless István had a change of heart when Álmos died and he married his blinded son Béla to Jelena and made him his heir.

Béla was crowned in 1131 and Jelena had the sixty-eight boyars accused of blinding her husband executed and made her brother, Belos, commander of the army. But Könyves's dispossessed son, Boris, decided it was time to reclaim the throne with Polish and Russian support and Belos threatened to execute any boyar who refused to declare him a bastard. Boris and Bolesław III invaded in 1132 only to be defeated along the Sajó River. But Béla had drunk himself to death by 1141 and he left the throne to young Géza who was governed by his mother and uncle.

Boris was still after the throne but he and his new supporter, Henry II of Austria, were defeated by the Hungarians in 1146. The following year Konrad III led his German Crusaders through Hungary without trouble but Lajos VII of France followed, taking Boris with him, and refused to hand him over, angering Géza.

Géza supported his uncle Uroš II when the Byzantines invaded Serbia but the country soon fell under Constantinople's rule. He then tried to help his brother-in-law Iziaslav II hold Kiev against the Prince of Halych but had to return home when Boris invaded

Hungary, this time with Byzantine help. Géza defeated Boris and declared a truce with the Byzantines, ending the usurper's quest for the throne. Having dealt with one claimant, Géza had to defeat two more by his brother István and his brother László, forcing them both to flee to the Byzantine Empire.

Géza died in 1161 and the teenage István III returned to be crowned. But Emperor Manuel I thought he was too strong a leader so he invaded and bribed the Hungarian boyars to accept his brother László as a compromise. László was proclaimed king but Archbishop Lukas excommunicated him because he was loyal to István; László died soon after, probably poisoned. István III returned only to find László's followers had proclaimed his brother István IV king. Archbishop Lukas also excommunicated István instead of crowning him and then the Hungarian boyars turned on him because he was pro-Byzantine. István III saw his chance and he captured István IV at the Battle of Székesfehérvár in 1163, with Emperor Friedrich I's help.

István IV returned to the Byzantines when he was released, and while Manuel attacked Hungary on his behalf, he soon realised he lacked support. Meanwhile, István III sent his brother Béla to Constantinople to make the peace by marrying Manuel's daughter. The emperor promised to drop his support for István IV but invaded Hungary in 1164, pretending he was fighting for Béla's inheritance. The following year István IV made a comeback only to be besieged in Zimony, where he was poisoned by his own men after refusing to surrender.

Manuel continued his campaign against Hungary, capturing Croatia and Dalmatia after the Battle of Sirmium in 1166. István III divorced his wife so he could marry Henry II's daughter to get Austrian support but their combined army was still defeated near Zimony. István would die (possibly poisoned) on a pilgrimage to the Holy Land in 1172, leaving Béla as his heir.

The problem was Manuel had taken Béla's lands for himself. His second wife, Maria, had also given birth to a son, Alexius, in 1166 so he married Béla to his sister-in-law instead. While Béla was still heir to Hungary, his mother and many boyars preferred his brother, Géza. So Manuel gave him money to agree a truce, allowing Béla to arrest Géza knowing he had Byzantine support. Béla took over one of the richest countries in Europe, because new technology allowed Hungarian mines to produce over 20 tons of silver per year.

Meanwhile, Géza had escaped to Austria and Henry II refused to hand him over, so Béla and Sobéslav II of Bohemia allied and invaded. Béla also recaptured Hungarian lands lost to the Byzantines when Manuel died in 1180 and then made peace with Emperor Isaakios II.

Béla looked north-east after a dethroned Vladimir II of Halych sought refuge in Hungary in 1188. He conquered Halych but arrested Vladimir instead of reinstating him and placed his own son, András, on the throne. Vladimir would escape later on and recapture his principality.

Béla welcomed Friedrich I as he headed for the Holy Land in 1189 but died before fulfilling his promise to lead his own Crusade and Imre inherited the throne. His brother András inherited money to fulfil his father's oath, but instead he hired mercenaries, allied with Leopold VI, Duke of Austria and defeated Imre at the Battle of Mecsek in 1197. He then claimed Croatia and Dalmatia and Imre had to defeat András at the Battle of Rad in 1199 before peace was restored.

In 1200 Pope Innocent III urged Imre to stamp out the Balkan-based Bogomilism, a Christian based religion which shunned Roman Catholic trappings and worshipped in the open. He helped Vukan take the throne from Nemanjić of Serbia, only to use the title King of Serbia himself. He then made Kulin of Bosnia, another Bogomil supporter, accept his suzerainty. Imre also captured lands in Kaloyan's Bulgaria around 1203. But András rebelled again and this time Imre knew he was outnumbered. When their armies met, Imre approached his brother's camp alone, wearing his crown and the sceptre, reminding his brother who was king, and András surrendered.

A sick Imre crowned his young son László III in 1204 but András seized power as soon as the king died. Queen Constance and László escaped to Austria where the child king died in 1205. András II was anxious about his borders and although he gave lands along the south-east border to the Teutonic Knights to stop Cuman invasions, they established an independent territory instead. András also invaded Halych east to secure rule for the child prince Danylo but Volodymyr III bribed him to leave. He would capture Halych and install Danylo in 1208, when it was clear Volodymyr was an untrustworthy neighbour.

Meanwhile, the boyars were scandalised by András's generosity towards his wife's family and friends. Conspirators murdered his queen while he was visiting Nicaea in 1213. Though he caught them, he only executed the leader, something his son, Béla, would hate him for. In 1215 András married Yolanda, a niece of Henry I of the Latin Empire. He had hoped to inherit the territory but his father-in-law, Peter of Courtenay, was declared emperor when Henry died a few months later. Instead András finally fulfilled his father's promise and went on a Crusade and returned with relics after failing to capture any cities. András had to avoid assassination attempts by his cousins in Nicaea on the journey back and returned to find his kingdom in anarchy.

András initially agreed and then refused to divide Halych with Poland so Leszek I allied with Mstislav of Novgorod and they captured Halych. Hungary and Poland later divided Halych and although András made his son, Könyves, prince he was expelled from Halych in 1226. Hungarian rule ended in 1234 after Halych had exchanged hands several times. András married the teenage Beatrice and they had a son, to the disgust of his older sons, Béla and Könyves, and then died. Béla burnt his advisers' seats so they had to stand in his presence and then accused his stepmother and his father's adviser, Denis, of adultery. He ordered their arrest and called her baby son, István, a bastard.

An influx of Cumans escaping the Mongols warned Béla of the coming invasion so he granted asylum to 40,000 of them, hoping they would fight for him. While the hordes crossed Hungary's border in 1241, the country's boyars wanted rid of the Cumans and raided the village where Khagan Koten and his princes were being held as hostages. Koten killed his wives and committed suicide during the massacre. The Cumans then went on the rampage and withdrew to Bulgaria, allowing the Mongols to defeat the Hungarians at the Battle of Mohi, on the Sajó River. Béla fled to Austria where Friedrich II seized his treasury and forced him to hand over lands. He then fled to Zagreb and asked Emperor Friedrich II and Pope Gregory IX to help him fight back; none came. The Mongols continued into Austria but then surprised everyone by turning around after hearing the grand khan had died; they were heading home to elect a new one. Their withdrawal allowed Béla to return to Hungary and begin rebuilding it. He also recaptured lands lost to Friedrich II and gave territories to the Cumans.

Friedrich II invaded and defeated the Hungarians on the Leitha River in 1245 only to die soon after, so Béla retaliated by marching through the Vienna Basin in 1252. Ottokar II of Bohemia claimed the Austrian throne and concluded a peace in which Béla was given Styria. But Ottokar supported a Styrian rebellion and helped to defeat Béla and his son, István, at the Battle of Kressenbrunn in 1260. Old Béla and his favourite son, young Béla, turned their attentions on Bulgaria in 1261, while old Béla's daughter, Anna, took István's wife and son prisoner. István retaliated by defeating young Béla at the Battle of Isaszeg in 1265 and was awarded the eastern part of the kingdom. When young Béla died in 1269, old Béla sent Anna to Ottokar II of Bohemia for safe keeping.

Old Béla died in 1270 and Anna and Ottokar escaped to Prague only to be arrested. István's first move was to ally with Bolesław V of Poland against Bohemia and they defeated Ottokar in May 1271. István was heading to Dalmatia to meet Károly I of Sicily the following year when he heard that Joachim Gut-Keled of Slavonia had kidnapped his young son, László. He was organising a rescue when he died. Gut-Keled crowned László with a crown of thorns and would soon control both of István's sons, aiming to divide the kingdom between them. But László allied with Rudolf I of Germany when he came of age and defeated Ottokar II at the Battle on the Marchfeld in 1278.

László IV favoured his Cuman concubines over his wife and he imprisoned a papal legate who came to excommunicate him in 1279. The *voivode* of Transylvania forced him to reconcile and the Cumans revolted, so László defeated them in battle in 1282 and they left. A civil war ended when the Mongols raided in 1285 and some claimed László invited them into Hungary to help him regain power. He was eventually excommunicated·for arresting his wife so he could live with his Cuman mistress, Edua. The Cumans would serve their revenge cold, eventually murdering him.

The claim of András II's grandson, András III, was questioned because his father had been declared a bastard. He faced three other claimants: someone pretending to be László's brother, László's sister Mária and Albrecht I of Austria. He defeated the pretender and fought off an invasion by Rudolf I of Germany but Mária's supporters arrested András and handed him over to Albrecht I of Austria.

András promised to demolish fortresses along his western border to keep the peace but their owner, Miklos Koszegi, rebelled and imprisoned András until he paid a ransom. András then secured his alliance with Albrecht by marrying his daughter Agnes in 1296 and they united to defeat the Hungarian rebels. András supported his father-in-law's revolt against Adolf of Germany but he faced a final rebellion by the boyars supporting Mária's grandson, Károly Róbert, before he died in 1301.

András III's only child, Erzsébet, had been betrothed to Wenceslaus Premyslid. Although Wenceslaus was crowned László V, Pope Boniface VIII encouraged everyone to support Károly Róbert instead. László asked his father, Wenceslaus, to help and he took his young son and the Hungarian crown back to Bohemia for safety. Young Wenceslaus broke off his engagement and renounced the Hungarian throne when his father died in 1305 but he had not learnt his lesson. He married Mieszko I's daughter, Viola, and claimed the Polish throne only to be assassinated in 1306, trying to secure it.

Otto III of Bavaria was crowned Béla V but he too was unpopular and Károly of Anjou occupied part of the country. László of Transylvania imprisoned Béla in 1307 while Károly was proclaimed king but he refused to hand over the crown, undermining Károly's position. A papal legate made a new crown so Károly could be crowned in 1309 and László then handed over the original crown under threat from Rome so there was a second coronation. Károly fought rebel boyars for the next ten years but he enjoyed the considerable wealth generated by the Hungarian gold mines.

Basarab I of Wallachia refused to acknowledge Hungary in 1330, so Károly invaded Wallachia only to become lost in the Carpathian Mountains. Basarab offered to lead Károly out but ambushed his army at Posada and Károly had to exchange clothes with one of his knights so he could escape. Hungary allied with Poland and Bohemia at the 1335 Congress of Visegrád and they then attacked the Holy Roman Empire and Austria.

Lajos succeeded his father in 1342 and he immediately made Wallachia and Moldova his vassals. He also wanted the port of Zadar on the Dalmatian coast but the Venetians twice bribed his generals not to take it until a furious Lajos made them capture it in 1346.

Lajos's son, András, had been betrothed to Joanna I and 5 tons of gold was donated to Rome to guarantee he would be crowned King of Naples. But András was murdered by conspirators and his body was hung out of a window by its genitals. Although Joanna was suspected of murder, Pope Clement VI did not call for a trial because she had sold Avignon to the papacy for a good price. So Lajos invaded and defeated Naples at the Battle of Capua in 1348. The conspirators escaped and Lajos lost his popularity in Italy after he executed an innocent man. Lajos withdrew his army as the Black Death swept through Italy while Joanna fled with her new husband. Pope Urban VI then allowed Lajos to decide her fate so his nephew, Károly of Durazzo, seized the throne of Naples and suffocated Joanna.

Hungary repelled Dušan's Serbian army in 1349 and 1354 and then forced the Serbs, the Bosnians, Wallachians, Bulgarians and Moldavians to become his vassals, so they would be ready to face the Ottomans. The Byzantine Emperor John V asked Lajos to ask for help against the Ottomans but they parted on bad terms and John V was forced to leave a son behind as a hostage. Lajos would defeat the Ottomans at Nicapoli in 1366 and again in Wallachia in 1374.

Lajos had appointed his uncle Casimir III of Poland his successor but Casimir died in 1370. The Poles elected Lajos as their king but he sent his mother Elizabeth to be their regent, to remove her from his court. The Poles hated her tax rises and they eventually killed her Hungarian bodyguards and forced her to flee to Hungary in 1375. Lajos appointed Władysław of Opole regent in Poland. Lajos the Great died in 1382, leaving a huge empire to his young daughter Mária.

The Hungarian nobles did not want a female monarch so they supported Károly the Short of Naples instead. But the Polish nobility accepted Mária and she was crowned king rather than queen, with her mother Elizabeth as regent. But the Poles wanted their monarch to live in Poland and Mária refused so the Poles accepted her sister, Hedwig, as their queen instead. The sisters also agreed if one died childless, the other would succeed her as queen.

Károly had been living in Hungary since Lajos died. Elizabeth wanted to stop him claiming the throne so she betrothed Mária to Károly's enemy, Lajos of Orléans, in 1384, causing an outrage. Károly was secretly invited to take the throne and he then secured the boyars' support before forcing Mária to abdicate and marry Sigismund. Károly was crowned while Mária and Elizabeth looked on but Elizabeth had him stabbed in Mária's apartments soon after and he died three weeks later. Mária was restored to the throne, with Elizabeth as regent. The boyars seized control when John Horvat imprisoned mother and daughter and Elizabeth took the blame for Károly's murder as she begged for her daughter's life. They did spare her but she had to watch her mother being strangled when Sigismund sent troops to rescue them. Sigismund was crowned and although Mária kept out of state affairs, she had John Horvat tortured to death. She fell pregnant and then died in a suspicious horse-riding accident in 1395.

Sigismund immediately led a Crusade against the Ottomans but Sultan Bayezid I raised the Siege of Constantinople and defeated him at the Battle of Nicopolis. Instead Sigismund concentrated on improving his position over his neighbours, starting with Croatia. He invited István Lackovic to meet him in Sabor in 1397, a town where Croatian law dictated no one could carry arms. He ignored the law and his men slaughtered István and his followers in the Bloody Sabor of Krizevci. Sigismund supported a Bohemian uprising against Wenceslaus in 1401, taking him prisoner and ruling the country for nineteen months. He founded the Order of the Dragon after this victory and it became an influential society which many of Europe's monarchs joined.

Sigismund then defeated and executed 170 Bosnian nobles at the Battle of Dobor in 1408. He also allied several times with the Teutonic Knights against Poland, a union which ended following their decisive defeat at the hands of the Polish–Lithuanian alliance at the Battle of Grunwald (Tannenberg) in 1410. Sigismund was elected emperor twice the same year because his rival died after three months. He was then elected King of Germany in 1411 and campaigned against the Venetians in Italy.

Sigismund was present when three popes were forced to abdicate at the 1414 Council of Constance, ending the Western Schism. He also promised safe-conduct to the Bohemian religious reformer, Jan Hus, and protested when the Council of Constance burned him at the stake for heresy in 1415. The death of Wenceslaus IV in 1419 left Sigismund titular King of Bohemia but they accused him of betraying Hus, so he entrusted the government to the dead king's widow, Sofia. The Hussites continued their protests so he declared war on them, only to see all three of his campaigns end in disaster.

The German princes did not help when the Ottomans invaded Hungary and it left him powerless to pursue his campaign in Bohemia until the Hussites threatened Germany. The situation led to the Union of Bingen and Germany eventually joined the indecisive campaign against the Ottomans in 1428. Sigismund received the Iron Crown of Italy in 1431 and was crowned emperor in Rome in 1433 by Pope Eugenius IV. He then returned to Bohemia where he was finally recognised as king in 1436.

Sigismund had no sons, so he married his daughter, Elizabeth, to Albrecht V of Austria and named him his successor. Albrecht moved his court of Hungary when his father-in-law died in 1437 but the Bohemians did not accept him when he was crowned their king. He also refused to accept the offer to be King of the Romans in 1438. Despite all his accolades, Albrecht was defeated and killed by the Ottomans at the Battle of Neszmély in 1439.

Władysław III of Poland was offered the crown of Hungary even though Albrecht's pregnant widow, Elizabeth, wanted her unborn child to be king. She stole Hungary's crown and fled to Austria with her newborn son only for Friedrich V to imprison her baby and take the crown himself. Cardinal Oleśnicki ran Hungary while Władysław and János Hunyadi concentrated on fighting the Ottomans.

János Hunyadi was a *Voivode* of Transylvania who employed professional soldiers and mobilised the peasants, rather than paying mercenaries. He stopped an Ottoman invasion in 1441 and then conducted the Long Campaign across the Balkan Mountains at the end of 1443. But Władysław and Hunyadi were defeated at the Battle of Varna in 1444 and Murad II displayed Władysław's head on a pole as the Hungarian army fled.

Hunyadi supported László the Posthumous against the young László V in the early 1440s and was appointed his regent in 1446. Although he was defeated at the Second Battle of Kosovo in 1448, he stopped the Ottomans at the gates of Belgrade in 1456. Hunyadi resigned a rich man in 1452 but died three weeks after his triumph when an epidemic swept the Crusaders' camp. Pope Pius II called him 'Christ's Champion' because he held the Ottomans back for so long.

Ulrich II of Celje was made governor of Hungary but Mátyás Hunyadi and László Hunyadi were imprisoned for his murder. The nobles were so angry when László was executed, that the teenage King László fled to Prague and died suddenly in 1457. Although poison was suspected, he had died of leukaemia, an unknown disease at the time.

László's early death left four positions open. Lower Austria went to Leopold's descendants, Friedrich succeeded him in Austria and Bohemia appointed Jiří of Poděbrad. Hungary's electors wanted Mátyás Hunyadi and Jiří of Poděbrad freed him while his uncle Michael Szilágyi deployed an army to support his election in 1458. Mátyás's friends wanted him to marry the daughter of László Garai to appease the boyars, but he refused to marry into the family which had murdered his brother, and married Poděbrad's daughter instead.

But teenage Mátyás was in a difficult position. The Ottomans threatened his east border, the Venetians were to the south and both Emperor Friedrich III to the west and Casimir IV of Poland to the north were claiming his throne. So Mátyás raised the mercenary Black Army, invaded Serbia in 1458 and then reasserted Hungarian rule over Bosnia. The boyars continued to conspire against the commoner but Emperor Friedrich turned down their offer of the throne and recognised Mátyás as King of Hungary instead. Mátyás allied with Wallachia against the Ottomans but he spent the crusade money sent by Rome and then forged a letter saying Vlad the Impaler had offered Mehmed support. Mátyás imprisoned Vlad, recovered Bosnia from the Ottomans on his own and his treachery was rewarded with a Holy Crown in 1464.

Pope Paul II excommunicated Hussite leader Jiří of Poděbrady when he became King of Bohemia and he asked neighbouring princes to depose him. But Mátyás was busy in Moldavia and was defeated and wounded at the Battle of Baia in 1467. Mátyás eventually invaded Bohemia and was elected king in 1469 while Poděbrad died soon after.

Mátyás stopped a rebellion designed to place Casimir on the Polish throne so the Poles retaliated by attacking Bohemia. The Hungarian army built an entrenched camp and forced a peace at Breslau (Wrocław) in 1475. Mátyás then recognised László as King of Bohemia, in return for Moravia, Silesia and Lusatia. He then attacked Emperor Friedrich and forced him to accept peace. The emperor failed to pay the promised war indemnity so Mátyás attacked for a third time. He then defeated an Ottoman army at the Battle of Breadfield in 1479, as it returned from ravaging Transylvania.

Relief from the Ottoman threat came when Sultan Mehmet II died in 1481 and his sons squabbled. Mátyás took Cem hostage but Pope Sixtus IV and the Venetians would not let him deal with Bayezid, so an opportunity to end the Ottoman threat was missed. His final campaign was against Austria and he captured Vienna in 1485 to become their king. Despite his successes, Mátyás could not have children with Queen Beatrice and she stopped him making his illegitimate son, John, his heir. He died in 1490, heirless and crippled by gout.

THE PRINCIPALITY OF WALLACHIA

The ruination of Hungary by the Mongols led to the formation of a new principality, Wallachia. The *voivode* (warlord), Litovoi, refused to pay tribute when László IV claimed his lands. He was killed in battle in 1285 fighting Hungary and his brother Barbat was imprisoned until he recognised Hungarian rule. But when Hungary forced all the Wallachian nobles to become Roman Catholics in 1289, Radu the Black crossed the Carpathian Mountains and founded Wallachia between the mountains and the River Danube.

Basarab became a vassal of Károly I of Hungary but he angered him by marrying his daughter into the Bulgarian royal family and then allied with Bulgaria against Serbia. He ambushed Károly at the Battle of Posada in 1330 and the Hungarian king barely escaped with his life. The result was an independent Wallachia with Basarab as its founder. Lajos of Hungary's first action after succeeding Károly in 1342 was to invade Wallachia.

Nicholas Alexander was crowned in 1352 and he became a Hungarian vassal, returned captured lands to Lajos and allowed the Roman Catholic Church to establish missions across Wallachia. Vladislav I, whose name meant 'to rule with glory', was crowned in 1364 and he became a vassal to both the Hungarians and the Bulgarians. Radu accepted the situation but his son Dan went to war with Bulgaria and was killed in 1386.

Dan's brother, Mircea the Elder, faced a new problem from the Ottoman Empire. He made a truce with Poland to secure his northern border and then allied with Hungary and Bulgaria to face the common threat. Mircea defeated Beyazid the Thunderbolt's army at the Battle of Rovine in 1395 but then had to flee to Hungary while Vlad the Usurper was put on the throne. Wallachia and the Hungarians fought back, and while they were beaten at the Battle of Nicopolis, Mircea was restored to the throne. They defeated another Ottoman invasion in 1402 and then counter-attacked to take advantage of the anarchy following Beyazid's capture.

Mircea helped Musa seize the Ottoman throne and then bribed him to keep Wallachia safe. Mircea's son drove Mehmed's army as soon as he was crowned, but Michael was killed when they returned in 1420. Civil war ensued and Dan II proved to be the better commander, beating Radu II the Empty Head despite his Ottoman support. The throne changed hands eight times in seven years and the anarchy finally ended when Radu died in 1427. Dan was killed when the Ottomans invaded in 1432 and another of Mircea's sons, Alexander I, died of illness soon after.

The power vacuum allowed Vlad II to return from exile and he murdered members of the rival Dănești family to seize the throne in 1436. János Hunyadi of Hungary defeated Vlad Dracul, or Dragon (because he was a member of the Order of the Dragon), at the Battle of Marosszentimre (or Hermannstadt) in 1442 so he went to the Ottomans for support. Hunyadi forced his son, Mircea II, to flee and placed Basarab II on the throne instead.

Vlad secured Emperor Mehmed's support by promising tribute and a steady supply of Wallachian boys for his Janissary army. He also left his two sons, Vlad and Radu, as hostages in the Ottoman court. Although Radu converted to Islam, served the sultan's son and commanded the Janissaries, Vlad hated his father for leaving him and refused to co-operate.

Vlad the Dragon was able to retake the throne with Ottoman support and took his revenge by burying Basarab alive. Mircea also returned from exile to attack the Ottomans, and while Vlad did not help his supporters, he made sure his sons were safe. Hunyadi invaded again but the Ottomans defeated his army at the Battle of Varna in 1444 and again Vlad refused to get involved.

Hunyadi escaped but he was blamed for the defeat and was furious with Vlad for refusing to help. In 1447 his supporters captured Mircea II, blinded him and then buried him alive. They then murdered Vlad II and placed Vladislav II on the Wallachian throne. Young Vlad did not give up and he had reconquered Wallachia in July 1456, killing Vladislav II in hand-to-hand combat. Young Vlad then executed many of Wallachia's boyars, blaming them for the province's wretched state, and replaced them with loyal subjects.

Mehmed II captured Constantinople in 1453 meaning mainland Europe was under threat from the Ottoman Empire once more. When Mehmed's envoys visited to collect the overdue tribute, Vlad made his point by nailing their turbans to their heads when they refused to raise their 'hats' to him. He ambushed the first Ottoman invasion and impaled all the prisoners, with their leader Hamza Pasha on the highest stake. Vlad the Impaler's Wallachians struck back over the winter of 1462 with raids and ambushes, including the Night Attack when 15,000 Ottomans were killed.

Vlad's brother Radu led the Ottoman Janissaries on another raid and they besieged Poenari where Vlad's wife was hiding. When an archer shot a message into the castle reporting Vlad's death, she said she would rather be eaten by the fish than be an Ottoman prisoner and threw herself into the moat. But Vlad was still alive and Radu turned back when he found 20,000 impaled corpses outside Târgoviște.

Pope Pius II had sent money to Mátyás Corvinus so Hungary would help fight but Vlad discovered Corvinus had already spent the money on himself. Corvinus also forged a letter which stated Vlad was proposing peace with the Ottomans and he arrested Vlad in 1462, accusing him of high treason, to cover his tracks. Mehmed II made Radu Bey of Wallachia and he took the boyars' families hostage to keep their support. But Radu lost Mehmed's backing in 1473 so he appointed Basarab the Old, starting a civil war in which the two exchanged power several times before Radu died in 1475. A free Vlad III seized the throne only to be assassinated soon afterwards and his head was delivered to Constantinople. A prolonged civil war, in which Basarab the Old, Basarab the Young (known as the Little Impaler) and Vlad IV the Monk were elected and re-elected several times, lasted for over twenty years.

THE PRINCIPALITY OF MOLDAVIA

According to legend, the warlord Dragoș was hunting in the Moldavia region, east of the Carpathian Mountains, and decided to claim the area. It had the Dniester River to the east, the Danube River to the south-west and the Black Sea to the south-east. He ruled in the name of Lajos I of Hungary after 1352 and was succeeded by Sas. Eleven years later, Bogdan entered the region and rebelled against Hungarian rule, defeating Balc, son of Sas. He declared his independence and was known as the founder of Moldavia.

Lațuc succeeded Bogdan in 1365 and he converted to Catholicism to gain equal status with the Polish and Hungarian kings. Unfortunately, Pope Gregory XI's first act was to tell him he could not divorce his infertile wife, leaving him without an heir. Yuri Koriatovich was invited to rule only to be poisoned, so Lațuc's grandson, Petru, became *voivode* and he made Moldavia a Polish fief.

Roman I became *voivode* in 1393 and he supported Prince Fyodor of Podolia against Władysław II of Poland and Vytautas of Lithuania. He was defeated at Bracław in 1394 and both his sons, Ștefan and Iuga the Crippled, died soon after. A third brother, Alexandru, allied with Poland against Hungary and fought alongside Jogaila during the defeat of the Teutonic Knights at Grunwald (Tannenberg) in 1410 and at Marienburg in 1422. He also supported Radu II and Alexandru during the Wallachia civil wars. Jogaila had defaulted on the vassal agreement when the Ottomans invaded Moldavia in 1420 so Alexandru retaliated in 1431, while Poland was embroiled in the Lithuanian Civil War. Peace was restored with the Treaty of Suceava.

Alexandru's son Iliaș renewed Moldavia's vassalage to Poland but his illegitimate half-brother, Ștefan, offered land to Władysław II and he enrolled the help of Vlad II of Wallachia, hoping to take the throne. Iliaș was imprisoned until his Polish supporters convinced their new king, Władysław III, to withdraw his support for István in favour of Moldavia's legitimate heir. The half-brothers fought until Władysław intervened following the indecisive Battle of Podraga in 1435. Iliaș and István II shared power until Iliaș breached the agreement in 1443, so he was blinded and imprisoned while his wife, Maria, fled to Poland with her sons. Ștefan ruled with another illegitimate brother, Petru II, until Iliaș's son Roman murdered him in 1447. Petru and Roman then ruled together until Roman was forced to flee to Kraków.

Bogdan II had only been ruler for two years when he was beheaded by his stepbrother, Petru Aron, at a wedding in Rauseni in 1451. His son Ștefan was lucky to escape and Alexandru II forced him to take refuge in Cetatea Albă castle in 1455. Petru succeeded him and he became a vassal to Poland to secure his northern border and paid the Ottomans tribute to secure his southern border. But the Moldavian civil war rumbled on and Petru was eventually forced to flee to Poland, while Ștefan became *voivode* in 1457 with Wallachian help. Ștefan III the 'Great and Holy' submitted to Kazimierz IV so he could enter Poland to find him in a search which ended with Petru's execution ten years later.

But Ștefan's troubles were far from over. He had to defeat Mátyás Corvinus's Hungarian army at Baia in 1467 and a Tatar invasion at Lipnic in 1471. Four years later the Ottomans invaded, and while Ștefan won the Battle of Vaslui in 1475, Mehmed II defeated him at Valea Albă the following year. It took an outbreak of the plague in the Ottoman camp to force them to retire.

Ștefan helped to oust the Muslim Radu the Handsome and installed Basarab the Old on the Wallachian throne, hoping it would return to Christianity. But Basarab turned to the Ottomans for protection, so Ștefan replaced him with Vlad the Monk in 1482. Mehmed's son, Bayezid, renewed the attacks into Europe, and the Moldavians had to defeat the Ottomans at Cătlăbuga Lake in 1485 and Șcheia in 1486. Ștefan had raised Moldavia to the height of its power during his forty-seven-year reign.

THE SECOND BULGARIAN EMPIRE

The First Bulgarian Empire ended when it was conquered by the Byzantine Empire in 1018. Following the disastrous rule by Andronikos, Emperor Isaakios II raised taxes for his wedding. Brothers Theodore and Ivan Asen asked him to reduce taxes but Ivan was slapped in the argument when Isaakios II refused. The brothers returned home and Theodore was crowned Petar IV the Glorious in 1185, first king of the Second Bulgarian Empire. The offended emperor marched into Bulgaria and captured Queen Elena before a truce was agreed. Petar sent his young brother Kaloyan as a hostage to Constantinople in exchange for his wife.

The Bulgarian Empire was on the south bank of the River Danube, with Hungary (later Wallachia) to the north, Serbia to the west and the Black Sea to the east. Its biggest threats were from the Cuman hordes to the north and the Byzantine Empire to the south. The Third Crusade passed through the area in 1187 and Petar offered help to Friedrich when relations between the Byzantines and the Crusaders soured. The ailing king was succeeded by Ivan I and he started a rumour that the Cumans were about to attack when Emperor Isaakios II invaded Bulgaria. He then ambushed the Byzantines as they withdrew through the mountains and Isaakios barely escaped with his life.

Ivan punished Ivanko for having an affair with his sister-in-law so the general retaliated by murdering the king and then tried to take control of the country. Ivan's brother, Peter, forced Ivanko to flee to the Byzantines, but Ivanko soon returned and murdered Peter. Kaloyan allied with Ivanko and they took control of Bulgaria only to face an invasion by Hungary. Pope Innocent III made peace between the two countries and he gave Kaloyan an imperial crown and sceptre, hoping to unite the Bulgarian Church with Rome.

The Byzantines asked Kaloyan for help when the Fourth Crusade sacked Constantinople in 1204 so his Cuman allies ambushed the Crusaders and imprisoned Emperor Baudouin of the Latin Empire. Kaloyan would dismember Baudouin after his wife falsely alleged that Baudouin had propositioned her; he had probably spurned her advances.

The Bulgarians defeated the Latin Empire at Serres in 1206 and Rusion in 1207, and while they captured Thrace and Macedonia, they failed to take Adrianople. Kaloyan turned on the Byzantines when they conspired against his rule and he became known as 'the Roman slayer'. Kaloyan allied with Theodōros I of Nicaea against the Latin Empire and then killed Bonifacio of Montferrat, ruler of Thessalonica. But Kaloyan's luck ran out when he was assassinated by his Cuman commander during the Siege of Thessalonica.

Boril was crowned in 1207 and some suspected him of ordering Kaloyan's murder, even more so when he married Kaloyan's Cuman widow. The following year Emperor Henri de Flanders defeated Boril at Plovdiv and northern Thrace fell to the Latins. Boril handed over Belgrade to get Hungarian help when the Cumans rebelled. Henri died in 1216 and András II of Hungary left to join the Fifth Crusade, leaving Boril without any support. His cousin Ivan then returned from exile and captured Boril, blinding him and imprisoning him in a monastery.

Ivan Asen II set about recovering the lands Boril had given away. He married Anna Maria to reclaim territories along the Danube back from Hungary and married his daughter to Theodōros of Epirus's brother. But Theodore reconquered Thessalonica, captured Adrianople, threatened Constantinople and then invaded Bulgaria in 1230. He then blinded Theodōros and conquered his lands.

The Latin Emperor, Robert de Courtenay, died in 1228 and Jean of Brienne was made guardian and co-emperor with young Baudouin II, breaking another of Ivan's alliances. Ivan married his daughter Elena to Iōannēs III of Nicaea's son, Theodōros, in 1235 and they campaigned together against the Latin Empire.

Jean of Brienne died two years later and Ivan suggested marrying his daughter to Baudouin II to get control of the Latin Empire. He kidnapped Elena from her husband and was attacking Nicaea when he heard his wife, one of his children and the Patriarch of Tarnovo had died. He took the deaths as a sign from God, broke off the siege and sent Elena back to her husband. Ivan's final battle was against the Mongols in 1241, as they passed through Bulgaria, heading home to elect a new khan.

Kaliman's regent abused his power, losing Bulgaria's influence over Thessalonica and Serbia. The Mongols returned but promises to pay an annual tribute stopped them devastating the country. Young Kaliman died in 1246, possibly poisoned, and he was replaced by his even younger brother, Michael II, who was controlled by his mother Eirene. Hungary, Nicaea and Epirus took the opportunity to capture large areas of Bulgaria.

The Bulgarians recovered lands from Nicaea when Iōannēs III died in 1254 but Michael was injured escaping through a forest when Emperor Theodore II counterattacked. Michael struck back with an army of Cumans and then married one of Prince Rostislav of Russia's daughters. Rostislav arranged a truce with Nicaea in 1256 but the Bulgarian nobles rallied around Michael's cousin, Kaliman. Kaliman II murdered Michael during a hunting trip, married his widow and seized the throne. But when Prince Rostislav advanced on Tarnovo, Kaliman fled and he too was assassinated. Rostislav claimed the title of emperor and returned home with his daughter only for Michael's brother-in-law, Mitso, to seize the throne in 1256.

Bulgaria's nobles rebelled when Mitso's campaign against Nicaea failed and they proclaimed Konstantin their emperor in 1257. Mitso fled and offered Emperor Mikhaēl VIII lands in exchange for asylum in Nicaea. Konstantin I was then kept busy fighting off the Hungarians. Michael VIII deposed and blinded the Nicaean Emperor Iōannēs IV in 1261. Constantine got his revenge by helping the Mongols raid Byzantine territory. He then remarried Mikhaēl VIII's niece, Maria, to restore the peace but arguments over the dowry spoiled the relationship.

Mikhaēl married his illegitimate daughter, Euphrosyne, to the Mongols' leader, Nogai Khan, and joined forces to invade Bulgaria in 1274. Konstantin's troubles increased when he was badly injured after falling off his horse and Maria's poor management of the kingdom while he was ill led to a peasant uprising in 1277. Constantine was killed in battle and a pig farmer called Ivaylo the Radish seized control of the kingdom.

Mikhaël initially offered his daughter, Irene, to Ivaylo but he changed his mind when he became worried about his style of rule. So he betrothed her to Mitso's son, Ivan III, who was in Constantinople, instead. Mikhaël wanted to put Ivan on the throne and he found support from George Terter. George divorced his first wife Maria and sent her and their son to Constantinople to confirm Byzantine support before marrying Ivan's sister, Maria. Ivaylo, meanwhile, married Mikhaël's mother, Maria, to oppose them. Maria would soon find out her son had been right to distrust Ivaylo because he was an abusive husband.

Ivaylo stopped the Byzantine invasion only to become trapped inside Drastar by the Mongols. Rumours of his death circulated so the nobles crowned Ivan emperor but Ivaylo was alive and well enough to stop the Byzantines rescuing Ivan from the capital. Ivan and Irene fled to Constantinople in 1280, leaving his brother-in-law, George Terter, free to seize the throne. The Mongols murdered Ivaylo when he asked for help and then refused to help Ivan, leaving him to die in exile.

The new King George allied with Sicily but Charles was too busy with the War of Sicilian Vespers to help Bulgaria fight off another Mongol attack. So George engaged his daughter Anna to Uroš II to get Serbian support instead. Emperor Mikhaël also died and George sent his second wife to Constantinople, in return for his first wife, to get Andronikus II's support.

All George's efforts did not stop the Mongols invading a third time in 1285 and he had to marry his daughter to the Nogai Khan's son, Chaka, and handed his son over as a hostage for a second time. The raids only stopped when the Nogai Khan appointed Smilec tsar of Bulgaria in 1292. George went to Constantinople but Andronikus refused to help him and he was sent into exile in Anatolia.

Smilec waged an unsuccessful war against the Byzantine Empire but trouble was brewing in the Mongol Hordes. Toqta of the Golden Horde defeated and killed Nogai in 1299 and his son Chaka headed into Bulgaria taking his wife, Elena, and his brother-in-law, the exiled Teodore with him. Teodore convinced the Bulgarians to accept Chaka as their ruler and Smilec disappeared.

In 1300 Toqta besieged Tarnovo looking for Chaka, so Teodore strangled him and sent his head to the khan to make the peace. The Mongols withdrew from Bulgaria, and while there was a sigh of relief as Teodore was crowned emperor, he punished all who stood in his way. Teodore defeated the Byzantines at the Battle of Skafida, forcing co-emperor Mikhaël IX to flee and the war ended with Teodore marrying Mikhaël's daughter, Theodora, in 1307. He also negotiated his father's release and George was settled in a life of luxury.

The teenage George II was crowned emperor in 1321 only to die a year later and Andronikos III took the opportunity to recapture Thrace from his successor Mihail Šišman. Mihail re-entered the area in 1324 but refused Andronikos's offer to duel to settle ownership. Mihail divorced his Serbian wife, Anna Neda, and married Theodora, widow of Emperor Theodore to make peace. Mihail became involved in a Byzantine civil war in 1327. He hoped his troops might take the emperor by surprise and capture Constantinople, but Andronikos was warned and he sent them back.

Mihail's ex-wife, Anna, asked her brother Urós to fight for her honour but he was too busy fighting his cousin Vladislav II for the Serbian throne. Instead Mihail invaded Serbia in 1330 and he met the Serbian army at Velbazhd, expecting Andronikos to join him. They agreed a one-day truce but the Serbians attacked as soon as their reinforcements arrived and defeated the Bulgarians. Mihail was mortally wounded and Anna was sent to Tarnovo so that her son Ivan could be proclaimed emperor. Mihail's second wife, Theodora, took her sons to Constantinople and Andronikos abandoned his war with Serbia so he could attack Bulgaria and reclaim his nephew's inheritance instead. The Byzantines invaded Thrace, sparking a coup in 1331, and Anna and Ivan fled to Serbia.

Ivan's sister, Helena, was married to Urós IV, to seal an alliance with Serbia. They defeated the Byzantine army and captured Andronikos, with the help of Mongol mercenaries, at the Battle of Rusokastro in 1332. The betrothal of Ivan's son, Mihail, to Andronikos's daughter, Maria, sealed their alliance. Ivan demanded the extradition of Mihail's son Shisman from Constantinople in 1340 but the Byzantines sent a fleet to ransack the Danube Delta instead. The Bulgarians immediately countered but their army was beaten near Adrianople as the Black Death ravaged their kingdom.

Ivan sided with Iōannēs V in his Byzantine civil war with Iōannēs VI but both his sons were killed in battle. Iōannēs VI immediately asked for Serbian and Bulgarian help against the Ottomans when the war was over and Ivan's daughter Keraca was married to Iōannēs's son, Andronikos IV, to seal the alliance. Unfortunately for Ivan, Iōannēs VI abdicated soon afterwards in favour of Iōannēs V. Hungary invaded because Bulgaria refused its demands to become his vassal, so Ivan was captured and his people were forced to accept Roman Catholicism in 1365.

Ivan Aleksandǎr died in 1371, and while his second wife, Sarah-Theodora, made sure Ivan Šišman was crowned, Ivan Sratsimir declared himself rival emperor. Ivan Šišman refused to help when the Ottomans invaded Serbia but Bulgaria was their next target and Ivan had to submit to Murad I in 1373. The marriage of Ivan Šišman's daughter, Kera Tamara, to Murad I, secured peace until the Ottomans captured Sofia in 1385.

Serbia and Bosnia defeated the Ottomans at the Battle of Pločnik in 1387 so Ivan Šišman decided not to send any more tribute. Murad invaded to get his money and he besieged Ivan in Nikopol; Ivan Sratsimir refused to rescue him.

The Serbs and Bosnians were defeated at the Battle of Kosovo in 1389, but while Ivan looked to Hungary for help, Bayezid I pretended to make peace to prevent them joining forces. The Ottomans then devastated Bulgaria in 1393 and captured Ivan Šišman; he died in captivity. Ivan Sratsimir joined Hungarian king Zgismond's Crusade only to be defeated at the Battle of Nicopolis in 1396. He also died in captivity.

Ivan Sratsimir's son, Konstantin II, allied with Serbia and Wallachia but he failed to take advantage of the civil war raging in the Ottoman Empire and Sultan Musa brought the final area of Bulgaria under Ottoman rule in 1413. Constantine supported Musa's brother and rival, Mehmed I, in his bid for the throne and was allowed to keep Bulgaria when he became sultan. Konstantin II died while living at the Serbian court in 1422, bringing the Second Bulgarian Empire to an end.

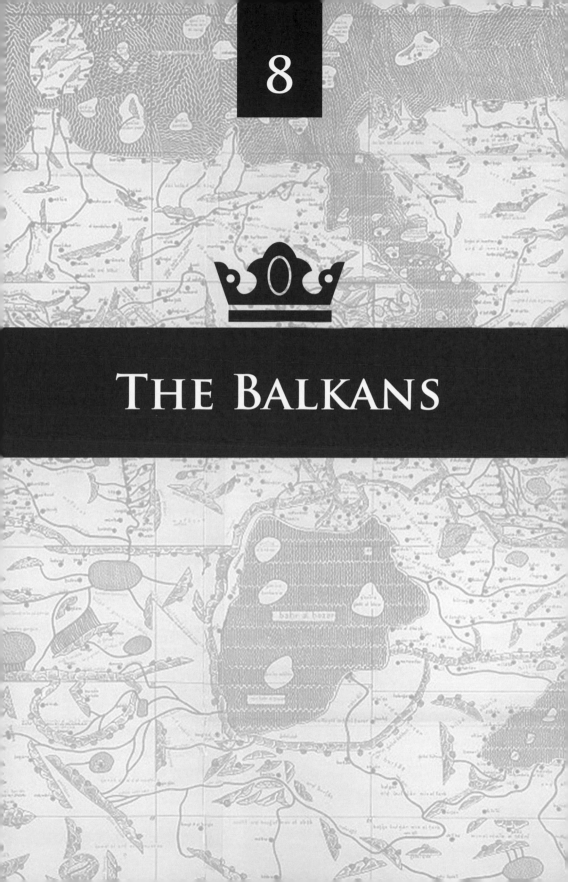

8

THE BALKANS

CROATIA, BOSNIA AND SERBIA LIE along the east coast of the Adriatic Sea and they constantly fought each other and Hungary. While Bosnia and Serbia weathered the storm, Croatia came under Hungarian rule in 1102 and Bosnia declared its independence in 1154. Bosnia and Serbia faced Hungarian attacks from the north and fought the Byzantines to the east. The Mongol hordes crossed the area in the 1240s but the final battles were against the Islamic Ottomans, once they had defeated the Byzantines.

THE KINGDOM OF CROATIA

Péter I of Hungary had imposed new taxes, taken Church money and imprisoned two bishops. The final straw was when he arrested his wife, Queen Giselle, and the Hungarian barons exiled him. Stjepan I of Croatia used the opportunity to further secure his independence along the Adriatic coast. Petar IV was crowned in 1058 and he expanded Croatian territories both inland and along the Adriatic coast, gaining the nickname 'the Great'. The Sicilian Normans invaded Croatia and captured Petar in 1075 and he died in prison even though a large ransom was paid and cities were handed over. But Venice expelled the Normans and secured the Croatian cities for themselves.

Petar's cousin Zvonimir was renamed Dmitar at his coronation and he took an oath of allegiance to the pope. He also supported the Norman attack against Byzantine territory in 1084. An elderly Stjepan II was persuaded to take the throne in 1089 but he remained in his monastery until he died. Dmitar's widow, Jelena the Beautiful, wanted her brother, László I of Hungary, to inherit the crown but the people elected Petar instead and he stopped the Hungarian invasion at Mount Gvozd. László's nephew Kálmán also invaded, Petar was killed at the second Battle of Mount Gvozd and Croatia had fallen under Hungarian rule by 1102.

THE BANATE OF BOSNIA (KINGDOM AFTER 1377)

The Byzantines fought Hungary over Bosnia until Emperor Manouël I agreed a truce, so he could turn on Sicily. Borić took the opportunity to declare Bosnia an independent state along the Adriatic coast in 1154 before helping Serbia and Hungary defeat the Byzantines. Manouël retaliated by hiring German mercenaries to depose Borić in 1163 and Bosnia fell under Byzantine control until Hungary claimed it in 1180.

Kulin was initially a vassal to Constantinople but he switched allegiance when the Hungarians advanced on Sofia in 1183. After sixteen years of peace, the Serbian Duke Vukan told Pope Innocent III that Kulin supported the Bogomil faith, to cause trouble. Although a papal legate was sent to Bosnia to root the heretics, their efforts only made the cult stronger. Kulin's son, Stjepan, ruled from 1204 and he too did nothing to stamp out the Bogomils. Although Pope Honorius III asked András of Hungary to crusade against them in 1221, he was too busy fighting a civil war. Archbishop of Kalocki organised a Crusade instead and the Bogomils deposed Stjepan in 1232 for failing to protect them.

His successor, Matej, tried to appease Rome but the pope appointed a zealous German bishop to stamp out the heresy. András II of Hungary deposed Matej and appointed Prijezda in 1234, handing his son to the Dominican Order as a guarantee he would crusade against the Bogomils. He would become known as 'Prijezda Our Faithful' for burning many at the stake.

The Mongol hordes rode through Hungary in 1241 and then headed south-east through Bosnia after clashing with the Croatians. Matej was reinstated after the Mongols defeated Hungary and he re-established control over Bosnia. Béla was unable to reassert Hungarian rule over Bosnia, so he asked Pope Innocent IV to launch a new Crusade against the Bogomils. It was cancelled after Matej convinced Rome he was a Catholic supporter.

Matej died in 1250, Prijezda returned to power in Bosnia and the pope returned his son because he renewed the campaign against the Bogomils. Béla gave Prijezda new territories in return for Bosnian troops which were used to support the Hungarian invasion of Bohemia in 1260.

An elderly Prijezda retired in 1287 leaving Prijezda II and Stjepan I to share power until Prijezda II died three years later. András III was crowned King of Hungary when László IV of Hungary died childless.

Pavao Šubić of Croatia was one of many who helped young Charles Martel seize the throne in 1297. Charles allowed Pavao to seize Bosnia from Stjepan as a reward and he appointed his brother, Mladen, to hunt down the Bogomil sect. Mladen was murdered by Stjepan's supporters in 1304 so Pavao appointed Mladen II in his place. Pavao and Stjepan died soon afterwards.

Stjepan's son, also Stjepan, was taken to Dubrovnik for safety but Malden recalled him and made him his vassal. Károly Róbert of Hungary and the Venetians refused to help Mladen crush a Bosnian rebellion in 1322. Instead they imprisoned him following the Battle of Bliska and gave Bosnia to Stjepan II. Stjepan helped his uncle Vladislav II regain Serbia, taking areas for himself, and would take more when Vladislav died.

Károly of Hungary wanted to increase his influence over Stjepan and while he offered the hand of a relative in 1323, Stjepan waited sixteen years before he divorced his wife and married Elizabeth. Stjepan had captured all of Serbia by 1329 and when Petar of Tolien rebelled he was put in irons, sat on his horse and pushed off a cliff. But while Stjepan was increasing his power in the Balkans, Pope Benedict XII wanted a Crusade to end the Bogomil heresy forever. But Stjepan convinced Rome he was a loyal Roman Catholic in 1340.

Károly died in 1342 and his heir, Lajos of Hungary, ordered Stjepan to seize Croatia and hold back the Venetians while he mustered his own army. But Stjepan told the Venetians that the Hungarians were coming, earning him the nickname 'the Devil's Student' for his deceit. Lajos still defeated the Venetians but Stjepan played Venice and Hungary off against each other, to keep control of Bosnia. Stjepan then invaded Serbia in 1349 while its army was attacking the Byzantines. Dušan turned back home and bribed Stjepan's generals to withdraw before attacking Bosnia.

Stjepan died in 1353 leaving no sons, so Lajos of Hungary appointed Vladislav's teenage son Tvrtko as Ban of Bosnia and held his brother, Stjepan Vuk, as a hostage. The Ottoman's had recently established a foothold on European soil Lajos was anxious to ally the Balkan countries against the new threat. Unfortunately, Tvrtko failed to restore control in Bosnia, so Lajos seized his royal seal in 1363. He then told Pope Urban V that Tvrtko supported the Bogomils so Stjepan Vuk could invade in 1370. But the Bosnians called on Serbian help to drive him out and Tvrtko was crowned king in 1377.

Tvrtko declared independence from Hungary, making Bosnia a kingdom, when Lajos died in 1382. He was appointed protector of Lajos's widow Elizabeta and her daughters Queen Mária of Hungary and Queen Jadwiga of Poland. He did a poor job because Mária and Elizabeta were imprisoned in 1386 and Elizabeta was strangled in front of her daughter. The Ottomans finally invaded Bosnia in 1388, beating Tvrtko at the Battle of Bileća. Bosnian troops helped the Serbs fight the invaders but Prince Lazar was killed at the Battle of Kosovo in 1389. Tvrtko's last action was to capture an invading Hungarian army.

As well as the threat from the east, his successor Dabiša faced an unruly nobility and he had to defeat the Sanković brothers, who wanted their areas under Hungarian control. Dabiša defeated an Ottoman invasion only to die of disease in 1395, after nominating Zgismond, who was married to his cousin Mária, his heir. But Mária died and the Bosnian nobility refused to recognise Zgismond and installed Jelena the Ugly instead. They expected to be allowed to rule their own lands but she died only a few months later.

Ostoja attacked Hungarian-controlled Dubrovnik in 1403 to assert his control but the barons soon forced him to flee to Hungary. Tvrtko's son, Tvrtko II, was appointed Ban but Ostoja refused to stand down, resulting in a war between Zgismond and László, claimant to the Hungarian throne. Zgismond won a decisive victory in 1408 and he had 170 Bosnia noblemen thrown from Doboj's city walls to end the anarchy. Zgismond then restored Ostoja to the throne but he still had no support.

A young Tomaš was appointed Ban and his mother, Kujava, made sure Jelena was sent to prison where she was probably murdered. Ostojić was opposed by his half-brother Radivoj until his uncle Tvrtko II seized power with Ottoman support in 1421. Radivoj eventually returned to the Ottoman court but Murad II withdrew his help because he wanted Bosnia to remain divided.

Meanwhile, Tvrtko II made a trade treaty with Venice and he had to pay the Ottomans to stop them raiding. At the same time a revengeful Kujava failed to put Vuk Banic on the throne. Tvrtko asked Hungary for an alliance against the Ottomans, but Zgismond wanted him to make his father-in-law, Hermann, his heir and Tvrtko accepted him to stop Vuk's claim. Both Tvrtko and Vuk died soon after and Tvrtko's half-brother, Tomaš, was appointed Ban.

The barons rebelled when Tomaš married Vojaca, a woman of low status, and he was forced to divorce her when she gave birth to a son. Bosnia was unable to help Hungary fight another Ottoman invasion and Władysław was killed at the Battle of Varna in 1444. Young László V became King of Hungary and his regent, János Hunyadi, recognised Tomaš and he converted to Roman Catholicism. The civil war ended when Tomaš married Katarina, the senior Bosnian noble's daughter.

Serbian kings Đurađ and Lazar died in quick succession, so Tomaš seized their lands and married his son, Tomašević, to Lazar's young daughter, Jelena, in 1459. Another Ottoman invasion forced Tomašević to flee to Bosnia and he was accused of selling the keys to Smederevo Fortress to the Ottomans. But the Serb garrison had handed them over, asking Mehmed for religious tolerance. Thomas asked Pope Pius II for help against the Ottomans but Rome wanted the Bogomils crushing first. He was murdered in 1461 and Tomašević was crowned, the only time a Bosnian monarch received a crown from Rome, even though he had to pay Hungary to support him.

Vladislav Hercegović invited the Ottomans to invade Bosnia during a civil war but Tomašević defiantly told their ambassador he would rather use his money to defend his kingdom than hand it over. An outraged Mehmed invaded in 1463 and both Tomašević and his brother, Radivoj, were captured. Mehmed ignored a promise not to harm them because it had been made without his knowledge and Tomašević, Radivoj and their cousin Stjepan were beheaded. Bosnia fell in weeks. Their nephews were taken to Constantinople while Queen Katarina unsuccessfully campaigned in Italy for the restoration of the kingdom.

Mehmed the Conqueror named Matija his puppet King of Bosnia in 1465 but Nikole of Ilok led the opposition with support from László of Hungary and Emperor Friedrich III. Nikole was named titular King of Bosnia in 1471, even though the Ottomans ruled Bosnia, and he was succeeded by Damian Horvat. Matija Vojsalić was the sultan's next choice but he was deposed around 1476 for conspiring with Hungary.

THE SERBIAN GRAND PRINCIPALITY
(KINGDOM FROM 1346)

Serbia had the Adriatic Sea to the west, Hungary to the north and Bulgaria to the east. Stefan divided his principality between his five sons when he died and their mother acted as their go-between. But the barons killed Gojislav; Domanek and Saganek fought; and Radoslav murdered Domanek. Mihailo was appointed Knez in 1050 and he married Kōnstantinos IX's niece to make peace with the Byzantine Empire. Bulgaria asked Mihailo I to help him attack the Byzantines, following their defeat by the Seljuk Turks at the Battle of Manzikert in 1071. They even gave the Bulgarian throne to his young son Bodin (who was renamed Petar III) to secure the alliance. But Petar was captured in 1073 and the Byzantine general who was released to rescue him defected.

Mihailo improved relations with the west and he was granted a royal title in 1077 while Duklja became a kingdom. Venetian sailors rescued Bodin and his first act was to support the Byzantine attack on the Normans at Durazzo in 1081. His second was to do nothing when the Normans seized the city. He married the daughter of a Norman nobleman and backed Pope Urban to get Rome's support but Queen Jakvinta executed, murdered and exiled all claimants to the throne, plunging Duklja into a civil war. The Byzantines recaptured Durazzo, defeated the Pecheneg hordes and then turned on the Serbians in 1090.

Vukan, Grand Prince of Rascia, defeated the first invading Byzantine army but asked for peace when a larger army approached. Emperor Alexios had to accept because the Cumans were raiding his lands. Vukan broke the treaty when he seized Byzantine territory and then offered his son Uroš as hostage when Alexios retaliated. Vukan the Great invaded Macedonia as Alexios faced the First Crusade and invaded Byzantine territory when the Normans attacked the Byzantines in 1106. This time he was defeated and finally had to submit to Alexios; he died in 1112.

Vukan's nephew, Uroš I, was immediately attacked by the Byzantines so he married his daughter, Jelena, to the blind Béla II to get Hungarian help. Her first act was to execute the sixty barons who had supported the blinding of her husband.

Uroš II was crowned grand prince in 1145 and his brother Beloš brought a Hungarian army to help him defend Serbia. The Byzantines defeated their combined army at the Battle of Tara River in 1150, and while Uroš II swore loyalty to Byzantine Emperor Manouēl I, the emperor abandoned his fight against the Normans in Sicily and concentrated on Hungary. Desa was made co-ruler in 1153 but he ousted Uroš because he refused to be a Byzantine vassal. Emperor Manouēl re-instated Uroš but soon grew tired of him. He appointed his brother Beloš in 1162 but he gave the crown to Desa and returned to Croatia to rule. Emperor Manouēl then appointed Stephen IV, but Beloš took him prisoner and sent him to the Byzantines. The emperor forced Desa to meet him, making him swear humiliating public oaths over his diplomacy with Hungary. He then appointed Tihomir and his brothers as rulers of Serbia in 1162. But one of them, Nemanja, rebelled and deposed the others in 1166, taking the throne for himself.

The emperor wanted Tihomir back on the Serbian throne because he was the weakest leader, so he gave him an army. But Nemanja defeated Tihomir at Pantino and Tihomir was drowned in the River Sitnica. His brothers were captured but they were given land after promising to keep the peace. Nemanja maintained his anti-Byzantine stance by joining the coalition with the Holy Roman Empire, Hungary and Venice in 1172. Unfortunately, Venice left the alliance when an epidemic devastated its fleet and then István II died, leaving the Hungarian throne to the pro-Byzantine Béla III. Emperor Manouël's troops defeated the Serbian army and Nemanja was forced to hand his sword over and was taken to Constantinople as a slave.

Nemanja befriended Manouël and he was recognised as Serbia's Grand Zupan after vowing never to attack the Byzantine Empire again. Instead he concentrated on dealing with the Bogomil heresy until Manouël died in 1180. He then allied with Béla III of Bulgaria and advanced to Byzantine-held Sofia until a rebellion forced the Bulgarians to withdraw, leaving the Serbians to fight on alone. Nemanja invited the Third Crusade to stay in Serbia in 1188 but Emperor Friedrich Barbarossa rejected his plan and attacked the Byzantines instead. Both Nemanja and Béla followed the Crusaders until Friedrich made peace with Isaakios II. The Byzantines attacked Serbia as soon as the Crusaders left for the Holy Land. The Byzantines forced Nemanja to relinquish his conquests, recognise Byzantine rule. Emperor Isaakios II also made Nemanja marry his son to the Byzantine Princess Eudokia to split the Serbs from the Bulgarians.

Nemanja became a monk in 1196. He favoured his second son, Stefan, but his first son, Vukan, pledged allegiance to Emeric and seized the throne with Hungarian help. Kaloyan of Bulgaria retaliated by conquering the eastern part of Serbia before Stefan could retake the Serbian throne in 1204. Boril succeeded Kaloyan and while his brother, Strez, took refuge in the Serbian court, Stefan refused money to help him retake the Bulgarian throne. Instead Stefan reclaimed lost Serbian territories while the Latin Empire attacked the Bulgarians.

Stefan the First-Crowned received a crown from Pope Honourius III in 1217, making him the first Serbian king acknowledged by Rome. Although Radoslav succeeded him in 1228, he was rejected because his mother, Eudokia, had been exiled for adultery; a rebellion forced him to retire to a monastery five years later. Vladislav was married to Belošlava, daughter of Ivan Asen II of Bulgaria, but both their countries were ransacked by the Mongols in 1242. Ivan was killed and his successor, Kaliman, made Bulgaria a Mongol vassal. The move ruined Vladislav's reputation and the nobles replaced him with his brother.

The development of silver mines made Uroš I the Great so rich he invaded Hungary in 1268. But he was captured and had to hand over all his wealth to pay the ransom. Uroš was also forced to marry his eldest son, Dragutin, to Katalin, daughter of the Hungarian heir, and he was outraged when his younger brother was named heir. Uroš was given a Hungarian army to defeat the Serbs at the Battle of Gacko in 1276 and forced his father to retire to a monastery.

Dragutin broke his leg while out hunting and he had to pass the throne to his brother Uroš II (also called Milutin) when he fell ill in 1282 but he continued to rule Syrmia until he died. Meanwhile, Uroš captured parts of Macedonia and Albania from the Byzantines but Emperor Mikhaël VIII died before he could counterattack. Instead it was the Bulgarians who attacked Serbia first. Although Dragutin and Uroš defeated them, a Bulgarian boyar convinced the Mongols to attack Serbia and Uroš had to hand his son Dečanski over to the Golden Horde as a hostage to stop them.

Uroš made peace with the Byzantine Empire in 1299 and helped them defeat the Ottomans on the Gallipoli Peninsula. When Dragutin died in 1314, Dečanski rebelled when Uroš took control of his father's lands. Decanski was exiled to Constantinople and partially blinded, while his younger brother Kōnstantinos was made heir. Dečanski soon returned from exile and was pardoned but his brother refused to submit. Uroš II died in 1321 and Vladislav II was freed to rule Syrmia with Hungarian help. Kōnstantinos was captured in battle in 1322. According to some stories, he may have been nailed to a tree and cut in half; it is known for certain that his skull was turned into a wine goblet for the new king Uroš III (the same name Dečanski had taken).

Uroš III was challenged by his cousin Vladislav II, but Vadislav was defeated in battle in 1324 and forced to flee, despite Hungarian support. Uroš was angered to hear Mihail Asen III of Bulgaria had divorced his sister Anna so he could marry the Byzantine princess Theōdora. The Bulgarians and the Byzantines then invaded Serbia in 1330 but Mihail was killed at the Battle of Velbazhd and Andronikos III withdrew. Despite driving off the invaders, Uroš's advisers convinced his son (also Uroš) to imprison and strangle his father in 1331.

Ivan Aleksandăr of Bulgaria married his sister, Jelena, to Uroš IV to secure a peace but Serbia continued to raid Byzantine. Lajos the Great's huge army caused him most trouble when it invaded and defeated him in the Šumajida region in 1336. Uroš struck back by defeating both the Croatian and Hungarian armies and then exploited a Byzantine civil war, conquering most of their Balkan territory by 1342. The Byzantines retaliated, defeating the Serbs with Ottoman help, at the Battle of Stephaniana in 1344. Uroš, or Dušan the Mighty as he was known, fought back by conquering Byzantine lands and attacking Bosnia. Uroš was excommunicated by Constantinople when he took over the kingdom's churches and he died in 1355, possibly from poison.

Uroš V was a weak ruler who depended on his mother, Jelena, and his advisers. His uncle Simeon (renamed Siniša) made an unsuccessful attempt to seize the throne in 1356 and the empire fragmented as Serbia's nobles assumed control. Vukašin was made co-ruler in 1365 but he and most of the Serbian nobility were defeated and killed by the Ottomans at the Battle of Maritsa in 1371. Uroš died childless soon after. The surviving Serbian nobles refused to recognise Marko as their ruler and when Nikola Altomanović emerged as the most powerful noble, Prince Lazar and Tvrtko of Bosnia worked together to capture and blind him in 1373. Although Tvrtko became titular king, Serbia's nobility stopped Lazar reunifying the kingdom.

Lajos I of Hungary died in 1382 and both Prince Lazar and Sultan Murad were killed at the Battle of Kosovo Field in 1389. Serbia was left with too few men to defend its lands and Lazar's brothers, Andrijas and Dmitar, fled to Hungary with the countries treasury before the kingdom became an Ottoman vassal. The surviving Serbian nobles joined the Bayazid invasion of Wallachia only to be defeated and killed at the Battle of Rovine in 1395.

Stefan the Tall's Serbian army fought alongside the Ottomans when they defeated Zgismond's Catholic alliance at the Battle of Nicopolis in 1396. However, Bayezid's empire began to collapse when the Timurs invaded from the east and they were defeated at the Battle of Ankara in 1402. Stefan had fought well and Bayezid granted him the title of Despot. But Stefan accepted Hungarian suzerainty after his nephew Đurađ Branković and Bayezid's son, Suleyman, defeated him at the Battle of Tripolje in 1402.

Zgismond died suddenly in 1427, leaving no children, and the throne went to Đurađ. The Ottomans captured Thessalonica in 1430, and while Đurađ paid a ransom to rescue the area's people, he could not afford the annual tribute and had to hand over his son as a hostage. He fled to Hungary when the Ottomans invaded in 1439 but two years later he was back in Serbia, trying to raise an army.

Đurađ played an important part in the 1444 Peace of Szeged between Hungary and the Ottomans. He married his daughter, Mara, to Sultan Murad II and gave János Hunyadi lands and in return was allowed to rule Serbia. The truce did not last long and Đurađ distanced himself from Hungary when it allied with Poland and attacked the Ottomans. Their Crusade ended with an Ottoman victory at the Battle of Varna in 1444. Hunyadi was again defeated by Murad II's forces at Kosovo in 1448 but he beat Mehmet II at the Siege of Belgrade in July 1456, allowing Đurađ to reoccupy Serbia before he died.

Lazar's older brothers, Grgur and Stefan, had been blinded in 1441 for plotting against Murad II. Lazar exiled them both and then poisoned his mother to secure his position. He offered to be an Ottoman despot in 1457 but died the following year. The blinded Stefan became co-ruler with Lazar's widow, but Jelena married her young daughter Maria to Tomašević, Prince of Bosnia, to hold onto the power.

Mátyás Corvinus of Hungary and Tomaš of Bosnia dethroned Stefan in 1459. Two months later, Tomašević surrendered the Serbian throne to the Ottomans and fled to his father's court where he became the Ban of Bosnia in 1461. Mehmed the Conqueror invaded Bosnia after he refused to pay tribute to the Ottomans; he captured and beheaded Stephen.

The imperial crown worn by the emperors of the Holy Roman Empire.

Roger II of Sicily depicted in an Arabic-style fresco.

The race to rescue the Birkebeiners' leader, Haakon IV of Norway.

Saladin's Ayyubid army captured the Christian Kingdom of Jerusalem.

Emperor Friedrich II
Barbarossa's death led to
the collapse of the Third
Crusade in 1190.

The Mongols swept across
Eastern Europe in 1248
and then asked for gold to
prevent more raids.

Jaime I ruled Aragon for
sixty-three years and he
conquered large areas of
Almohad territory.

The fall of Acre in 1291 ended
the crusader presence in the
Holy Land.

Pope Clement V had Jacques de Molay, head of the Knights Templar, burnt as a heretic in 1307.

The Battle of Kosovo in 1389 marked the start of Ottoman rule over Serbia.

A Polish and Lithuanian alliance defeated the Teutonic Knights at Grunwald in 1410.

Emperor Sigismund of Luxembourg eventually ruled Hungary, Croatia, Germany, Bohemia and Italy.

Vlad III of Wallachia terrified his Ottoman opponents by impaling prisoners on spears.

Mehmed II conquered Constantinople in 1453 and then swept across south-east Europe.

Ivan the Great united the principalities of
Russia into one huge empire.

Emperor Maximilian I in a highly
decorated suit of armour.

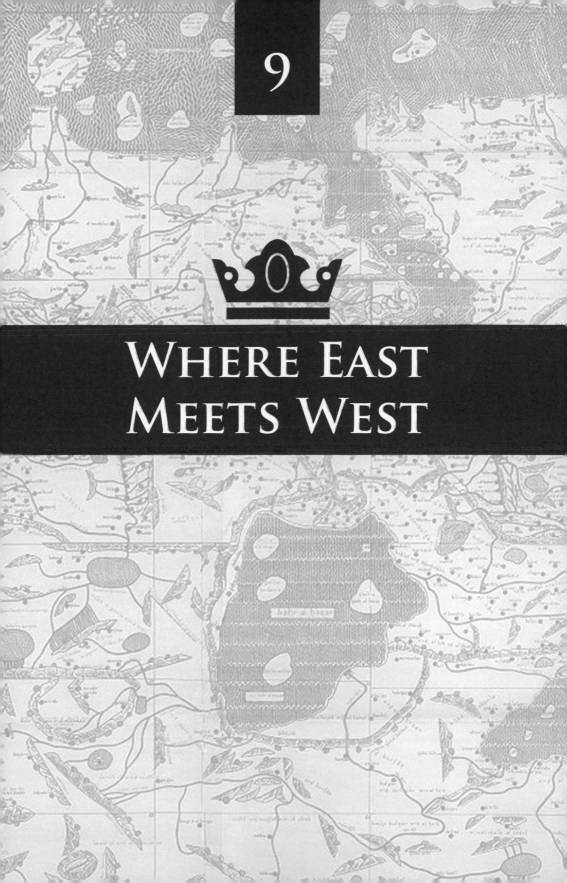

9

WHERE EAST
MEETS WEST

THE BYZANTINE EMPIRE COVERED WHAT is now Greece, Bulgaria, Thessalonica and Macedonia to the east of the Sea of Marmara and the Aegean Sea. It also ruled over all of Asia Minor (most of modern-day Turkey) and the island of Cyprus.

THE BYZANTINE EMPIRE

When Mikhaël IV was dying his brother, Iōannēs the Eunuch, forced Zōē to adopt their nephew Mikhaël, hoping to keep power. But Mikhaël V seized power in 1041 and banished Zōē to a convent, accusing her of killing the emperor. Four months later the people stormed the palace, releasing Zōē and her sister Theōdora. Theōdora guaranteed Mikhaël's safety to calm the crowds and then had him blinded, castrated and imprisoned in a monastery. Zōē did not want to be empress but she did not want Theōdora to be either, so she married Kōnstantinos IX only to discover he preferred his mistress, Maria. The stand-off ended when Zōē died in 1050 and Theōdora returned to her convent.

Pope Leo IX's legates and the Patriarch of Constantinople, Mikhaël Keroularios, fell out in 1054 and they excommunicated each other, marking the final separation of the Greek and Roman Churches, called the East–West Schism. It also meant Kōnstantinos could not ally with the pope in his fight for southern Italy and he became known as 'the One who Fights Alone'. Kōnstantinos died in 1055 and Theōdora left her convent, Nikephoros was exiled and she was proclaimed empress. She only employed eunuchs, to keep all the power, and she appointed her finance minister her successor.

Mikhaël VI humiliated General Bryennios so the army proclaimed their commander their new emperor. After defeating the imperial army at the Battle of Petroe, Mikhaël wanted to adopt the general to settle the matter. But a riot in Constantinople overthrew Mikhaël the Old and Bryennios was crowned with the name Isaakios I. The Byzantines successfully fought off András I of Hungary and the Pechenegs along their north frontier but Isaakios was nearly hit by lightning and fell ill. He thought his bad luck were signs of God's displeasure and retired as a monk in 1059.

Kōnstantinos X reduced the size of the army and disbanded the militia, spending his money on mercenaries instead. So the generals tried to assassinate him when the Seljug Turks and their Turcoman allies attacked the empire in 1061. But it did not end there. Most of the Italian mainland was lost to the Normans, Alp Arslan raided through Asia Minor, Oghuz Turks invaded the Balkans and the Hungarians captured Belgrade.

Kōnstantinos made his wife, Eudokia, promise she would not remarry on his death-bed, to make sure his young sons succeeded him in 1067. Eudokia had her promise revoked when Rōmanós tried to seize the throne and she married him because she was infatuated with him. Her actions upset the Doukas family and the Varangian Guard so Rōmanós IV raised a mercenary army only to be captured by Seljug Turks at the Battle of Manzikert in August 1071.

Rōmanós was ransomed and allowed to retire but his uncle Iōannēs Doukas had not forgotten his treachery and had him blinded; he died of his infected wounds in exile. Teenage Mikhaēl VII was crowned but he relied on incompetent advisers and became known as 'Minus a Quarter' as the empire collapsed and the army mutinied. Iōannēs Doukas seized power in 1074 and banished Eudokia to a convent but Mikhaēl raised a new army which defeated Doukas's mercenaries and captured Iōannēs.

The elderly Nikephoros rebelled in 1078, besieged Constantinople and forced Mikhaēl to become a monk. He was crowned Nikephoros III and married Mikhaēl's wife but there were uprisings when he promoted his nephew Synadenos over Mikhaēl's son, Kōnstantinos. The Norman Roberto of Apulia then declared war on the Byzantine Empire because young Kōnstantinos was engaged to his daughter, Helena. Nikephoros was forced to abdicate and he retired to a monastery, leaving his wife Maria to adopt Alexios.

Alexios escaped to raise an army and returned to capture Constantinople by bribing the guards. But he upset his wife Irene by crowning his mother Anna as his queen and the two were constantly at odds. Alexios made his adopted brother Kōnstantinos co-emperor and although he betrothed him to his daughter Anna, the engagement was dissolved when Alexios had a son in 1087. Alexios faced attacks from Sicily so he paid the German king Heinrich IV to counterattack in Italy, forcing the Normans to withdraw. The Pechenegs allied with Thracian heretics and although they fought the Byzantines to a standstill, Alexios allied with the Cumans and defeated them at Levounion in 1091.

Alexios asked Pope Urban II for help against the Seljugs in 1095 and the First Crusade was organised. It was an unruly affair and the first group pillaged the Balkans as they marched to Constantinople. Alexios then sent Peter the Hermit's rabble of Crusaders to Asia Minor where they were massacred in 1096. Godefroy de Bouillon, Boemondo de Taranto and Raymond IV de Toulouse followed and Alexios made each Crusader leader promise to turn over conquered lands to the Byzantine Empire in return for provisions. His son Iōannēs would establish Byzantine rule across large areas through treachery and deception while his father fought and defeated the Seljuqs at the Battle of Philomelion in 1117.

Alexios favoured Iōannēs, but his wife Irene wanted their son-in-law Nikephoros to rule. So Iōannēs crept into the monastery and took the imperial signet ring from his dying father and then rode to the Great Palace where the mob forced the guards to let him in so he could be proclaimed emperor. Iōannēs the Good soon uncovered a family conspiracy and while his mother Irene was retired to a convent, his sister Anna was stripped of her property.

The Pecheneg hordes attacked again in 1121, and though Iōannēs had promised a peace treaty, in fact he revoked the truce and made a surprise attack on their camp. Iōannēs was wounded in the Battle of Beroia but he had ended the Pechenegs' independence. Although Iōannēs was married to the Hungarian Princess Piroska, he gave asylum to the blinded Álmos, claimant to the Hungarian throne, in 1127. István II's Hungarians invaded but the Byzantines won the Battle of Haram and counterattacked, capturing large areas of Hungary including Belgrade. The death of Álmos two years later solved the problem.

Iōannēs cut off the Crusaders' overland route to mainland Europe when he conquered part of Cilicia in 1137 so Raymond of Antioch and Josselin of Edessa allied with him. They all refused to fight Syria because none of them wanted any of the others to gain anything from the campaign. The alliance was ruined when the Emir of Shaizar bribed Iōannēs to call off his attacks. Raymond and Josselin conspired to delay the handover of Antioch when they learnt of the treachery and Iōannēs had to withdraw in the face of a large Syrian force.

Iōannēs called off his attacks on Seljuqs in 1142 when his eldest son and heir, Alexios, died of fever. He then turned on the Crusader states until Fulk of Jerusalem persuaded him not to attack Jerusalem. The Byzantine army went to Edessa instead where Josselin II handed over his daughter as a hostage. The emperor then went to Antioch but Raymond delayed negotiations over the winter and Iōannēs died of an infected wound caused by a poisoned hunting arrow.

Iōannēs chose his youngest son, Manouēl, as his heir, and his bad-tempered brother Isaakios was imprisoned to stop him interfering with the coronation. Raymond of Antioch asked for the emperor's protection when the Syrian Zengids overran Edessa. Manouēl responded by attacking Rûm in 1146. He then had to deal with Roger II of Sicily capturing Corfu and the Adriatic Coast while the Second Crusade passed through the empire. Manouēl secured an alliance so the Crusaders and the Venetians to attack Roger. But Roger in turn convinced the Serbs to invade Byzantine territory but they were beaten and forced to be a Byzantine vassal.

The death of the Holy Roman Emperor Konrad in 1152 changed everything because his successor, Friedrich I, revoked his alliance with the Byzantines and captured Apulia from Sicily. Pope Hadrian IV also allied with the Byzantines because Manouēl had hinted at a union between the eastern and western Churches. But the Byzantine mercenaries deserted when the Sicilians won the Battle of Brindisi in 1156. The Byzantine army returned home two years later, having wasted a huge amount of money on their Italian campaign.

Meanwhile, Renaud of Antioch claimed the Byzantines had failed to pay him tribute, so he ransacked Cyprus and mutilated the islanders. Once the Byzantine army returned from Italy, Manouël used it to capture Cilicia and attack the Rûm Empire. Renaud was made to appear before the emperor in sackcloth with a rope around his neck and forced to beg for forgiveness. Manouël also captured Antioch.

Manouël attacked Hungary in 1163 and overran Transylvania three years later with help from Yaroslav of Galicia. Bosnia and Dalmatia were also taken after decisive victories at Sirmium and Syrmiain in 1167. The Hungarian heir, Béla, had been educated in Constantinople and Manouël intended to marry his daughter to him so he could claim the country. However, Manouël no longer needed Béla after his wife gave birth to a son in 1169, and he was sent home.

Manouël had allied with Jerusalem by marrying his grandniece Maria to Amalric I in 1167. They planned to attack Egypt and although it was agreed the Byzantines would clear the coast while the Crusaders captured the interior, the generals refused to co-operate and their armies turned back. Egypt fell to Saladin in 1171 and Amaury made Jerusalem a Byzantine satellite state to get Constantinople's protection. Manouël's final attack was against Rûm but he was ambushed and defeated at the Battle of Myriokephalon in 1176.

Young Alexios II was crowned in 1180 and his mother, Maria, made sure her lover, Alexios, controlled the empire even though she was a nun. Alexios's supporters rebelled and his father's cousin returned home to take advantage of the disorder. Andronikos had spent over twenty-five years in exile after conspiring against Manouël and he had had a scandalous time. First he fled to Antioch where he seduced Raymond's daughter Philippa. Then he escaped to Jerusalem where he seduced Baudouin III's widow Theodora. The couple eloped but were captured and taken to Constantinople in 1180 where he appeared in chains before Manouël only to be banished a second time.

Andronikos took the Byzantine throne, overthrew the government and massacred 80,000 Latins across Constantinople. He allowed young Alexios II to be crowned but poisoned his half-sister and her husband before they had any children. He then imprisoned Maria and forced Alexios to sign his mother's death warrant; he also murdered her lover. Andronikos was proclaimed co-emperor and he had young Alexios II strangled with a bowstring when he came of age in 1183. He then married Alexios's bride-to-be, young Agnès of France, daughter of Louis VII.

Andronikos reduced the power of the Byzantine nobles but remained paranoid and executed many of them. After Hungary captured Syrmia and Bosnia and the Venetians seized Dalmatia in 1185, he murdered all prisoners, exiles and their families for alleged collusion with the invaders. Isaakios Angelos was one of those condemned to death but he killed the imperial agents' leader, took refuge in a church and stirred up a rebellion. Isaakios was pronounced emperor while Andronikos, his wife Agnès and his mistress were captured while attempting escape and handed over to the mob. They tied Andronikus to a post and mutilated him before hanging him by his feet in Constantinople's Hippodrome where the crowds tore him apart. His son Iōannēs was also murdered by soldiers in Thrace.

Isaakios II took the throne in 1185. He defeated Guglielmo (William) of Sicily at the Battle of Demetritzes in 1185 but he raised taxes and squandered the money on buildings and gifts to the churches. Several tried to depose him and were punished: Isaakios Komnenos (nephew of Andronikus) was tortured to death while Basil Chotzas and Kōnstantinos Tatikios were blinded and imprisoned.

Emperor Friedrich I had obtained permission to march the Third Crusade through the Byzantine Empire, but Isaakios allied with Saladin in 1189 and they tried to stop them. The Crusaders defeated the Byzantines and Isaakios had to let them pass through while he struggled to put down with a Bulgarian uprising. He failed and the founding of a second Bulgarian Empire was secured after a disastrous defeat at Arcadiopolis in 1194.

While the emperor was away hunting in Thrace, the generals proclaimed his older brother Alexios emperor, with the help of Isaakios's wife, Euphrosyne. Isaakios was captured, blinded and imprisoned. The following year Holy Roman Emperor Heinrich VI threatened to invade the Byzantine Empire if Alexios did not hand over the gold Isaakios had promised, so he plundered imperial tombs and increased taxes to raise the money. But Heinrich died in 1197 and Alexios squandered the money on palaces instead of paying his debts. As Alexios practised architecture, Hungary, Bulgaria and Wallachia were invading the Balkans and the Seljug Turks were overrunning the east of the empire. He gave tax concessions to his nobles in return for promises to protect the frontiers but they used their bonuses to increase their independence instead.

By 1201 it was time for a change and Pisan merchants smuggled Isaakios's son, Alexios, out of Constantinople and took him to Philipp of Swabia, King of Germany. The teenager wanted to be emperor and he offered Bonifacio of Montferrat troops, ships and money if he organised a Fourth Crusade to claim his inheritance. He also promised Pope Innocent III to bring the Greek Orthodox Church under Rome. The Crusade reached Constantinople in 1202 but the citizens ignored Alexios IV camped outside their walls. The Crusaders attacked the following summer and Alexios III fled with one daughter and headed for Thrace, leaving his wife and two other daughters behind.

Blind Isaakios II was released and proclaimed emperor again with his son Alexios IV as co-emperor. While Alexios IV ran the empire, Isaakios hid the fact that they could not pay the Crusaders because Alexios III had escaped with most of Constantinople's gold reserves. The Crusaders refused to leave without their money, even after Alexios IV told them Alexios III had stolen it. All the while, Isaakios spread rumours that Alexios was homosexual, hoping to seize the throne for himself. Eventually a court official called

Alexios Doukas imprisoned both of them in 1204 and ended the rivalry by strangling Alexios. Isaakios II died soon after, either from shock or from poison.

Alexios Doukas thus became Alexios V the Sullen. But he could not persuade the Crusaders to hunt down Alexios III, so he married Alexios III's daughter, Eudokia, and went to Thrace himself. Alexios III had his new son-in-law ambushed and blinded. Alexios V was soon taken to Constantinople and thrown from the top of the Column of Theodosius. Bonifacio's Crusaders captured Alexios III in Thessaly and he was eventually sent to his son-in-law, Theodōros of Nicaea. Alexios was captured at the Battle of Antioch in 1211 and Theodōros confined him to a monastery where he soon died.

THE THESSALONICAN, LATIN AND NICAEAN EMPIRES

The Byzantine Empire split into three small empires. The Thessalonican Empire covered the west coast of the Aegean Sea while the Latin Empire covered both sides of the Sea of Marmara; they both bordered on the Bulgarian Kingdom. The Empire of Nicaea covered the north-west part of Asia Minor while the Sultanate of Rûm covered the centre. The Empire of Trebizond held the Black Sea coast and the Kingdom of Cilicia covered the north-east part of the Mediterranean coast.

The Empire of Thessalonica

Bonifacio I of Montferrat wanted to lead a Fourth Crusade and he travelled to Rome in 1201 to ask for Pope Innocent III's blessing. Although he was instructed not to attack any Christians (including the Byzantines) Enrico Dandolo made him capture several rebellious cities before the Venetian fleet would take his Crusaders. Although Egypt was the target, Bonifacio marched into the Byzantium Empire when Alexios IV offered him a huge amount of money to capture Constantinople. The Crusaders were successful in 1204 but the Venetians chose Baudouin (Baldwin) instead of Bonifacio to head the Latin Empire.

Bonifacio founded the Kingdom of Thessalonica along the Aegean coast instead and married Emperor Isaakios II's widow, Margaret. But the Bulgarians ambushed his army in September 1207 and Bonifacio's head was sent to Kaloyan. The Bulgarian emperor then besieged his son, Demetrius, in Thessalonica until he was murdered by his Cuman ally. Demetrius's regent, Obert, planned to replace the young king with his half-brother, Guglielmo. The Latin Empire's army advanced on Thessalonica in 1208 but Emperor Henry only supported Guglielmo long enough to enter the city and then crowned Demetrius and imprisoned Obert.

Obert got his revenge by poisoning Henry in 1216 and he convinced his brother-in-law, Pierre II de Courtenay, to make the absent Guglielmo of Montferrat king. Pierre was soon captured and executed by Theodōros of Epirus and he then conquered the kingdom. Guglielmo of Montferrat agreed to lead a Crusade to Thessalonica in 1222 and Demetrius fled to the Holy Roman Empire for support. Emperor Friedrich II helped him recapture the kingdom and he inherited Thessalonica when Demetrius died in 1230.

THE LATIN EMPIRE

Baudouin embarked on the Fourth Crusade in 1202, intending to go to the Holy Land, but he was diverted to Constantinople. Alexios III refused to pay him to leave, so his army besieged and ransacked the city. Enrico Dandolo of Venice refused the crown so Baudouin defeated a rival candidate, Bonifacio of Montferrat, for the crown. The Bulgarians sponsored a Greek rebellion in Thrace and Baudouin was captured at the Battle of Adrianople in 1205. Kaloyan later murdered Baudouin and made his skull into a drinking cup either because he tried to seduce his wife or because he refused her advances and she lied to get her revenge.

Baudouin's brother Henri was crowned and although he married Maria of Bulgaria, he went to war against her country. He was poisoned in 1216, possibly by revengeful Maria. Henry's brother-in-law, Pierre II de Courtenay, marched from France and was crowned emperor by Pope Honorius III in Rome. He was captured en route to his new empire by Theodōros of Epirus and murdered in prison.

After Pierre's death, his wife Yolande ruled Constantinople until his brother Robert de Courtenay arrived in 1221. Robert planned to marry the late emperor's daughter, Eudoxia, but his sister was married to Theodōros I and he could not be both brother-in-law and son-in-law to the emperor. Instead he married a nobleman's fiancée and the angry husband-to-be chased Robert from Constantinople. He went to Rome, and although the pope convinced him to return, he died before he made it back.

The King of Jerusalem, Jean of Brienne, was invited to become emperor-regent in 1229 on condition that Pierre's youngest son, Baudouin de Courtenay, would marry his daughter and succeed him. But Jean had to fight off Iōannēs III of Nicaea and Ioan Asen II of Bulgaria before he died. Young Baudouin was crowned in 1237 but he only ruled the city of Constantinople and had to pawn the Crown of Thorns to pay for an army. When that failed, he sold religious relics to raise money and eventually handed his son Philippe to Venetian merchants to secure a loan. He finally sold his inheritance in Flanders, but even that did not raise enough money to get his lands back. Byzantine soldiers entered Constantinople via a secret passageway in 1261 and recovered the city for Mikhaēl VIII. So Baudouin fled leaving his crown and sceptre behind and headed for France but he again failed to raise any more help. Baudouin died in Naples in 1273, the last emperor of the Latin Empire.

The Nicaean Empire

Theodōros I had distinguished himself at the Siege of Constantinople before fleeing to Nicaea where he became a rallying point for his people. While he stopped the Latin Empire advancing further east across Anatolia, Kaloyan of Bulgaria stopped it spreading north at the Battle of Adrianople in 1205. But Emperor Henri de Flanders kept trying until the Latin Empire captured both shores of the Sea of Marmara. Theodōros made peace with Henri in 1214, but made one final attack just before he died in 1221.

Iōannēs III was a soldier chosen to marry Emperor Theodōros I's daughter, Irene, but he had to fight off the rest of her family, who were supported by the Latin Empire, to keep the throne. He allied with the Bulgarians and counter-attacked the Latin Empire in 1235, annexing Thrace before trying to capture Constantinople. Iōannēs would also expand his empire into Europe and across the Aegean.

The Bulgarians turned on Theodōros II but he defeated Mikhaēl Asen I at another Battle of Adrianople in 1255 and continued to expand west. But Theodōros's decision to favour the middle classes caused problems with the nobles, especially when he exiled their favourite, Mikhaēl VIII, for conspiring with the Seljugs of Rûm. Theodōros's epilepsy worsened and he died in 1258, leaving the throne to his young son Iōannēs IV.

The nobles murdered Iōannēs's regent, Geōrgios Mouzalōn, and recalled Mikhaēl to be regent and co-emperor. Mikhaēl recaptured Constantinople from the Latin Empire in 1261 and then turned the Empire of Nicaea into a new Byzantine Empire. He blinded Iōannēs on his eleventh birthday and imprisoned him as a monk. He also married his sisters to foreign nobles so their children could not claim to be heirs to the throne of Nicaea.

THE BYZANTINE EMPIRE RESTORED

The restored Byzantine Empire reunited the empires of Thessalonica, Latin and Nicaea. The Sultanate of Rûm still held the centre of Asia Minor while the Empire of Trebizond held the Black Sea coast and the Kingdom of Cilicia covered the north-east part of the Mediterranean coast.

Emperor Mikhaēl VIII was excommunicated for blinding and imprisoning young Iōannēs, and while one of the envoys sent to Pope Urban IV was flayed alive, the other barely escaped with his life. The emperor responded by invading Morea in 1263 but his army was routed at Prinitza and Makryplagi while his fleet was defeated by the Venetians at the Battle of Settepozzi. The Byzantines' problems increased when the Mongols ravaged Thrace and nearly captured Mikhaēl in 1265. He had to make alliances with the Venetians, the Mamluks and the Kipchak Khanate to fight them off.

Mikhaēl appealed for help against the Mongols, when he learned Louis IX of France was planning a new Crusade to the Holy Land in 1270. However, Charles of Anjou convinced Louis to invade Tunisia instead, only for the Crusade to end in disaster. Byzantine envoys attended the Second Council of Lyons in 1274 and although the western and eastern Churches agreed on many matters, there was a huge backlash to the meeting and nothing changed.

Mikhaēl fought Ivaylo the Radish, Emperor of Bulgaria, and his own son-in-law, Ioan Asen, over Thessaly in 1275. While his armies were defeated at the battles of Neopatras and Devina, his fleet was successful in the Battle of Demetrias. The Byzantines were also successful against Charles d'Anjou in western Greece but the new Pope Martin IV excommunicated Mikhaēl in 1281. The Sicilian Vespers revolt flared up again the following year and both Pedro III of Aragon and Mikhaēl were excommunicated for getting involved.

Andronikos II was crowned in 1282, and while he rejected his father's union with Rome, it took until 1310 to resolve the split in the Orthodox Church. His son and co-emperor Mikhaēl IX was defeated by the new Ottoman Empire at the Battle of Bapheus in 1302 so Andronikos hired mercenaries to get his revenge. But the leader of the Catalan Almogavars, Roger de Flor, was murdered in 1305, and they occupied southern Greece with deserting Ottoman troops. Theodōros of Bulgaria then defeated Mikhaēl IX and conquered north-east Thrace.

Mikhaēl's son Andronikos accidentally killed his brother Manouēl in 1320 and their father Mikhaēl IX died of grief. Andronikos II disowned his wayward grandson and the two ruled as rival emperors. Mihail Asen III of Bulgaria had offered to help Andronikos II against his grandson, but then treacherously tried to capture the emperor instead. Eventually Andronikos III concluded the 1327 Treaty of Chernomen, allying with Mihail Asen III against Serbia.

Andronikos III captured Constantinople in 1328 and Andronikos II abdicated and became a monk, leaving his grandson as emperor. The Ottomans besieged Nicaea a year later and Sultan Orhan defeated Andronikos's relief army at the Battle of Pelekanon. When Nicaea fell in 1331, Andronikos offered the Ottomans money to turn back but they wanted more money than he could afford and continued their conquest of Anatolia.

Meanwhile, Andronikos III's attempts to annex Thrace were stopped at the Battle of Rusokastro in 1332 so he married his daughter to a Bulgarian prince to restore the peace. Instead he conquered Serbia by sending a Byzantine general posing as a deserter into the Serbian camp to murder the governor of Thessalonica. The Serbian army fell back in disarray and Dŭsan of Serbia sued for peace.

Andronikos died in 1341 and there was a civil war between the rival regents of his young son Iōannēs V, until his mother, Anna, took control. Mikhaēl's son, Iōannēs, left for Morea only to be declared emperor by the generals after they ignored an order to disband the army. Anna pawned the Byzantine crown jewels to get Serbian and Bulgarian help for Iōannēs V but Iōannēs VI rallied greater support from the Ottomans. The two Iōannēs called a truce when the Black Death struck Constantinople in 1346 and they ruled as co-emperors. But the plague subsided and hostilities resumed when Iōannēs V and Dŭsan of Serbia attacked Iōannēs VI in 1352. The Ottomans helped to defeat the Serbs at the Battle of Demotika in 1352, but they had seized their first territory on European soil.

Iōannēs VI made his son, Matthaois, a co-emperor in 1353 but he was under attack from all sides. He lost two fleets supporting Venice against the Genoese. He lost north-west territories to the Serbs and his Ottoman allies seized Adrianople and Philippopolis. The Byzantine Empire was bankrupt by the time Iōannēs V captured Constantinople in 1354 and Iōannēs VI retired to a monastery, leaving his son in his enemy's hands.

Iōannēs V had promised to end the schism with Rome in exchange for help against the Ottomans. But in 1366 he offended the Hungarians by remaining seated on his horse, while Louis I approached him on foot. The deal was Iōannēs had to convert to Roman Catholicism or recognise the pope's supremacy before the Hungarians would help. Iōannēs refused and roamed Europe looking for help, even though he had no money to pay for any. He was imprisoned as a debtor in Venice, held prisoner in Bulgarian territories and was finally forced to be Murad I's vassal when he returned to Constantinople in 1371.

Iōannēs's son Andronikos rebelled against his father and allied with Murad's son, who was defying his own father. Both failed and emperor and sultan agreed their sons should be blinded. But while Murad blinded his son, Iōannēs only partially blinded Andronikos, leaving him eligible to rule in future. The Genoese helped Andronikos to escape prison in 1376 and he went to Murad I, promising him support if he attacked Gallipoli while he captured Constantinople. Andronikos captured the city and imprisoned his father and brother but they soon escaped and Murad helped them get their throne back.

The partially blinded Iōannēs VII usurped his grandfather, Iōannēs V, in 1390 but Manouēl defeated his nephew with Venetian help. Five months later Iōannēs V was restored, also with Venice's help, and his son Manouēl was sent as an honorary hostage to Bayezid I's court. Iōannēs VII also sought refuge with Bayezid. Iōannēs strengthened Constantinople's Golden Gate but Bayezid threatened to blind his son and go to war unless he knocked it down; so he removed it before he died in 1391.

Manouēl had to take part in the Ottoman capture of the last Byzantine enclave in Anatolia but he fled to Constantinople when he heard his father had died. Bayezid placed the city under siege in 1394, so Manouēl II entrusted it to Iōannēs VII while he went in search of help from Western Europe. A Crusade by Sigismund of Hungary was stopped at Nicopolis in 1396 but the Ottomans were finally defeated at the Battle of Ankara in 1402.

Manouēl remained on friendly terms with Mehmed I but he interfered in the Ottoman succession in 1421 and Murad II attacked the following year. Manouēl again went looking for help but he found none because Hungary was in a civil war and Bohemia was engaged in the Hussite Wars. Instead Manouēl offered tribute to the Ottomans to make the peace before he died in 1425.

His successor Iōannēs VIII visited Pope Eugene IV looking to get help against the Ottomans, and while they consented to the union of the Greek and Roman Churches, it was opposed in both camps. A childless Iōannēs nominated his brother Kōnstantinos as his heir so their brother, Dēmētrios, planned a coup, which was stopped by their mother, Helena. The brothers asked Murad II to arbitrate in 1448, and while Kōnstantinos was crowned, Dēmētrios and another brother, Thomas, were given Morea to rule as Ottoman vassals, removing them from Constantinople.

The teenage Mehmed II was appointed sultan in 1451 and he immediately wanted to conquer Constantinople. Kōnstantinos threatened to release Prince Orhan, a pretender to the Ottoman throne, so Mehmed built a fortress on the European side of the Bosporus, cutting the route to the Black Sea. Kōnstantinos XI appealed to the west as the Ottomans besieged Constantinople but none came. Mehmed offered to spare Kōnstantinos's life if he surrendered the city but he refused and died in the last charge.

The Fall of Constantinople in 1453 left Dēmētrios ruling Morea, the last part of the Byzantine Empire, but he handed it over in 1460 rather than fight the Ottomans. The pope recognised his brother Thomas as the new claimant so the brothers fought until the Ottomans chased Thomas out. Mehmed II refused to return Morea to Dēmētrios, saying 'he is not man enough to rule any country', and he was held in his palace until he upset Mehmed II and was exiled in 1467. The final Byzantine claimant was Andreas but he preferred to live beyond his means in the Papal States where he married 'a lady from the streets' in 1480. He sold the rights to the Byzantine crown to Charles VIII of France in 1494 and again to Fernando and Isabel of Aragon and Castile. He died a pauper in 1502.

THE RÛM SULTANATE

The Rum Sultanate was in the Anatolia region of modern Turkey. Qutalmish fought his brother Alp Arsen (Heroic Lion) for control of the Seljuq state and his four sons were forced to hide in the mountains after he died in 1064. Only Suleiman survived and he founded an independent sultanate in Anatolia in 1077, naming it Rûm, the Persian word for Roman.

Emperor Mikhaēl VII asked Rûm for help when he was challenged by Nikephoros, and while Suleiman captured the usurper, he switched sides because he was made a better offer. Nikephorus seized the Byzantine throne and rewarded Suleiman with territory east of the Bosporus. Suleiman also helped Nikephoros capture Byzantine Asia Minor and was given Nicaea as a reward in 1080. He captured Antioch only to be killed by the Syrians in 1085.

Suleiman's son Kilij Arslan (Lion Sword) was taken hostage when his father died but he was released in 1092 and he re-established the Sultanate of Rûm with Nicaea as his capital. When Emperor Alexius I told him that Tzachas was planning a rebellion, Kilij invited the rebel to a banquet in his tent, got him drunk and murdered him.

The Peasants' Crusade reached Nicaea in 1096 but Kilij besieged and starved one group in Xerigordon castle, executing those who refused to renounce Christianity. The rest of the Crusaders were ambushed and slaughtered near Dracon.

The First Crusade followed a year later and the Byzantines captured Nicaea, taking Kilij's wife and children hostage, but Emperor Alexius returned them without asking for a ransom – against the Crusaders' wishes. Kilij defeated two more Crusader armies before he was killed fighting against Mosul in 1107. His son Malik became sultan when he was released from prison in 1110 only to be defeated, blinded and murdered by his brother Masud in 1116. After enjoying thirty years of peace he faced the Second Crusade in 1147; he defeated Emperor Konrad III at Dorylaeum and King Louis VII at Laodicea in 1148.

Kilij II was crowned sultan in 1156 and three years later he attacked Emperor Manouēl I as he returned from negotiations with the Atabeg of Aleppo. Manouēl's nephew, Iōannēs, in turn defeated Kilij and he had to go to Constantinople and submit. Kilij later refused to hand over territory so Emperor Manouēl invaded only to be defeated at Myriokephalon in 1176. Three years later Kilij captured Henri de Champagne, and while Manouēl paid the ransom, Henri died just after his release.

Manouēl died in 1180 and Kilij allied with Saladin, allowing him to capture the south coast of Anatolia from the Byzantines. The ageing sultan transferred power to his nine sons in 1186 only to see them squabble as the Third Crusade approached. Fortunately the Crusaders returned when Friedrich Barbarossa drowned in 1190.

Kilij's youngest son Kaykhusraw was chosen, but he was overthrown by his brother, Suleiman II, who expanded his territories against the Byzantines. Kilij III was appointed sultan but Kaykhusraw married the daughter of a Byzantine nobleman and he helped him regain Rûm. He captured Antalya in 1207 only to be killed at the Battle of Alaşehir in 1211, fighting Theodōros I of Nicaea.

His successor Kaykaus I negotiated a peace with Theodōros, but his brothers challenged him until they were imprisoned by the emirs. Rûm then joined with the Fifth Crusade to fight the Ayyubids. Kaykaus was captured was out hunting by Emperor Alexios of Trebizond in 1214 and he had to hand over the Black Sea port of Sinop as a ransom.

Kaykaus died in 1220 and his brother, Kayqubad, was appointed sultan. He conquered the Mengujek and Mingburnu tribes before expanding further east, as the Mongols and Georgians withdrew. Although Kayqubad the Great preferred his younger son Izz al-Din, the emirs wanted Kaykhusraw II to rule and they helped him seize the throne. Kaykhusraw married a Georgian princess to stop them invading. Baba Ishak was busy preaching Islam to the immigrant Turkmen and they eventually rebelled and destroyed Kaykhusraw's army in 1240. Baba Ishak was soon captured and executed and the Turkmen were defeated. But Kaykhusraw's troubles were far from over because the Mongols routed his army at the Kose Dag pass in 1243 and he had to escape with his treasury and harem. His vizier, Muhadhdhab, fought off the hordes but Kaykhusraw still became a Mongol vassal.

Kaykhusraw had designated Kayqubad, the sickly infant son of his favourite wife, but the emirs appointed his eldest son, young Kaykaus, in 1246. Kaykaus delayed a payment to the Mongols in 1254 and they were soon seen assembling ready to attack. Kayqubad was sent to negotiate with them but he was murdered en route and some believed his brothers had killed him. The impatient Mongols overran the Rûm Empire and Kaykaus fled to the Balkans where he was imprisoned by the Byzantines.

His brother, Kilij IV, was strangled by his stepfather because he was becoming too powerful. Kayqubad asked for help from the Golden Horde so the Mongol hordes invaded the empire in 1265. He then went into exile in the Crimea and ignored his sons' appeals to return.

The emirs preferred Kilij's young son, Kaykhusraw, but Ahmad Tekuder continued to rule after he came of age in 1283. The Mongols encouraged the teenage heir to stage a rebellion but he was executed by Ahmad and he installed Kaykaus II's son, Masud II. Although Ahmad's successor, Arghun, seized control and gave half the empire to Ahmed's two young sons, Masud had them both executed. The Mongols and Turkmen soon grew tired of Masud and implicated him in a plot in 1297 so he could be imprisoned.

Kaykaus's nephew, Kayqubad III, was appointed in 1298 but he was also implicated in a plot and executed. Although Masud returned to power both he and the Sultanate of Rûm disappeared around 1306.

THE OTTOMAN EMPIRE

The Mongols invaded the area now known as Turkmenistan and enslaved or massacred the majority. A few hundred horsemen escaped and their leader, Ertuğrul, was granted lands after helping the Seljugs of Rûm fight the Byzantines. Osman the Bone Breaker became their leader in 1281 and refugees escaping the Mongols and the Caliphate of

Damascus joined him until he announced his independence in 1299. Three years later Osman defeated the Byzantines near Nicaea, forcing them to withdraw from Anatolia.

Orhan was appointed Bey in 1326 but his brother Alaeddin ran the empire and created a loyal army called the Yaya. A worried Orhan built his own army of Janissaries, captured Christian children raised as soldiers. Only three years later, this new army defeated Emperor Andronicus III at the Battle of Pelekanon and the Byzantines surrendered the city of Nicaea. Orhan's two sons quarrelled in 1345, so he executed one and imprisoned the other. He took sides in the Byzantine civil war by marrying the daughter of Emperor Iōannēs V's regent and then switched allegiance by sending Ottoman soldiers to help Iōannēs VI become co-emperor.

Ottoman troops occupied the Gallipoli Peninsula after an earthquake struck in 1354 and Orhan turned down Iōannēs VI's offer of money to withdraw because he had a bridgehead into Europe. Orhan was devastated when his eldest son, Pasha, died following a riding accident in 1357 and he died five years later.

Murad I the Sovereign established the title of sultan in 1383 but his youngest son Savcı saw an opportunity to seize power when Andronicus refused to pay his father's ransom. An angry Emperor Iōannēs V disinherited Savcı so he staged a joint rebellion with Andronicus against their fathers. After it failed Murad murdered Savcı and insisted Iōannēs imprison and blind Andronicus.

Murad campaigned against the Serbs, the Bulgarians and the Hungarians with his Janissaries, bringing most of the Balkans under Ottoman rule; he also forced the Byzantine emperor to pay tribute. The Serbs were defeated at the Battle of Kosovo in 1389 but Murad was assassinated after the battle and Bayezid strangled his older brother, Yakub, to become sultan.

Bayezid I the Thunderbolt conquered Bulgaria and northern Greece only to lose the Battle of Rovine in 1394. Unable to capture Wallachia, he besieged Constantinople. Zgismond of Hungary answered Emperor Manouēl II's call for help, but he was defeated at the Battle of Nicopolis in 1396. A Timurid army (the Muslim dynasty ruling the Persian area) would break the siege six years later and imprison Bayezid and his son, Mustafa.

Bayezid died in 1403 and his four remaining sons fought each other. Musa had Isa assassinated in a public baths in 1406, Suleyman was murdered in 1411 and Musa was killed at the Battle of Carmulu in 1413. Mehmed I the Gentleman was appointed sultan in 1413 and he became known as the 'second founder' of the Ottoman Empire because he conquered parts of Albania and large parts of Anatolia. Mustafa demanded part of the empire when the Timurids finally released him but Mehmed exiled him; his nephew Orhan was also blinded for plotting.

Murad II was appointed sultan in 1421 and he faced long wars in the Balkans and Anatolia. His uncle Mustafa then escaped from exile and Emperor Manouēl II acknowledged him as the heir. After capturing Adrianople, he crossed the Dardanelles only to be captured and executed so Murad retaliated by besieging Constantinople. The Byzantines supported a rebellion in Anatolia by his teenage brother Mustafa and Murad was forced to abandon the Siege of Constantinople so he could catch and execute his brother. But Murad II continued to capture territories in the Balkans and the Holy Roman Empire and Poland joined the Serbian–Hungarian coalition after the Ottomans annexed Serbia in 1439.

Murad abdicated in favour of his young son Mehmed II in 1444 but he had to return to the throne when the Janissaries revolted against the child's unpopular teacher. Murad stopped János Hunyadi's invasion at the Battle of Varna in 1444 and then abdicated again. Mehmed then defeated another Christian alliance at the Second Battle of Kosovo in 1448 and he took control of the Bosporus Strait over the next three years. He then captured Constantinople in 1453 and made it his capital. Mehmed would become known as 'the Conqueror'.

Vlad III refused to pay the Ottomans' tribute and Mehmed's first envoys to Wallachia had their turbans nailed to their heads because they refused to raise their 'hats' to him. The next group of peace makers were impaled. Vlad the Impaler then went on the offensive, massacring two Ottoman armies in Bulgaria and impaling thousands of prisoners as a warning. But Vlad was betrayed and he had to hide in the mountains while the Ottomans invaded Wallachia; around 2,000 heads were delivered to Mehmed after one force was massacred.

The Ottomans went to war with the Venetians in 1463 after a Muslim slave stole a large quantity of silver from Koroni and he then converted to Christianity. Mehmed was furious when the Venetians failed to execute him so he built a fleet to face them. Civil wars in the Balkans allowed Mehmed to capture Morea, the southern part of Greece, Serbia and Bosnia. He would execute the last Bosnian king, Stjepan Tomašević. But Mátyás Hunyadi's Hungarian counter-invasion of Bosnia undermined Ottoman power while the Venetians seized part of the Aegean Sea.

Petru III of Moldavia had paid the Ottomans tribute to secure his southern border but his successor, Stephen the Great, refused. The Ottomans invaded only to be defeated at the Battle of Vaslui in 1475. The Tartar hordes attacked the following year and after being turned back in Moldavia, they rode through Albania.

The 1479 Treaty of Constantinople eventually stopped the Ottomans at the gates of Venice but the Venetians had to pay a huge indemnity and tribute on Black Sea trade to turn them back. Mehmed marched his army back to the Constantinople area in 1481 only to fall sick on the Field of the Sultan. Whether he died or natural causes or was poisoned, Europe rejoiced because the 'Great Eagle' was dead.

Bayezid II the Just defeated his brother Cem and his supporters, the Mamluks of Egypt. Cem fled to Rhodes but the Knights of St John handed him over to Pope Innocent VIII and he died in prison. In 1492 Fernando and Isabel expelled the Jewish population from Aragon and Castile, followed by the Moors a few years later. Bayezid sent his navy across the Mediterranean Sea to rescue them all, swelling anti-Christian support across the Ottoman lands.

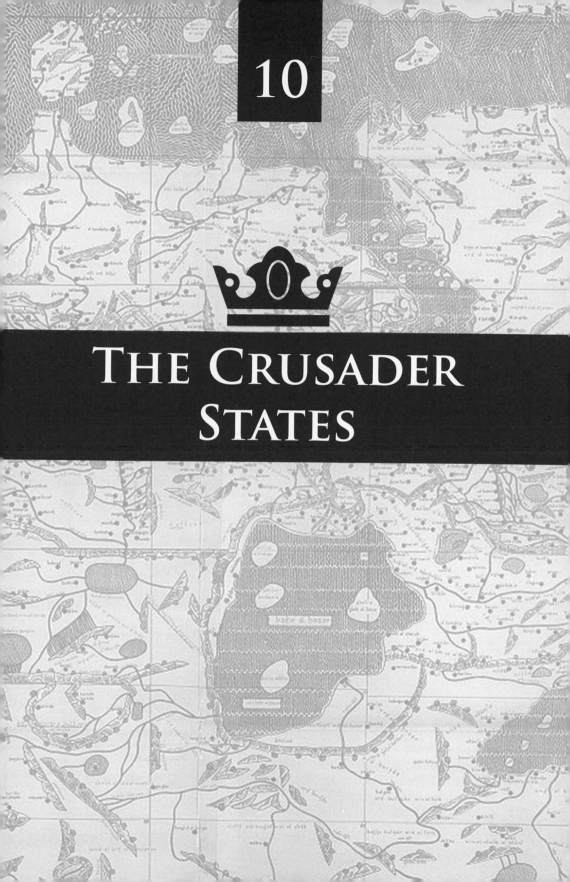

10

THE CRUSADER STATES

THE PROPHET MUHAMMAD, THE FOUNDER of Islam, died in 632 and two years later his companion, Umar, captured Jerusalem from the Byzantines. In 1095 Pope Urban II called for a Crusade to recapture Jerusalem and help the Byzantine Empire drive back the Seljug Turks. Godefroy de Bouillon, Boemondo de Taranto, Raymond IV de Toulouse and Roberto de Flanders travelled across Europe separately, reaching Constantinople in November 1096. Alexios I asked for help to recapture Byzantine lands and although Godefroy agreed, the emperor failed to give him support. While Godefroy's brother Baldwin and Tancred headed east into Edessa, Boemondo captured and claimed Antioch for himself in 1098. The rest of the Crusaders captured Jerusalem the following year.

THE KINGDOM OF JERUSALEM

Raymond refused to become king of the new kingdom. Godefroy accepted but he rejected the title king, believing Christ was the true King of Jerusalem, and declined 'a crown of gold where his Saviour had worn a crown of thorns'. Godefroy defeated an Egyptian Fatimid army at the Battle of Ascalon and then stopped Raymond of Saint-Gilles and Dagobert of Pisa capturing Jerusalem. He died in 1110 after a mystery illness, possibly caused by a poisoned apple.

Count Baldwin of Edessa was invited to Jerusalem and he immediately invaded Fatimid territory. He returned to be crowned king and, unlike his brother, he had no qualms about holding the ceremony in Bethlehem on 25 December 1100. Baldwin captured Acre, north of Jerusalem, meaning he did not need Armenian support to hold Edessa. So he abandoned his Armenian wife, Arda, in a monastery claiming she had been raped by pirates (or she had been unfaithful, versions differ). He then married Roger I of Sicily's widow, Adelaide.

The Caliph of Baghdad ordered attacks on the Crusaders and, while Edessa held out and the Battle of Shaizar was a draw, the Abbasids defeated Baldwin at the Battle of Al-Sannabra in 1113. He fell sick and blamed his illness on his bigamous marriage so he sent Adelaide back to Sicily and his faith was restored when he recovered. It was not restored for long. He marched into Egypt the following year and died after eating a fish dinner.

The throne was offered to Eustace III but Count Josselin of Edessa insisted the crown was passed to Baldwin II the Thorny and he accepted. After fighting off the Syrians and Egyptians, he defeated Roger of Salerno on the Field of Blood in 1119 and recovered Antioch. Hugues de Payens captured Temple Mount and called it the Temple of Solomon so his knights became known as the 'Knights of the Temple' or Knights Templar. The

Crusaders also captured Tyre in 1124 but they could not take Damascus. Baldwin intended to take over Edessa after Josselin was captured but he too was taken prisoner. They were both rescued but Baldwin was recaptured and ransomed in exchange for Josselin's son and one of Baldwin's daughters.

Melisende was crowned queen in 1131 but she had to share the crown with Count Fulk of Anjou, a short, ugly man who was twice her age. He spread rumours that Melisende was having an affair with her cousin, Hugh of Jaffa, so the count rebelled and defeated Fulk's army in 1134. Fulk made peace but he tried to get Hugh murdered in exile. He then turned away Byzantine help, telling Emperor John II the area could not support a large army.

Fulk died out hunting in 1143 and Melisende told everyone her son, the teenage Baldwin III, was simple-minded so she could remain in control. The new Zengid dynasty of Mosul soon posed a threat. They captured Edessa in 1144, then allied with Damascus and defeated the Crusaders at the Battle of Bosra in 1147. The Second Crusade reached Jerusalem the following year and Louis VII of France and Konrad III of Germany made an ill-advised attack on Damascus before returning home. Mosul then invaded Antioch and killed Raymond at the Battle of Inab in 1149. Although Melisende became regent for the principality, in Baldwin's name, Jerusalem had to cede Edessa to the Byzantines in 1150.

Baldwin wanted to take charge and he paraded through Jerusalem with a laurel wreath on his head to prove his point, but he was banned from holding a second coronation. The high court gave Baldwin the north of the kingdom to rule and Melisende the south, to settle the matter, but Baldwin went to war with his mother. Jerusalem opened its gates to him and his mother and brother, Amalric, were besieged in the Tower of David until mother and son reconciled in 1154. Baldwin married Manuel's niece, Theodora, to make peace with the Byzantines, so he could concentrate on defeating Mosul. He then married his cousin Maria to the emperor to further seal their alliance.

Melisende died in 1161 and Baldwin was poisoned by his doctor two years later, dying after a long illness. Amalric immediately invaded Egypt, claiming it had not paid tribute, but the Fatimids flooded the Nile and forced him to turn back. Boemondo III of Antioch and Raymond III of Tripoli were captured at the Battle of Harim in 1164, and while Amalric paid the ransom for Boemondo, Raymond remained a prisoner.

Control of Acre reverted to Jerusalem when Baldwin III's widow, Theodora, eloped with her cousin Andronicus. Amalric renewed the alliance with Byzantium by marrying Manuel's great-grandniece, Maria, allowing him to attack Egypt. Although Amalric and Manuel united to besiege Damietta, they withdrew when their food supplies ran out. Saladin, leader of the new Egyptian Ayyubid dynasty, invaded Jerusalem in 1170 and Amalric made peace while desperately trying to get help from Europe.

Amalric died in 1174 and his sickly teenage son, Baldwin, was crowned. His regent, Raymond of Tripoli, ignored the treaty with the Ayyubids and he defeated Saladin at the Battle of Montgisard with the help of the Knights Templar. Raymond married his sister Sibylla to William of Montferrat but he died soon after, leaving her pregnant.

The ailing Baldwin, now suffering from leprosy, married Sibylla to Guy of Lusignan in 1180 and made Guy his regent following the Battle of Belvoir Castle.

Guy was at the wedding of Baldwin's young half-sister Isabella in 1183 when Saladin attacked the venue, Karak fortress. Guy refused to help lift the siege so Baldwin made his young nephew co-king and was working to annul Guy's marriage when he died.

Henry II of England and Philip II of France both turned down the throne so young Baldwin V was proclaimed king instead. The Patriarch of Jerusalem, Heraclius, and the Grand Masters of the Knights Templar and Knights Hospitaller agreed the kings of England and France, the Holy Roman Emperor and the pope would decide whether his mother Sibylla or his aunt Isabella would claim the throne if he died. Baldwin died a few months later and Sibylla annulled her marriage to Guy on condition she could choose her next husband. She divorced, was crowned queen, and immediately announced she would remarry Guy and gave him the crown. Her enemies claimed she was illegitimate and they fought to get Isabella crowned instead.

Meanwhile, Saladin was seeking his revenge and he beheaded Raynald of Châtillon and imprisoned Guy after winning the Battle of Hattin in 1187. Jerusalem was lost and Sibylla escaped to Tripoli with her two daughters, marking the end of the first Kingdom of Jerusalem. Saladin thought Guy was a poor leader so he released him so he and Sibylla could head for the only Crusader city, Tyre. But Conrad of Montferrat refused them in, announcing he was waiting for the kings of Europe to arrive and choose the King of Jerusalem. Guy and Sibylla attached themselves to the Third Crusade and they joined Philip II of France and Richard I of England at the Siege of Acre. Unfortunately, Sibylla and her daughters died in an epidemic which swept the Crusader camp. It was the chance her half-sister Isabella had been waiting for.

Isabella had already had an eventful life. She had been betrothed to pay a debt of honour in 1183 and Saladin had besieged her wedding venue, Karak fortress. Richard's cousin, Henry of Champagne, then kidnapped her and annulled her marriage on the grounds she had been under-age. She then had to marry Conrad to get the throne of Jerusalem, even though the Church said their union was incestuous.

Guy refused to relinquish his crown and in 1191 he joined Richard's attack on Cyprus, even saving Conrad's life during the battle.

Richard wanted to head home in 1192 but he needed a decision over the throne before leaving and Conrad was elected. Four days later he was murdered by the Assassins and Richard became the chief suspect after one of the murderers confessed under torture.

Richard left at once, selling Cyprus to Guy so he would stay behind, only to be captured by Conrad's cousin in Austria and accused of murder. He was ransomed for a huge amount when a forged letter, stating the Assassins had a vendetta on Conrad, appeared.

Meanwhile, Henry of Champagne had married the pregnant Isabella only a week after Conrad's assassination. In 1197 Henry fell from a palace window when the railing broke; his servant dwarf tried to catch him but fell on him, finishing his master off. Isabella then married Amalric II, who had recently inherited Cyprus from his brother, and he secured a ten-year truce while Saladin's brothers and sons argued over the inheritance. Unfortunately, he died in 1205 possibly poisoned; Isabella died four days later.

Conrad and Isabella's teenage daughter, Maria, became queen with John of Ibelin as her regent.

Philip II of France was asked to find Maria a husband and he and Pope Innocent III paid John of Brienne to marry her in 1210. Two years later she died following childbirth and her daughter, Isabelle, was proclaimed queen with her father as regent.

Although John of Brienne was prominent during the Fifth Crusade, it failed because the leader, Pelagius of Albano, was defeated after refusing to accept the sultan of Egypt's favourable terms. John met the emperor in 1223, to ask for help, and Friedrich II promised a Crusade on condition he was made King of Jerusalem. He married John's daughter Isabella in 1225 but immediately demanded the kingdom. He then delayed the Sixth Crusade, until Pope Gregory IX excommunicated him.

Friedrich reached Jerusalem, crowned himself king and then imprisoned Isabella in his harem in Palermo, where she died giving birth to their son, Conrad. Friedrich offered John the position of emperor-regent to placate him, and while he ruled Constantinople, he had to fight off Emperor John III of Nicaea and Ivan Asen II of Bulgaria in 1235.

The title of Jerusalem had passed to Friedrich's son in 1228. Conrad and his son, Conrad the Younger, held the title from 1254 until the elder died in 1268. Conradin, as he was known, never married, so the title passed to Hugh III of Cyprus. Hugh died in 1284 and his son, John, died a few months later, possibly poisoned by his brothers. Henry II of Cyprus was the last King of Jerusalem but the title was abolished after the fall of Acre, the last Crusader stronghold, in 1291.

THE KINGDOM OF CYPRUS

Guy of Lusignan became King of Jerusalem when he married Sibylla in 1186 and he was crowned King of Cyprus in 1192. He was succeeded on both thrones by his older brother Aimery, who was in turn followed by his son, Hugh. The line of succession became even more tenuous when Hugh died young in 1218 and his infant son inherited the throne. Henry's mother was regent, but her uncle Philip of Ibelin ruled and he crowned young Henry because Emperor Friedrich II had arrived in the area. The regency passed to Philip's brother, John, but Friedrich forced him to hand over Henry and Cyprus in 1228.

But Friedrich soon left the island and John regained control, resulting in the War of the Lombards between their supporters. Henry the Fat, as he would be known, took control of the kingdom when he came of age in 1232 and took his turn to serve as regent, this time for Conrad of Jerusalem from 1246. Henry's death in 1253 meant Cyprus was left with the infant Hugh II as its king.

John of Ibelin took Hugh and his mother to Acre in 1258 but teenage Hugh died and his regent, Hugh III the Great, claimed Jerusalem on his behalf following the execution of Conradin in 1268. But Hugh fell out with factions in Jerusalem and left for Cyprus in disgust. Hugh died in 1284 and Charles of Anjou opposed the succession of his son, John II; he too died soon after, probably poisoned by his brothers.

Henry II escaped from the Siege of Acre in 1291, leaving the Jerusalem title empty, and became so unpopular that Hugh III's son, Amalric, planned to retake the Holy Land with help from the Mongols. Ghazan failed to turn up so he called on the Knights Templar and they helped him capture Hugh. But Pope Clement V made Amalric arrest the Knights Templar in 1307, making him unpopular and he had to crush an uprising, exile his brother Henry and arrest many nobles. Amalric was murdered soon afterwards and Henry was restored to his throne; he would reign until 1324.

His successor, Hugh IV, allowed Venetian merchants to settle in Cyprus and Genoese merchants wanted the same as soon as Hugh had settled Henry's debts. While he was nominally King of Jerusalem, he just wanted to rule Cyprus and stopped his two sons heading to Europe to recruit support for a Crusade to Jerusalem. Peter founded the Order of the Sword in 1347, dedicated to the recovery of Jerusalem, and the brothers left without their father's permission so he imprisoned them on their return and executed the man who helped them escape. Hugh resigned in 1358.

Peter had more ambition and he invaded Cilicia and conquered Antalya while the Ottomans attacked the Byzantines. He then invaded Egypt and, while he sacked Alexandria in 1365, no one would help him capture Cairo, so he returned home. Peter travelled across Europe, failing to get support for a new Crusade, and returned home to find his wife, Eleanor, had been unfaithful. So he persecuted her favourite nobles until three of them murdered him in his bed in 1369.

Eleanor conspired against teenage Peter II's regent, his uncle John of Lusignan, believing he had organised her husband's (and his brother's) murder. The Venetians and Genoese argued over who should hold the left and the right reins of the king's horse, symbolising who was senior, and many Genoese were arrested during the fight at the feast. Venetians sailed their ships into Famagusta's harbour, on the pretence of negotiating, but they captured the port and imprisoned Peter and his mother instead. Peter II the Fat was forced to pay a ransom and he left Cyprus in 1374 while his estranged wife Eleanor was sent back to Spain after causing many scandals.

Peter's uncle James had been arrested in Rhodes and most of his twelve children were born in captivity. He promised the Genoese commercial privileges to secure his release and he was greeted enthusiastically on his return to Cyprus in 1385.

In 1398 James was succeeded by Janus, who had been left behind as a hostage when his father was elected king. Janus planned to recapture Famagusta in 1402, using duplicate keys to open the gates, but he was betrayed and his accomplices were executed. The Mamluks attacked Cyprus and Janus was captured at the Battle of Khirokitia in 1426. He was taken to Cairo, tied in chains and forced to ride a donkey before being made to kneel and worship in front of the sultan. Alexis started a rebellion and was declared king but he was captured and tortured when news arrived that Janus was returning, having agreed a ransom. Alexis was executed the day Janus landed.

Janus's son John III was crowned in 1432 but he was controlled by his wife, Helena. She cut his mistress's nose off and then fought his illegitimate son, James, for control of the king. John died in 1458 and was succeeded by his daughter, Charlotte, who had been widowed age 13. Her mother may have murdered her husband, leaving her free to remarry Louis of Savoy, in exchange for Genoese assistance.

Charlotte's half-brother, James the Bastard, arrived in 1460 and he blockaded her in a castle until Mamluks helped her escape to Rome. James was crowned, and while Charlotte initially adopted Alfonso of Aragon as her heir, she eventually ceded her claim in exchange for a pension.

James married the teenage Caterina Cornaro of Venice by proxy, but it was four years before they met. She fell pregnant but James died in 1473, possibly poisoned. His son, James III, died under suspicious circumstances before his first birthday and Venice forced Caterina to abdicate in 1489. Cyprus then became a Venetian colony.

THE COUNTY OF EDESSA

The Byzantine Empire recovered Edessa from the Ayubbid dynasty but it was still in danger. Thoros asked Baldwin of Boulogne for help in 1098 so he broke off from the

Crusade to Jerusalem and headed to Edessa. He convinced Thoros to adopt him as a son and heir only for the king to be assassinated soon after, so Baldwin took the title of the Count of Edessa.

Baldwin was crowned King of Jerusalem in 1100 so his cousin, Baldwin of Bourcq, became Count of Edessa and he took an Armenian wife to ally with her family. However, both Baldwin and Josselin of Courtenay were captured when Mosul attacked in 1104 and Boemondo's brother Tancred was Edessa's regent until they were ransomed three years later. Even then, Baldwin had to defeat Tancred to regain control of his city. But the Ayyubids kept up the pressure, capturing all the lands east of the Euphrates by 1110.

Eustace was offered the title when Baldwin died in 1118 but he did not want to leave France, so Baldwin II became King of Jerusalem while Josselin took over Edessa. But Josselin was captured in 1122 and Baldwin was captured trying to rescue him. Josselin was able to escape in 1123 and he organised Baldwin's release.

Josselin was killed fighting the Danishmends in 1131 and his son, Josselin II, argued with the counts of Tripoli rather than improving the county's defences.

Josselin II allied with Antioch and the Byzantines against Aleppo in 1138 but stirred up riots so that Emperor John II left with his army. John II and Fulk of Jerusalem both died in 1143, so Aleppo attacked while Edessa had no strong allies. Edessa soon fell to Zengi, leaving Josselin holding the lands west of the Euphrates.

Zengi was assassinated in 1146 and Josselin was able to briefly recapture Edessa, losing it to Zengi's son, Nur ad-Din. The Second Crusade was organised to recapture Edessa but it travelled to Damascus instead while Josselin was captured in 1150, trying to get help from Antioch. He was taken to Aleppo, publicly blinded and died in prison nine years later.

Josselin's son, Josselin III, was captured at the Battle of Harim in 1164 and was not ransomed for twelve years. He joined Jerusalem's court and in 1185 became Baldwin V's guardian. The regent, Raymond III, did not want to be accused of murder if the baby died because he had a lot to gain. Young Baldwin still died in 1186.

Josselin III was present at the disastrous Battle of Hattin in 1187, where the Crusader army was decimated. Saladin would soon capture Jerusalem and Josselin's remaining estates.

ANTIOCH

While Baldwin of Boulogne headed east to set up the County of Edessa, the rest of the First Crusade continued south to Antioch and besieged the city over the winter of

1097–98. Boemondo of Taranto bribed a guard to let the Crusaders enter the city only a few days before an army from Mosul reached the city. Although the Crusaders weathered the siege, the Byzantine Emperor Alexius I turned back believing Edessa had fallen.

A mystic named Peter Bartholomew produced what he called the Holy Lance (the spear used on Jesus while he was on the cross) having planted it himself. Whatever the spear's history, Boemondo marched out of the city with it at the head of his troops and defeated the Mosul army.

Boemondo was captured in battle by the Danishmends in 1100 and his nephew, Tancred, became regent. He was with Baldwin II of Edessa when he was captured at the Battle of Harran in 1104. Boemondo was released in 1103 and raised troops in Italy which he used to attack the Byzantines. He was soon defeated by Emperor Alexius I at the Dyrrhachium in 1108 and was forced to sign the Treaty of Devol, making Antioch would be a vassal state of the Byzantine Empire after Boemondo's death.

When Baldwin and Josselin were captured, Tancred became regent of Edessa and Antioch while Boemondo returned to Italy where he died looking for help in 1111. Alexius wanted Antioch but Tancred's nephew Roger of Salerno refused to hand it over when Tancred died the following year, becoming regent to young Boemondo II. Roger was killed at the Field of Blood in 1119 and the imprisoned Baldwin II was made regent while Antioch became a vassal state of Jerusalem.

Boemondo II ruled for only four years and Baldwin II and then Fulk of Jerusalem were regents for his infant daughter Constance. At 10 years old she was married to Raymond of Poitiers (twenty-six years her senior) in 1136. But Raymond's attack on Cilicia failed and Emperor John II forced him to submit to him. John led the armies of Byzantium, Antioch and Edessa against Syria but Raymond and Josselin played dice while John conducted the Siege of Shaizar.

Once back in Antioch, Josselin II of Edessa stirred up resentment until the Byzantines were forced to leave. Edessa would fall in 1144 and Nur ad-Din captured the eastern part of Antioch soon after while Raymond was killed at the Battle of Inabin in 1149. His widow, Constance, married Raynald of Châtillon in 1153 but he too was soon a vassal to the Byzantines after arguing over Cyprus.

Raynald was captured by the Muslims in 1160, the Patriarch of Antioch took control, and while Manuel married Constance's daughter Maria, she was deposed and replaced by her son Boemondo III in 1163. Boemondo was taken prisoner at the Battle of Harim the following year but he was soon released and married one of Manuel's nieces. The Byzantine alliance ended with the death of the Emperor Manuel in 1180, leaving Antioch unable to stop Saladin's assault in 1187.

Boemondo's son (also Boemondo) became Count of Tripoli following the Battle of Hattin while his eldest son, Raymond, took control of Antioch in 1201. But the brothers fought and Boemondo seized control by 1207. Boemondo III's grandson, Raymond-Roupen, briefly ruled as a rival but Boemondo of Tripoli died in 1233 and his son Boemondo V (who was nicknamed 'One Eye' or 'the Cyclops') played no part in the Crusades across the Holy Land.

Boemondo VI married Sibylla, to ally with Armenia, but then became caught up in the conflict between the Mamluks and the Mongols. He eventually submitted to the Mongols, at his father-in-law's insistence, and fought alongside Hetoum I during their conquest of Syria. They captured Aleppo and Damascus but the Mongols were defeated at the Battle of Ain Jalut in 1260. The Mamluks then turned on Antioch and captured the city in 1268 before taking Acre in 1291. After nearly 200 years the Crusader states ceased to exist.

THE COUNTY OF TRIPOLI

After taking part in the failed First Crusade, Raymond IV of Toulouse sailed to Antioch only to be imprisoned by Tancred in 1102. He was released after promising not to create his own Crusader state, but he broke his promise and built a castle on Pilgrim's Mountain. In spite of help from Emperor Alexius I, he died before Tripoli was captured. The infant Alfonso-Jordan (so called because he was baptised in the Jordan River) by his third wife was named successor but his older brother, Bertrand, soon arrived and sent his brother back to France. He had soon captured Tripoli with the help of King Baldwin of Jerusalem.

Bertrand died in 1112 and six years later his son Pons allied himself with Baldwin II of Jerusalem. Their plan was to help Roger of Salerno in his wars against the Muslim states, but he went forward alone and was slaughtered at the Battle of Ager Sanguinis. Pons and Baldwin wreaked their revenge at the Battle of Hab. They went on to capture Tyre and win the Battle of Azaz in 1125. But Pons argued with Fulk of Jerusalem and he was defeated at the Battle of Rugia.

The army of Damascus invaded Tripoli in 1137 and Pons was taken prisoner and executed. Raymond II of Tripoli blamed the Syrian Christians of Tripoli for his father's death so he imprisoned and tortured many to death. Raymond was captured by Zengi and had to hand over Barin castle in exchange for his release. He established the Knights Hospitaller in 1142 and gave them Krak des Chevaliers fortress. He would be murdered by the Assassins in 1152.

Young Raymond III of Tripoli's sister, Melisende, was offered to Emperor Manuel I as a potential wife. Although Raymond collected the huge dowry, the marriage was called off because of a rumour she might be illegitimate, so Manuel married Princess Maria of Antioch instead and Melisende died in a convent.

Raymond and Bohemond III of Antioch went to relieve Harim in 1164 but they were defeated and captured along with Josselin III of Edessa and taken captive. Amalric I of Jerusalem ruled Tripoli until Raymond was released from Aleppo in 1173, after a huge ransom was paid.

Amalric died in 1174 and he was succeeded by his young son Baldwin IV who was suffering from leprosy. Raymond arrived in Jerusalem and the king's regent, Miles of Plancy, was assassinated soon after in Acre. The ailing Baldwin came of age in 1176 while his sister, Sibylla, was widowed while she was pregnant. Although Raymond could have seized the throne of Jerusalem, he had no children of his own. Baldwin IV was succeeded by his nephew, Baldwin V, in 1185 only to die himself the following year. Raymond withdrew to Tripoli during the arguments over the succession of the throne of Jerusalem.

Although Raymond had made peace with the Ayyubids, he continued to attack their caravans, incurring Saladin's wrath. Tripoli reluctantly made peace with Guy of Jerusalem but they argued over what to do until they agreed to attack head on. But five of Raymond's knights had defected to Saladin's side, and the Ayyubids destroyed the Crusaders at the Battle of Hattin in 1187. Raymond was one of the few to escape and although his family was captured in Tiberias, they were allowed to return to him in Tripoli. Jerusalem fell soon afterwards.

Raymond died of pleurisy in 1187, and while he was succeeded by his godson, Raymond IV, Boemondo III sent his son, Boemondo IV, to replace him as count to Tripoli in 1201. Tripoli was ruled from Antioch until it fell to the Mamluks in 1268.

Young Boemondo VII took control of what was left of Tripoli, the port of Latakia, in 1275. His mother Sibylla was regent, and while peace was made with the Mamluks, the Bishop of Tripoli upset the Knights Templar, resulting in their indecisive attempts to take the port. The Embriacos family failed to take Tripoli by surprise in 1282 so he took refuge with the Knights Hospitaller. They handed them over to Boemondo and, though he promised to spare their lives, he buried them up to their necks in sand and starved them to death.

Boemondo left no children when he died in 1287 so his sister travelled to Tripoli to take control, despite opposition from the commune. Lucia allied with the Genoese so the Venetians and Pisans conspired with the Mamluks. Although she sought help from the Mongols, the Mamluks took it in 1289. Acre fell two years later, the last Crusader outpost in the Holy Land.

CONCLUSIONS

It is clear that kings played an important part in the growth and destruction of kingdoms between 1053 and 1492, the period encompassing the High and Late Middle Ages. A kingdom's fortunes reflected it ruler's characters because they had ultimate power, something we find difficult to come to terms with today.

There were a few strong characters like King Jaime I of Aragon, who ruled for sixty-three years, Jogalia who brought together Lithuania and Poland, and Zgismond who was King of Hungary, Croatia, Bohemia and Germany and who improved their kingdoms. Zgismond was also a Holy Roman Emperor, surely one of the most powerful men of the medieval era. But there were far more crazy characters, such as Emperor Henry IV, Carlos the Bold of Navarre, Giovanna of Naples and Andronikos of Byzantine, who brought their kingdoms into disrepute. They had absolute power compared with today's monarchs, and they had little if no checks against their megalomaniac tendencies. Democracy did not exist, and while the senior barons and Church leaders could advise their king, there were only a few occasions when they tried to overrule him. Magna Carta, signed by King John of England, is just one of a handful of examples.

Some kings were clever at forming alliances, at creating wealthy economies and at using the Church to their advantage. Some were good at taking opportunity of their neighbours' woes while others got lucky because their neighbour had self-destructed. The discovery of minerals or new mining technology sometimes gave a lucky king a windfall.

A monarch could start a war for the most trivial of reasons or conspire the most complicated of plots to pursue their territorial claims. They could form or break alliances at the click of a finger in their quest to defeat a neighbouring kingdom. They had no qualms about marrying their young children into foreign families and even had children murdered to end a claim to their throne. The monarch's supporters had to go along with these tyrannical methods or suffer the wrath of the king, which often ended in an execution and sometimes a gory one. The Scottish Black Dinner and the Danish Blood Feast are just two examples of multiple executions.

The royal family's bloodline came above all laws and the continuation of it, no matter how tenuous, was often a matter of life or death. Brothers and sons were killed, mutilated or imprisoned to end rival lines to the royal family. Sisters and daughters were married to protect the bloodline and they were expected to produce many children, no matter how old their spouse was. A few refused and were sent home in disgrace.

This putting together of couples in the name of an alliance rather than in the name of love sometimes resulted in complications when human emotions and needs interfered with politics. It was expected that a king would have affairs and barons often pushed their beautiful daughters under the nose of their king, in the hope that an affair would increase the importance of their family ties to the royal bloodline. A royal bastard, particularly a son, was the ultimate goal because it gave the family a chance to increase their power.

Some queens and princesses risked death by having an affair when their husband no longer took any interest in them. Some were poisoned, others were imprisoned and the lucky ones were sent home in shame. More often though, a king sought a royal divorce for one of two reasons. Either he wished to reverse the contract attached to the marriage or he had a new goal in his sights. Once discarded the best an ex-queen could hope for was to be sent home but the majority were confined to a convent, often a silent order where they could not divulge secrets about the king. The unlucky few were assassinated. Whatever the end result for the queen, the king usually had a new wife lined up and they were sometimes married only days after their spouse's demise, arranged or not.

It is obvious that love had little to do with most royal marriages. Some were just contracts and the royal couple were only seen together on official occasions. Sometimes the couple made an attempt to make the marriage work but it rarely succeeded. Some royal couples were married as children and would have grown up like brother and sister, exhibited like poodles for royal engagements. Only occasionally did a royal couple fall in love, have lots of children and create a strong and happy dynasty. Such a union was often the turning point in a kingdom's fortunes.

King Jaime I of Aragon is an excellent example. He was married at 13 to form an alliance with his neighbour, Castile. He divorced when he came of age and married for a huge dowry, only to have his new wife put her children ahead of her stepson. He married his third wife, a woman of low status, for love, but he had learned his lesson. The marriage contract had a clause which meant their children had no rights to the kingdom. He soon tired of her and he accused her of having leprosy before banishing her to a monastery.

Producing an heir to the throne was vital to continuing the royal line and it sometimes became an obsession. The most famous case in history is just outside the period covered in this book: that of Henry VIII of England who married six times to try to get a male heir. A preoccupation which led to him splitting with the Catholic Church because the royal line was so important to him. Then again some queens became baby-making machines, in a state of perpetual pregnancy as they produced a string of royal heirs.

The main problem with producing an heir was that paediatric science was non-existent beyond basic hygiene. The whole process of pregnancy and childbirth was considered more of a gift from God. The magic behind the creation of life was believed to be more dependent on religion than good midwifery skills. Once the infant survived, the mother then ran the risk of dying of internal infections related to the childbirth. It was known that the chances of giving birth to a healthy child reduced significantly with age. There was at least one case of an ageing queen giving birth in a tent in a marketplace, to prove that she was indeed the mother.

Whether infertility in a queen was seen as a sign of God's displeasure or a scientific matter, the end result was usually the same: divorce and banishment to a convent. No one dare say a king was infertile and all manner of things were done to check his condition, including his remarrying. But the king's enemies used rumours of homosexuality to undermine his position. A homosexual king was seen as a threat to the royal line and he would have to choose his friends wisely if he was to survive.

There were different views on legitimacy from kingdom to kingdom. Scandinavian countries were originally more concerned in crowning someone with a strong character and a magnetic charisma than about the child's mother. Other countries were very concerned about legitimacy. The kingdoms of modern day Spain had a multitude of problems due to the near-incestuous relations between cousins. From time to time the closeness of cousins, known as consanguinity (from the Latin for 'together' and 'blood') was used to initially support a marriage and then dissolve the same marriage. Rome agreed and disagreed according to the politics of the day or according to the amount of money which exchanged hands.

Every king wanted a supportive and mentally stable son to pass their kingdom on to. It was even better if he had plenty more sons to fight his enemies and give important titles to. Death was never far away, either through illness, battle or assassination, and it was useful to have reserves waiting in the wings because the loss of all a king's sons led to problems.

There were also different attitudes to female heirs and the female line, a subject known as Salic law. A few kingdoms were quite happy to accept a female ruler because it would avoid a potential civil war but there were only a handful of queens compared to hundreds of kings. The posthumous line, where the king died leaving a pregnant wife, was occasionally allowed in the hope she gave birth to a healthy son. Of course the odds of that happening were low, not least because there was always someone wanting to seize power from the vulnerable pregnant woman.

Kings were dying all the time, leaving their young sons to rule, and they needed a regent to act on their behalf and protect them until they reached the age of consent, which was typically 13. Regents were sometimes mothers, sometimes sisters, sometimes uncles and sometimes senior barons, depending on who was still alive. The young ruler was often lucky to reach adulthood because their protector often wanted to be king and they had no qualms about murdering their charge.

Queens were few and far between but they were notable. The two Joannas of Naples, Urraca of Aragon, Jadwiga of Poland, Mary of Hungary and Margaret of Denmark, Norway and Sweden. It was not unknown for a queen to use her sexuality in a male-dominated world.

While princesses never expected to rule, they would be used as pawns in alliances and offered as a potential spouse along with a huge dowry. Age had no meaning and young girls were sent hundreds of miles from home to meet their betrothed to stop or start wars. A queen's ability to produce a lot of children was a real plus. The refusal to consummate a marriage, either through religious vows or repulsion due to age ,was sometimes a problem. Domestic abuse was not unknown and, while queens were expected to take whatever their husband threw at them, a war could ensue if a king found out his daughter was married to a violent husband – for example, the war between Castile and Aragon.

The greatest natural disaster that shook Europe during this period was the bubonic plague, aptly named the Black Death. It was spread by fleas on rats, but this was not understood at the time. While neither doctors nor priests knew how to save people, it was soon realised that it indiscriminately killed peasant, baron and king alike. The disease moved seemingly randomly from country to country; no one knew that merchant ships and trade caravans were inadvertently transporting it around Europe.

On average the plague killed around one-third of people but in some countries it rose as high as 50 per cent, while others escaped the devastation altogether. Paradoxically, a few kings profited from the Black Death because it killed their enemies and creditors. They were then able to seize a dead baron's assets or write off their debts.

The biggest man-made event which cast a dark shadow across Europe was the carnage caused by the Mongol hordes in the 1240s. After decimating entire kingdoms riding back and forth, they chose the kings who would rule the Russian territories. They then forced them to pay huge amounts of tribute under the threat of another invasion.

Alliances were forged and enemies made for a host of reasons. Kingdoms grew and kingdoms came and went. Geography played a great part in shaping the kingdoms over the centuries and conflicts were restricted to neighbours. The isolation of what is now known as Spain by the Pyrenees and the oceans resulted in a back-and-forth series of Iberian conflicts. What we now know as the British Isles and France were attacking each other. The nations surrounding the Baltic Sea were often fighting or allying with each other. Landlocked nations had to choose their allies wisely and avoid enemies carefully if they were going to succeed and expand.

The Crusades show the importance of religion of the middle medieval age. Today travelling to the east side of the Mediterranean Sea is a journey that can be achieved without too much difficulty. Hundreds of years ago it involved travelling into the unknown for months on end. People's faith came ahead of the logistics, the cost and the danger for many.

As the Crusaders fought to seize and hold lands in the name of Christ in the Levante (Eastern Mediterranean) internal heretics were sometimes considered more of a problem than outside religions. There were the original pagans, like those in the Scandinavian and eastern territories. The Teutonic Knights were kept busy carving out an empire in north-east Europe with the Church's support. The Church supported Crusaders, both external and internal who fought to turn these countries over to Christianity, offering crowns as a sign of allegiance, to those who came into the Church's fold.

The reactionary heretics who had turned away from the Church were brutally dealt with. The Bosnian Bogomils shunned churches and preferred to worship outdoors. The Cathars of southern France believed that Earth was Hell and resurrection was a revival back to Hell. The Hussites of Bohemia wanted both reform and identification for their national Church but their leader, Jan Hus, was promised safe passage and then burnt at the stake, the preferred method of execution for heretics.

But Crusades were just one aspect of a religion which dominated many aspects of power and politics in medieval Europe. For as well as the battle for territorial power there was a battle for religious power as another kingdom spread its influence across Europe. That was the Kingdom of the Catholic Church with the pope at its head. Popes had many ways of influencing wars, alliances and politics and in the name of furthering the Church's influence.

The biggest conflict was the Investiture Controversy between the emperor and the pope, an argument which would ultimately decide who would appoint bishops. Popes also had a range of ways to reward and penalise kings. They could excommunicate them, banning their entrance into the Kingdom of God. They could approve or disapprove of marriages and divorces, affecting the outcome of alliances and wars. They could offer a king support through the offer of a crown or ignore a cry for help if it did not support the Church's plans. They could even confiscate a kingdom and make it a papal fief which could be given or sold to others.

The period covered starts with one of the most important events in the Christian Church: the Great Schism of 1054. It resulted in a constant war, both militarily and theologically, between west and east, Rome and Byzantium. The infighting between supporters of the two Churches would lead to the disintegration of the Byzantine Empire and the hostility between the splinter states. The same applies to south-east Europe, where Hungary, Wallachia and the Balkan states, were more interested in fighting each other than the growing threat from the Ottoman Empire. The constant in-fighting eventually resulted in the Islamic Ottomans conquering the Byzantine Empire and the defeat of the kingdoms of south-east Europe.

Kings were the judge and jury in a time when legal systems were in their infancy in some kingdoms and non-existent in others. They had the means to extract confessions under torture to get the truth, or the preferred truth. They also had the authority to pass any kind of sentence ranging from exiling, to imprisoning to execution. Some would even revel in murdering the accused themselves. While there were many different ways of execution, from beheading to burning, occasionally a king would think up some evil act, including dismembering, burying alive and pouring molten metal into orifices. Sometimes the humiliation continued after death with severed heads being displayed on a castle wall or boiled down so the skull could be used as a drinking vessel. But one of the cruellest of them all surely has to be Vlad the Impaler of Wallachia who thought nothing of killing thousands at a time by impaling them on stakes.

The unwritten law was a king could only be a king if he hadn't been mutilated. He could rule if he was born deformed because it was deemed to be God's will (foetuses with major deformities rarely survived childbirth at the time). The mutilation rule meant that blinding was very important because it simultaneously made a rival ineligible and avoided the 'Thou Shalt Not Kill' commandment. It also meant the mutilated challenger needed permanent assistance to carry out their daily duties.

Murdering a rival could cause as many problems as it solved. Taking a man's life could be used as an excuse to invoke an excommunication or the taking of a kingdom as a papal fief. The method of execution was sometimes chosen to avoid the drawing of blood, which was frowned on by Rome. Suffocation, strangulation and poisoning became the chosen methods of assassination.

Military technologies changed massively over 450 years. Sieges became more sophisticated as fortresses were improved and new weapons were invented to destroy them. There was also an arms race on the battlefield as muscle power was replaced by firearms. Hand-to-hand weapons, such as swords, lances and shields, were replaced by bows, longbows and cross bows soon to be replaced by firearms and gunpowder. There were also developments in personal armour as manufacturing methods led to it becoming more available.

All the new inventions and adaptions of existing technologies led to kings and generals having to adapt to new styles of warfare. The deployment of bodies of men and the different weapons had to be studied and understood if battles were going to be won. In many instances, the king was the general, and while some were masters of the battlefield, others were dangerously incapable. A king's fragile ego would often get in the way of a sensible strategy or interfere with battlefield tactics. An exasperated general would often become involved in a coup to rid the Kingdom of an incompetent ruler.

All in all, the years 1053 to 1492 were the time when kings and emperors had ultimate power and history was decided by how they wielded it. And then the New World of the Americas were discovered with the promise of new territories and great treasures. No longer would the Clash of Thrones be confined to the European continent.

Select Bibliography

General

Bartlett, Robert, *The Making of Europe: Conquest, Colonization and Cultural Change, 950–1350*, Princeton University Press, 1994.

Bishop, Morris, *The Middle Ages*, Mariner Books, 2001.

Davies, Norman, *Vanished Kingdoms: The Rise and Fall of States and Nations*, Penguin Books, 2012.

Jordan, William Chester, *Europe in the High Middle Ages*, Penguin Books, 2004.

Vauchez, Andre, *Encyclopaedia of the Middle Ages, Volume 1*, Fitzroy Dearborn Publishers, 2000.

North-West Europe

Best, Nicholas, *The Kings and Queens of Scotland*, Cassell, 1999.

Cannon, John, *Oxford Illustrated History of the British Monarchy*, Oxford University Press, 1988.

Crofton, Ian, *The Kings and Queens of England*, Quercus Books, 2007.

Davies, R.R., *The Age of Conquest: Wales 1063–1415*, Oxford University Press, 2000.

De La Croix, René, *The Lives of the Kings and Queens of France*, Alfred A. Knopf, 1979.

Fraser, Antonia, *The Lives of the Kings and Queens of England*, University of California Press, 1998.

Kings and Queens of Scotland: The Scottish Histories, Geddes and Grosset, 2002.

Law, Joy, *Fleur de Lys: The Kings and Queens of France*, McGraw-Hill, 1976.

Maund, Kari, *The Welsh Kings, Warriors, Warlords, and Princes*, Tempus, 2005.

McCaffrey, Carmel, *In Search of Ancient Ireland*, Ivan R. Dee, 2003.

McCullough, David, *Wars of the Irish Kings: A Thousand Years of Struggle*, Broadway Books, 2002.

Ross, Stewart, *Monarchs of Scotland*, Facts on File, 1990.

Starkey, David, *The Monarchy of England Volume 1: The Beginnings*, Chatto & Windus, 2004.

Wenzler, Claude, *Kings of France*, Editions Ouest-France, 1995.

The Iberian Peninsula

Disney, A.R., *A History of Portugal and the Portuguese Empire: From Beginnings to 1807, Vol. 1*, Cambridge University Press, 2009.

Lay, Stephen, *The Reconquest Kings of Portugal*, Palgrave Macmillan, 2009.

O'Callaghan, Joseph, *A History of Medieval Spain*, Cornell University Press, 1983.

Phillips Jr, William and Carla Rahn Phillips, *A Concise History of Spain*, Cambridge University Press, 2010.

Reilly, Bernard, *The Medieval Spains*, Cambridge University Press, 1993.

Central Europe

Abbott, John, *The House of Habsburg: A Short History of Austria from 1232 to 1792*, Quintessential Classics, 2015.

Italy and Sicily

Barbera, Henry, *Medieval Sicily: The First Absolute State*, Legas Publishing, 1994.

Brown, Gordon, *The Norman Conquest of Southern Italy and Sicily*, McFarland, 2002.

Matthew, Donald, *The Norman Kingdom of Sicily*, Cambridge University Press, 1992.

Norwich, John Julius, *Absolute Monarchs: A History of the Papacy*, Random House, 2012.

O'Malley, John, *A History of the Popes: From Peter to the Present*, Sheed and Ward, 2011.

NORTH-EAST EUROPE

Bideleux, Robert and Ian Jeffries, *A History of Eastern Europe: Crisis and Change*, Routledge, 2007.

Bushkovitch, Paul, *A Concise History of Russia*, Cambridge University Press, 2011.

Christiansen, Eric, *The Northern Crusades*, Second Edition, Penguin Books, 1998.

Davies, Norman, *God's Playground: A History of Poland, Vol. 1*, Columbia University Press, 2005.

Halperin, Charles, *Russia and the Golden Horde*, Indiana University Press, 1987.

Martin, Janet, *Medieval Russia, 980–1584*, Cambridge University Press, 2008.

Sienkiewicz, Henryk, *The Teutonic Knights*, Hippocrene Books, 1996.

Urban, William, *The Teutonic Knights: A Military History*, Greenhill Books, 2003.

Zamoyski, Adam, *Poland: A History*, Hippocrene Books, 2012.

SOUTH-EAST EUROPE

Bury, J.B. and Charles Diehl, *A History of the Eastern Roman Empire, Book III*, Didactic Press, 2014.

Forbes, Nevill, *The Balkans: A History of Bulgaria and Serbia*, Pyrrhus Press, 2014.

Nicolle, David, *Cross and Crescent in the Balkans*, Pen & Sword, 2012.

Perjes, Geza, *Fall of the Medieval Kingdom of Hungary*, Eastern European Monographs, 1989.

WHERE EAST MEETS WEST

Brownworth, Lars, *Lost to the West: The Forgotten Byzantine Empire that Rescued Western Europe*, Broadway Books, 2010.

Bury, J.B. and Charles Diehl, *A History of the Eastern Roman Empire, Book III*, Didactic Press, 2014.

Finkel, Caroline, *Osman's Dream: The History of the Ottoman Empire*, Basic Books, 2007.

Goodwin, Jason, *Lords of the Horizons: A History of the Ottoman Empire*, Picador, 2003.

Norwich, John Julius, *Byzantium: The Decline and Fall*, Knopf, 1995.

The Crusader States

Asbridge, Thomas, *The Crusades: The Authoritative History of the War for the Holy Land*, Ecco, 2011.

Madden, Thomas F., *The Concise History of the Crusades*, Rowman & Littlefield Publishers, 2005.

Riley-Smith, Jonathan, *The Crusades: A History Paperback*, Yale University Press, 2005.

Stark, Rodney, *God's Battalions: The Case for the Crusades*, HarperOne, 2010.

INDEX